A Guide to the Construction and Management of Workhouses: Together with the Consolidated Order ... of the Poor Law Board

Edward Smith

A GUIDE

TO THE

CONSTRUCTION AND MANAGEMENT

OF

WORKHOUSES;

TOGETHER WITH

THE CONSOLIDATED ORDER

AS AMENDED BY SUBSEQUENT ORDERS

OF

The Poor Law Board.

BY

EDWARD SMITH, M.D., LL.B., F.R.S.,

MEDICAL OFFICER OF THE POOR LAW BOARD, AND POOR LAW INSPECTOR;

Fellow of the Royal College of Physicians; Fellow of the Royal College of Surgeons; formerly Assistant Physician to the Hospital for Consumption, Brompton; Corresponding Member of the Academy of Science, Montpellier, and of the Natural History Society of Montreal, etc., etc.

LONDON:

KNIGHT AND CO., 90, FLEET STREET.

Publishers by Authority to the Poor Law Board.

———

1870.

LONDON:
PRINTED BY R. K. BURT AND CO., WINE OFFICE COURT,
FLEET STREET.

TO

THE RIGHT HONOURABLE

CHARLES PELHAM VILLIERS, M.P.,
&c. &c.

DEAR MR. VILLIERS,

The plan of this work was considered and some of the material collected under your administration as President of the Poor Law Board, and to you I owe the official position by which I have been enabled to gain the requisite information.

Knowing the deep interest which you still take in this subject, it will be a sincere gratification to me if the work should meet with your approbation.

I have the honour to be,

Dear Mr. Villiers,

Yours very sincerely,

EDWARD SMITH.

140, HARLEY STREET, W.,
March, 1870.

BY THE SAME AUTHOR.

1. *On Consumption in its Early and Remediable Stage.* 8vo, cloth. New Edition. Price 6s.

This work is especially written for those numerous cases in which the fatal characters of Consumption have not been recognised, or if known, the disease is in its first stage ; and its object is to show that at this early period further progress may be arrested, and health restored. It contains numerous researches by the Author on the effect of Consanguinity, and other subjects of general interest, and is especially occupied with practical details.

"The book is one which we can strongly recommend to our readers."— *Edinburgh Medical Journal.*

2. *Practical Dietary for Schools, Families, and the Labouring Classes.* 8vo. 4th Thousand. Price 3s. 6d.

The wants of the system, under a great variety of conditions, and particularly in early life and the important period of growth, are fully stated ; as are also the best and most economical kinds of food, and the proper modes of preparation. It is fitted for both public institutions and private persons, and by its aid the managers of public institutions may prepare dietaries for the inmates.

"Dr. Smith's book is by far the most useful we have seen upon all the practical questions connected with the regulation of food, whether for individuals or families."— *Saturday Review.*

"Heads of families, masters of boarding schools, or those who, whether clergy or laity, have to do with public kitchens, will find this a serviceable book."— *Literary Churchman.*

3. *The Cheapest and most Economical Kinds of Foods. A Handbill to be distributed to the Poor, or affixed to the Walls of Cottages.* Price 8s. per 100.

Many thousands have been purchased by ladies and clergymen for gratuitous distribution.

4. *The Present State of the Dietary Question ; being the Address delivered at Bath by the Author, as President of the Physiological Section of the British Association.* 8vo. Price 1s.

5. *The Periodical (or Cyclical) Changes of the Human System in Health and Disease.* 8vo, cloth. New Issue. Price 7s. 6d.

This work shows the changes which take place in the body with day and night, meals, temperature, seasons of the year, age, and exertion, and under almost all other circumstances which affect it in health ; and contains practical directions on the preservation of health, and the prevention of disease in daily life. It, moreover, contains the results of the very extended series of researches which the Author conducted, chiefly on himself, for a period of ten years.

"This is a remarkable book. It contains the result of a vast amount of original observation of facts, and a thoughtful application of the observed facts to practical purposes."— *Athenæum.*

"We said at the beginning of our review that we regarded this as a most remarkable, valuable, and useful work. We most earnestly recommend the book to all our readers."— *Dublin Quarterly Journal.*

"So thoughtful a work needs to be read with thought, and no work that we are acquainted with, at least of recent times, deserves more and will better repay attention in its perusal."— *British and Foreign Medico-Chirurgical Review.*

LONDON : WALTON, GOWER STREET.

PREFACE.

THE Management of Workhouses is a well-defined and difficult part of Poor Law Administration, and the changes of late years whereby those Institutions are now filled with aged, infirm, and sick rather than able-bodied inmates, have made it extremely important. It is, moreover, a subject which is not necessarily familiar to all administrators, but one which both Guardians and their officers must observe and consider attentively if they would discharge their duties efficiently.

Hence it is thought that a Guide, which should be restricted to this part of Poor Law work, would include a sufficiently wide field, and might be of service to those official persons who devote their time to this Department, as, also, to the public who now take interest in the provision which is made for the relief of the destitute poor. Such a Guide must obviously be based upon the legal requirements of the Poor Law Board, and be in conformity therewith; but as the Law has left much to the discretion of Guardians and their officers, it is needful to offer advice on all the subjects involved in their work, as well as on the proper mode of discharging duties which may be legally defined.

The Author has, therefore, prepared a Guide which, in a compendious form, includes sanitary, legal, and general observations, and supplies the requirements of the local executive on all the duties which devolve upon them. In effecting this it was deemed requisite to indicate those which are of legal authority by attaching to them the number of the article in the Consolidated Order, or the title of other Orders of the Poor Law Board on which they are based and to which the reader may refer.

Moreover, as on legal questions it is requisite that the exact terms of the provisions should be known, the Consolidated Order itself has been printed as the Third Part of this work, and those clauses which have been amended or superseded by subsequent Orders of the Poor Law Board have been indicated and altered.

The increased attention which has recently been given to this subject has led to improved administration, with an expenditure of very large sums of money, and has induced the Poor Law Board to express their views on certain subjects more definitely than heretofore, by the issue of " Instructions" and " Suggestions," all of which are printed in this work and will be at hand for reference.

Architects have long desired such " Instructions" when preparing plans; and it is hoped that those officially issued, with the remarks upon the selection of sites and the arrangement of the different blocks of buildings constituting the Workhouse, which are given in this book, will lead to the saving of time and expense in the performance of that duty. It may also be added that the subject of dietary and other medical and sanitary questions with which the Author is intimately associated, as well as the troublesome one of Book-keeping by the Master, have been duly considered.

Care has been taken in the arrangement of this work to render the references easy, by the preparation of an Index to the Consolidated Order distinct from that of the other parts of the work ; as, also, by an extended table of contents, and by lists of Acts of Parliament, Orders and Circulars of the Poor Law Board and the forms, official and non-official, which have been very largely introduced.

Whilst the Author cannot hope that some errors may not have crept in, he begs to add that great pains have been taken to ensure correctness by reference to the original documents, and that he is much obliged to his friend, Mr. Manwaring, for valuable aid in that direction. At the same time, he will be grateful for information which may lead to the correction of any errors and to the increased usefulness of the work.

The Author must add the expression of his gratitude to his esteemed friend, Mr. Hugh Owen, for much valuable advice, and to his other colleagues who have published works, from the perusal of which he has derived much advantage.

ERRATA.

Page 18, last line, for *challenged* read *challenge.*
  ,, 61, line 10, for *one-third* read *one-fifth.*
  ,, 63, line 3, read *should be more than 12 feet.*
  ,, 118, line 23, omit *his.*
  ,, 161, after *the University of London* add *Degree in Medicine and Degree in Surgery.*
  ,, 169, transpose 7th and 8th lines to end of 3rd line.
  ,, 175, omit heading, *Visits to the Schools.*

ACTS OF PARLIAMENT CITED.

LIST OF FORMS.

List of Forms.

NON-OFFICIAL.

ORDERS, CIRCULAR LETTERS, AND REPORTS
CITED.

TABLE OF CONTENTS.

Part I.

THE GENERAL MANAGEMENT OF THE WORKHOUSE.

Part II.

THE OFFICERS.

THE MASTER.

Part III.

THE CONSOLIDATED ORDER.

PART I.

THE GENERAL MANAGEMENT
OF THE WORKHOUSE.

Chapter I.

THE GUARDIANS.

CLASSES OF GUARDIANS.

1. There are two classes of guardians who administer the laws for the relief of the poor, viz. : the *ex officio*, who may act by virtue of powers conferred upon them as magistrates of the county in which the Union is situate [4 & 5 *Wm. IV. c.* 76, *s.* 38] or in the metropolis by the nomination of justices of the peace or other ratepayers, for a term of years, by the Poor Law Board [*Metropolitan Act*, 30 *Vict. c.* 6, *s.* 79]; and the *elected*, who are ratepayers, and are elected yearly by the ratepayers of the parishes in the Union for a period not exceeding one year [30 & 31 *Vict. c.* 106, *s.* 4; *G. O. Feb. 4th*, 1868], but there is no difference in the duties or powers of the two classes.

MEETINGS OF THE GUARDIANS.

2. A chairman and one or two vice-chairmen are elected by the guardians at their first meeting after the 15th day of April, and as often as vacancies may occur, from amongst the whole body of guardians, to hold office for one year

B

[*C. O. Art.* 29, 30], or for the remaining part of the year
[*C. O. Art.* 31], but they have no duties or powers connected with the management of the workhouse which are
not shared by the other members of the board.

3. Hence the responsibility of rightly conducting the
affairs of the workhouse devolves upon all the guardians
alike.

4. The powers intrusted to them are exercised only at
legal meetings of the board of guardians, and not by individual guardians at other times or places [4 *& 5 Wm. IV.*
c. 76, *s.* 38].

5. The chairman of the late board, if still a guardian,
takes the chair at the first meeting of the new board until
the chairman for the ensuing year shall have been elected,
and the late board of guardians discharges all the duties of
a board until the first meeting of the new board. Moreover, if on April the 15th the election shall not have been
concluded in respect of any parish or ward, the guardians of
the previous year will continue to be entitled to act for a
period of forty days after the 25th of March, or until his
successor shall have been elected [7 *& 8 Vic. c.* 101, *s.* 17].

6. The Poor Law Board cannot nominate or appoint
the chairman or any other member of the board of guardians
to represent the central authority, neither is the chairman
always selected from the magistracy. In umerous Unions,
however, a nobleman or gentleman of local influence is
chosen by the guardians as their chairman, whilst in others
an elected guardian is selected.

7, Having regard to the social status, landed possessions
and education of county magistrates, it has been observed
that a chairman who may have been selected from that
class exerts more authority than can usually be possessed by
an elected guardian, and is thus enabled to conduct the
business efficiently and harmoniously ; whilst such a selection
maintains the influence of the board amongst the ratepayers and the destitute poor, and gives dignity to the local
administration of the poor-laws.

8. The right selection of a chairman is very desirable, since a chairman who from any cause is feeble in authority and administrative powers is a hindrance to business and to progressive improvement.

9. Ordinary meetings of the guardians are held weekly or fortnightly, and the day, hour, and place of meeting may not be changed without the consent of the Poor Law Board [*C. O. Art.* 28]. In cases of emergency, however, the guardians may meet at any time at their ordinary place of meeting [*C. O. Art.* 36].

10. Extraordinary meetings are held at any time on the written requisition of two guardians addressed to the clerk, but only special business may then be transacted [*C. O. Art.* 34].

11. It is very desirable that the chairman and the senior vice-chairman (who in the absence of the chairman presides) should attend the meetings regularly and take interest in the management of the workhouse.

12. Three guardians must be present at a meeting of the guardians and concur in order that any act may be valid [*C. O. Art.* 32 ; 4 & 5 *Wm. IV. c.* 76, *s.* 38]. It is not required that each guardian should attend every meeting, but it is not desirable that any, much less the greater number, should frequently be absent, or that they should attend only at the election of officers, or when it is proposed to spend an unusual amount of money, or when other special business is to be transacted.

13. It is probable that the Legislature, by creating two classes of guardians, did not anticipate a somewhat frequent occurrence in certain Unions, viz., that the *ex officio* guardians would rarely take part in the business of the Union ; but, on the contrary, by selecting one class from those who are high in social position and familiar with judicial and administrative business, as also by constituting them the only permanent members of the board of guardians, indicated that the presence of those gentlemen at the meetings of the board was very desirable.

PROCEEDINGS OF THE GUARDIANS.

14. The chairman presides, and cannot act out of the chair as an ordinary member of the board. In his absence, the senior vice-chairman, or if both be absent, the junior vice-chairman, takes the chair, and may retain it or vacate it on the arrival of the chairman. In the absence of all these officers, the guardians present elect a chairman, who vacates the chair on the arrival of the chairman or vice-chairman.

15. The presiding chairman signs the minutes of the last preceding meeting, as to their correctness when read in his presence [*C. O. Art.* 41], and has all the powers of an ordinary member of the board as to speaking, making motions, and voting.

16. He votes with the other guardians, and afterwards declares that the motion is adopted or rejected, and in the event of an equality of votes, he gives a second or casting vote [12 & 13 *Vict. c.* 103, *s.* 19].

17. He is not bound to put a motion or an amendment, the effect of which would be illegal, and he may deal with amendments as he deems most fitting; but the usual practice is to dispose of one amendment before another is proposed, and if carried, to put it as an original motion, which will be subject to other amendments; but if lost, another amendment may be proposed and treated in the same way.

18. All resolutions are carried by a majority of the votes present [*C. O. Art.* 38], as determined either by show of hands or by ballot, at the option of the board, except when only three guardians are present, when they must be unanimous [*C. O. Art* 32]. At the election of officers, all the guardians who are present should vote, since to render an election valid there must be a majority, not only of those who vote, but of all who are present [*C. O. Art.* 155].

19. When the question is put to the meeting, the chairman takes the votes of the guardians present by show of hands, and declares the motion to be adopted or rejected as the case may be. If any guardian disputes the correctness

of the decision, he is entitled to claim to have the names of the guardians called over, and each guardian's vote taken down by the clerk, with a view to count them and thus to test the accuracy of that decision. If the result be to reverse the chairman's decision, the question must be determined by counting the votes consequent upon taking down the names, but so that any guardian who has held up his hand on one side of the question is to be counted to that side, even though on calling the names he may have given his vote the other way. It is not necessary that the names of the guardians who have voted should be recorded; but the number of the votes for and against, and whether challenged or not, should be entered upon the minutes.

20. It is desirable in order to insure uniformity of action, that modes of procedure which may not have been laid down by law, but are left to the discretion of the chairman or of the whole board, should be determined by the vote of the guardians, and thus become a bye-law, which would, however, be liable to be reversed at any other meeting of the board, unless previously approved by the Poor Law Board [4 & 5 *Wm. IV. c.* 76, *s.* 22].

21. Only such motions as may have been moved and seconded and put to the vote are recorded by the clerk.

22. All correspondence between the guardians or their officers and the Poor Law Board is conducted by the clerk of the guardians. The clerk does not reply to any communication from the Poor Law Board which is not on routine business, but which requires the decision and direction of the guardians, without having first submitted it to the guardians, and all letters and other documents received by the clerk, with copies of his replies to the same, are laid before the guardians at their next meeting. The clerk takes and keeps copies of all letters addressed by him to others.

23. No individual guardian, officer, or ratepayer, has the right to inspect or search the minute-books, or to take copies or extracts therefrom, without the permission of the board of guardians.

24. The guardians retain in their custody all books which are closed, and direct where they shall be kept.

25. Individual guardians have not the right to visit the workhouse, except to attend the meetings of the board, or of committees of which they are members, but the board of guardians may give them authority should they deem it right to do so.

26. The board may admit or exclude reporters for the press, and the general public, as they may deem to be desirable, but it is not desirable that they should ordinarily exclude the members of the press.

27. Resolutions which relate to the allowance of relief to any person, the punishment of paupers, to questions of emergency, or to any resolution or communication which the Poor Law Board requests the guardians to reconsider, may be reconsidered or altered at any time, but no other resolutions are rescinded or altered unless a guardian gives seven days' notice to the board (one day inclusive and one day exclusive) of his intention to move such alteration, which notice is entered by the clerk upon the minutes [*C. O. Art.* 39]. Hence notice is given only at a meeting of the guardians, and if sent to the clerk in the intervals of the meetings, it does not begin to operate until the next following meeting of the board. The clerk is not required to inform the whole of the guardians by letter, but he takes the direction of the board in reference thereto.

28. It is usually convenient at an ordinary meeting to take the business in the following order [*C. O. Art.* 41; *Instr. Letter,* 1842] :—

1. The minutes of the last ordinary, or of any extraordinary meeting which may have been held since the last ordinary meeting.
2. The business arising therefrom.
3. The continuance of relief, and the applications for relief made since the last ordinary meeting.
4. New applications for relief.

5. Reports upon the state of the workhouse, and all books and accounts.

6. The treasurer's account.

7. Any other business.

29. When there is special business it is sometimes convenient, or when the Poor Law Inspector is present to confer with the guardians, it is courteous to vary this order of procedure.

30. The minutes, if correct, are accepted, as to their validity, when they are read, and should any resolution contained in them be objected to by any guardian, he gives notice of his intention to move that it be reconsidered.

31. It is desirable that the entries in the rough minute-book should be full, legible, and intelligible, and be kept for future reference. The entries in the minute-book are made as soon after the meeting to which they refer as possible.

32. The guardians may make bye-laws on any subject connected with the management of the workhouse for which no legal enactment exists, provided that such bye-laws are not opposed to or inconsistent with the laws and regulations of the Poor Law Board [*C. O. Art.* 152].

Chapter II.

THE OFFICERS.

———◆———

ELECTION OF OFFICERS.

I. The guardians appoint, as often as it may be necessary for the management of the workhouse, but subject to the approval of the Poor Law Board, a master, matron, and assistant matron where required, a chaplain, one or more medical officers, and one or more nurses ; a schoolmaster or schoolmistress, or both, with such assistants as may be required, where there is a school for the children ; a porter, and one or more male or female industrial trainers where required [*C. O. Art.* 153], all of whom act in subordination to the board of guardians, but with powers and duties prescribed or sanctioned by the Legislature [*C. O. Art.* 154].

2. The assent of the Poor Law Board is not required for the appointment of assistant officers and servants [*G. O. Aug.* 19, 1867].

3. The guardians determine, subject to the approval of the Poor Law Board, the salaries to be paid to those officers, as also the dietary and other emoluments to be allowed to them, but they are not required to obtain the assent of the Poor Law Board to the wages which they pay to their servants.

4. Notice is given of the intention of the guardians to elect any of the above-mentioned officers (except for an assistant or temporary substitute) at one of the two ordinary meetings immediately preceding the day of election, or an advertisement notifying the intention of the guardians is inserted in a public paper by direction of the guardians, at least seven

days before the day fixed for the appointment [*C. O. Art.* 156]. The clerk sends a special notice to each of the guardians some days before the intended election.

5. The advertisement or notice need not mention the proposed salary (except in the case of a medical officer) or define the duties of the officer, and the guardians may not invite tenders for the supply of medicines, without mentioning the workhouse to be thus supplied [*C. O. Art.* 157]. Care should be taken that advertisements are not needlessly long and expensive, and it is desirable that the attention of the guardians should be called to the expense thus incurred with a view to its reduction.

6. The guardians may pay a reasonable sum as travelling expenses to such of the candidates as they may require to attend on the day of election [*G. O. Aug.* 19, 1867].

SALARIES AND WAGES.

7. The salaries of all officers are determined by the guardians, subject to the approval of the Poor Law Board, but the Poor Law Board has power to order that a greater or less salary shall be paid them than that proposed ; and when the guardians neglect or refuse to appoint officers, the Poor Law Board has power to appoint them, to fix their salaries, and to order that their salaries shall be paid out of the funds of the Union [4 & 5 *Wm. IV. c.* 76 *s.* 46].

8. The salaries are payable on the usual quarter days, viz., at Midsummer Day, Michaelmas Day, Christmas Day, and Lady Day, or to the day on which any officer or servant ceases to hold office, and the payment is reported to the Poor Law Board [*C. O. Art.* 173]. In the event of the suspension of any officer by the guardians being confirmed by the Poor Law Board, by the dismissal or by the resignation of the officer, the salary is payable only to the date of the suspension [*C. O. Art.* 175], but if the suspension be removed by the guardians or by the Poor Law Board, the salary is payable as though the suspension had not taken place.

9. The salaries of servants are paid daily, weekly, or otherwise, at the discretion of the guardians [*G. O. Aug.* 19, 1867]. The guardians may appoint a temporary substitute, and give him a reasonable remuneration, and they immediately report such appointment to the Poor Law Board [*C. O. Art.* 193].

10. The guardians are repaid from the consolidated fund one-half of the amount of the salaries of medical officers, and of the cost of drugs and medical appliances which may have been sanctioned by the Poor Law Board, as also a part or the whole of the salaries of the schoolmaster and schoolmistress, according to the proficiency of the teachers and the number of children in the school, and of the industrial trainer.

11. The payment from the parliamentary grant in respect of schoolmasters and schoolmistresses is according to the following scale [*Circular, 3rd June,* 1856.]

CERTIFICATES.		MASTERS.		MISTRESSES.		Sum to be allowed in respect of each Scholar in addition to the minimum allowance.
		Minimum Allowance from the Grant.	Maximum Allowance from the Grant.	Minimum Allowance from the Grant.	Maximum Allowance from the Grant.	
		£	£	£	£	*s.*
Efficiency	1	30	60	24	48	12
	2	30	55	24	44	11
	3	30	50	24	40	10
Competency	1	25	45	20	36	7
	2	25	40	20	32	6
	3	25	35	20	28	5
Probation	1	20	30	16	24	4
	2	20	25	16	20	3
	3	20	20	16	16	—
Permission		15	15	12	12	—

12. The payment in respect of industrial trainers is as follows [*Circular, 12th March,* 1867], viz.:—When the guardians provide board and lodging two-thirds of the officer's salary, and when they do not provide board and lodging one-half of the salary to be allowed. If the services of the officer are given solely for the instruction of the children, as in the case of a band-master or drill-master, the whole salary is allowed.

RESIGNATION AND REMOVAL OF OFFICERS.

13. The foregoing appointments, except as regards the porter, nurses, and assistants, cannot be made by the guardians for a term, or be determinable by them on their giving notice to the officer, but they continue until he resigns or dies, subject to the efficient discharge of the duties of the office, and the approval of the Poor Law Board, but the guardians may require the officer to give a month's notice of his intention to resign his office [*C. O. Art.* 187, *& Inst. Letter*].

14. In cases of neglect, misconduct, or inefficiency, the guardians have power to suspend any officer except the clerk, chaplain, and treasurer, and to appoint a temporary substitute, and on the communication of the facts to the Poor Law Board, by direction of the guardians, the Poor Law Board may remove the suspension, or require him to resign his office, or dismiss him from his office by order, either on a consideration of the facts of the case as presented to them by the guardians and the accused officer, or after an official inquiry on oath held by a Poor Law Inspector.

15. The guardians have power to remove the suspension which they had previously ordered.

16. The usual course in such a case is for the guardians to institute such a preliminary inquiry as they may deem necessary in order to determine the facts of the case, and if they should deem further action necessary, to submit the result of their inquiry to the Poor Law Board, with or without a request that the Board would order an official inquiry to be instituted. This statement is usually forwarded to the accused officer for his observations, and the Poor Law Board having in this preliminary manner informed themselves of the facts and explanations as offered by both parties, decide whether an official inquiry is necessary to enable them to arrive at a just conclusion, and inform the guardians of their decision accordingly.

17. Should a Poor Law Inspector be instructed to hold

an official inquiry, he gives due notice of his intention to the clerk of the guardians and to the accused officer, and forwards such copies of communications as may be necessary and summonses for the witnesses named by both parties. The place for holding the inquiry is usually the board-room of the workhouse, and it is therefore desirable that the inquiry should not be held on a board-day.

18. The summonses of the Poor Law Inspector do not run beyond ten miles from the nearest boundary of the Union in which the inquiry is to be held, but within those limits disobedience or neglect of them is punishable as a misdemeanour. It is the same whether the Poor Law Inspector be the Inspector of the district in which the Union lies or otherwise.

19. The guardians may dismiss the porter, nurses, assistants, and servants, without the assent of the Poor Law Board, in accordance with the following provisions of *G. O. Aug.* 19, 1867, but they should inform the Poor Law Board of the dismissal, and the grounds thereof, of the porter, nurses, and assistants [*C. O. Art.* 188] :—

" So much of any order as would require the guardians to report to this Board the appointment, salary, removal, or discharge of any such person employed by them as aforesaid, or as would provide for the quarterly or other periodical payment of any such person engaged at daily, weekly, or monthly wages, or by the piece or job, is hereby rescinded.

" The foregoing articles of this order (except so much thereof as relates to their quarterly or other periodical payments) shall not apply to the following officers or persons ; that is to say,—clerk to the guardians, chaplain, medical officer for the workhouse and his assistants, dispensers and persons engaged in preparing and dispensing medicines, master of the workhouse, matron of the workhouse, porter, nurse and assistant nurses, schoolmaster and schoolmistress, and other persons engaged in teaching or instructing pauper children."

Chapter III.

PURCHASES AND PAYMENTS.

———·———

PURCHASES AND CONTRACTS.

1. The guardians purchase food for the officers (where the officers are supplied with rations) and inmates, as well as clothing and such other articles as are allowed to the inmates and officers, and order and pay for such alterations and repairs as may be required in the structure of the workhouse and premises or the erection of a new workhouse, and direct and control the expenditure of money for all purposes connected with the management and maintenance of the workhouse.

2. All purchases of goods and materials the consumption of which is estimated to cost ten pounds monthly, or the cost of which is estimated to exceed £50 in a single sum [C. O. Art. 45], or work and repairs of the fabric and fixtures estimated to exceed £50 in one sum [C. O. Art. 46], are contracted for by sealed tenders obtained after advertising in a public paper which circulates within the Union, at least ten days prior to the day fixed for the opening of the tenders. The advertisement states the nature and conditions of the proposed contract, the amount of the articles required, the last day on which the tenders will be received, and the day on which the tenders will be opened [C. O. Art. 47].

3. The guardians are not bound to accept the lowest or any tender, and they may advertise again, or if there be no tender they may renew the old contract.

4. The contract is in writing and sealed, and contains all requisite particulars mutually agreed upon. The guardians may at their discretion require the contractor to provide one or more sureties for the due performance of the contract,

and the bonds are not liable to stamp duty [*C. O. Art.* 48].
If the contract should be informal, it is voidable under the
direction of the Poor Law Board, but is not necessarily void.

5. The guardians may in certain exceptional cases, and with
the consent of the Poor Law Board, dispense with sealed
tenders, and employ particular persons with or without
naming a specific sum as the purchase-money, or as the
charge to be made for the work to be done and materials
required [*C. O. Art.* 49]. It is, however, only in exceptional
cases that the general regulation of proceeding by tenders
after public advertisement should be departed from. The
guardians should be very watchful to prevent fraud or
excessive charge in such cases, and it is desirable that the
goods to be purchased and the work to be done should be
clearly specified in writing by the clerk.

6. The day on or before which the contractor or tradesman should send his bill or account is named in the contract,
and contractors, or other tradesmen or their agents, attend
on a day fixed by the guardians, and advertised in a public
paper, within twenty-one days after the end of each
quarter, to receive payment of the money due to them
[*C. O. Art.* 50 & 51].

7. No guardian may, directly or indirectly, whether in
his own name or in that of others (except in the case of his
being a member of a joint stock company), supply anything for use within the workhouse or upon the workhouse
premises for his own profit under pain of severe penalties,
and it matters not whether he do so under his contract or
at the verbal or written request of the master [55 *Geo. III.*
c. 137, *s.* 6 ; 4 & 5 *Wm. IV. c.* 76, *s.* 51 & 77 ; *Off. Cir.*
No. 10].

8. A guardian may supply goods without profit to himself, or supply work and labour in building or repairing
the workhouse, or he may act professionally for the
guardians, or purchase old stores from them, but the
object of the Legislature in prohibiting the guardians
from abusing their office to their own rofit is so clear

and reasonable, that it is not desirable that any guardian should be concerned in any transaction by which he may make a profit in the manner now indicated.

9. If it be desirable that a guardian should supply goods or labour for the workhouse he should first resign his office of guardian.

PAYMENTS.

10. The guardians may not remunerate themselves for their attendance at meetings of the board, neither may they reimburse themselves for their travelling or personal expenses in journeying to and from the workhouse, nor supply themselves with food at the charge of the rates of the Union.

11. Every bill against the Union exceeding one pound, except officers' salaries, is examined with the goods or items of work done, and cast up at the meetings of the guardians, or by a committee of the guardians, and noted upon the face of it if allowed [*C. O. Art.* 85].

12. All payments above £5 are paid by an unstamped order upon the treasurer, made payable to order, and signed by the presiding chairman and two other guardians, and countersigned by the clerk in the following form :—

———— [Date].

———— [Place of Meeting].

To A. B., treasurer of the guardians of the poor, of the ———— Union [parish or township], in the county of ————, at ————

Pay to C. D. or order the sum of ———— pounds, ———— shillings, and ———— pence, and charge the same to the account of the said guardians.

[Signed]

———— Presiding Chairman.

———— { Guardians of the poor of
———— { the said Union [parish or
———— { township].

Countersigned by ————
Clerk to the said guardians.

N.B.—The guardians request that this order may be presented for payment within fourteen days from the date hereof, to the treasurer at his house or usual place of business, and within the usual hours of business [*G. O. April* 7, 1857].

13. Every contributor's order is drawn up in the following form :—

Order for Contributions.

To A. B. and C. D., overseers [or* ———], of the parish of ———, you are hereby ordered and directed to pay to F. G., of ———, treasurer of the guardians of the poor of the ——— union, at ———, on the ——— day of———, the sum of ——— pounds, ——— shillings, and ——— pence, [or on the following days, that is to say, on the ———day of ———, the sum of ——— pounds, ——— shillings, and ——— pence, and on the ——— day of ———, the sum of ——— pounds, ——— shillings, and ——— pence], from the poor-rates of the parish fund of the Union, and for such other expenses as are chargeable by the said guardians on the said parish separately, and to take the receipt of the said F. G., endorsed upon this paper, for the said sum [or sums].

Given under our hands at a meeting of the guardians of the poor of the said ——— Union, held on the ——— day of ———, 18 .

<blockquote>
[Signed]   X. Y.,   Presiding Chairman.
           W. X., ⎫
           U. V., ⎬ Guardians.
</blockquote>

——— Countersignature of the clerk to the guardians [*G. O. Feb.* 26, 1866].

* Here insert the names of any parties in the parish authorised to make the poor-rate in p'ace of the overseers.|

14. Orders or cheques drawn upon the treasurer for a less sum than £5 are stamped.

15. The clerk may not pay to himself or to his account any cheque thus drawn to any one but himself [*C. O. Art.* 219], and no officer of the guardians may receive any allowance of any kind with respect to any contract made by or for any goods or labour supplied to the guardians [*C. O. Art.* 218].

16. The clerk pays or transmits the cheques to the proper persons within fourteen days, and produces the acknowledgment at the first ordinary meeting which follows his receipt of it [*C. O. Art.* 220], and every officer with all convenient speed pays to the treasurer of the Union all moneys received by him on behalf of the guardians, without any

deduction or account of money due to him from the guardians [*C. O. Art.* 221].

17. No officer may receive money on behalf of any non-settled pauper of other Unions [*C. O. Art.* 222], and if any should be sent to him, he enters it in his accounts, but pays it to the treasurer of his own Union, and reports to the guardians of that Union [*C. O. Art* 223].

CUSTODY OF BONDS.

18. The guardians provide for the safe custody of bonds; and the clerk, who has charge of all bonds, except his own, and the treasurer, who has charge of the clerk's bond, produce them to the auditor yearly for his inspection, and no person may have charge of his own bond [*C. O. Art.* 86, 87, 202]. The bonds of collectors and assistant overseers are unstamped [7 & 8 *Vict. c.* 101, *s.* 61].

BORROWING MONEY.

19. The guardians have power to borrow, to be repaid within thirty years, an amount not exceeding one-half in the metropolis and at Liverpool, and two-thirds elsewhere, of the poor-rate, calculated on the average of the preceding three years, for the construction or alteration of the workhouse, and for such land as they may require [31 & 32 *Vict. c.* 122, *s.* 35; 30 *Vict. c.* 6; 30 & 31 *Vict. c.* 106, *s.* 14]. In the metropolitan district they may further borrow a sum equal to the cost of the site of the workhouse, district schools, and other premises [7 & 8 *Vict. c.* 101, *s.* 30].

20. The cost of fittings, architect's commission, and the salary of the clerk of the works, as well as the cost of the repairs of the workhouse, may be paid out of the current rates.

Chapter IV.

COMMITTEES AND THEIR REPORTS.

APPOINTMENT OF COMMITTEES.

1. Committees of the guardians are appointed for various purposes at a meeting of the guardians, as occasion may require, but they have no power, except such as may be conferred upon them by the board of guardians [*C. O. Art.* 40].

MANAGERS OF SCHOOL DISTRICTS.

2. The guardians, at one of the two meetings of the board immediately preceding the 25th day of March in each year, elect members whose term of office has expired, to represent them at the board of management in those Unions where there is a school district.

VISITING COMMITTEES.

3. The guardians appoint one or more visiting committees, but ordinarily they appoint one only at a time, and determine the number of members and duration of office [*C. O. Art.* 148].

4. Each member has usually authority given to him by the board to visit the workhouse at any time, but the guardians may limit this privilege in any manner which they may see fit.

5. The number of members of the visiting committee is not prescribed by the orders of the Poor Law Board, and it may be so few as one, or so many as to include all the guardians. The guardians may and should prescribe a *quorum*.

6. It is not desirable that the committee should consist of only one member, since the duties are onerous, and allow, if not challenged, some difference of opinion in the

matters to be reported upon; whilst the whole board is too numerous to render it probable that all the members would regularly attend, and each feel his due share of responsibility.

7. It should consist of from two to five members, of whom two or more should be *ex-officio* guardians.

8. It is desirable that the chairman, or one of the vice-chairmen, should be a member of this committee, since it may be presumed that those officers take great interest in the management of the workhouse, and their regular attendance would tend to give uniformity to the mode of conducting the inquiries.

9. It may be appointed only until the next meeting of the board, or for any longer period within the year of office, but it is desirable that it should be limited to one month, and that a new committee should be appointed monthly.

10. The members are sometimes appointed according to a *rota* prepared by the clerk under the direction of the board of guardians, but as this includes members who differ much in leisure, inclination for the duty, and distance of residence from the workhouse, it is desirable that a selection should include those only who are able to discharge the duties of the office regularly and efficiently.

11. Those guardians will probably discharge the duties best who take interest in such inquiries, who have some sanitary knowledge and acquaintance with the structure and arrangements of workhouses, and the mode of management of public institutions generally, and who reside somewhat near to the workhouse.

12. It would be an error to assume that every guardian is well fitted for the discharge of this duty, since but few persons possess the requisite knowledge and leisure, and all require a certain amount of experience before they can perform the duty satisfactorily.

13. Hence it demands consideration whether the law should not direct that the management of the workhouse should devolve solely upon a committee to be elected yearly by the guardians on the ground of special qualification,

instead of, as at present, upon the whole board, many of the members of which rarely attend the meetings, and but few have the requisite qualifications.

14. The committee visits the workhouse at least once in each week, but it is not obligatory that all the members should attend at the same time. It seems, however, to have been contemplated by the Poor Law Board that they would attend and make their visit together.

15. It is desirable that the committee should meet at the workhouse at stated periods weekly, or that the members should agree amongst themselves as to the days in each week on which one or more of them would visit the workhouse.

16. It is not desirable that they should be always accompanied by the officers, and particularly when they offer the inmates the opportunity to make complaints; but it is desirable that the master, matron, and medical officer should attend them occasionally whilst inspecting their several departments. The medical officer would be of service to those members who wish to increase their sanitary knowledge.

17. They should visit every part of the workhouse once in each week; but if the workhouse be large, the visit may be conveniently divided into two or more parts, which together would include the whole workhouse.

18. The visit should not be made on a board day, or at any hour when the attendance of guardians may be expected by the officers, but at periods known only to the visiting committee.

19. They should observe—

The state of repair and cleanliness of the fabric and furniture.

The sufficiency of the accommodation as to space, furniture, fittings, and appliances for the different classes of inmates in the dormitories, day rooms, workshops, yards, baths, lavatories, and water-closets.

The state of the drains and drainage, and the water
supply.

The sufficiency of the linen, bedding, and clothing.

The sufficiency and fitness of the dietary, as well as
the efficiency of the mode of cooking and serving
food.

The evidence of waste in food, fuel, or other property.

20. They should inquire in every ward if any inmate has
complaint to make, and particularly ask those who are
blind, deaf, or bed-ridden, and if a complaint should be made
to investigate it.

21. They should inquire as to the conduct of every officer
and servant, including that of the nurses and the attendance
of the medical officer upon the sick.

22. They should inquire as to the general state of health
of the inmates, and particularly of the children, and as to
the existence of fever, or any contagious disease, or any
unusual amount of sickness or mortality.

23. They should in a general manner examine the stores
and judge of their sufficiency ; and from time to time they
should compare the stores with the entries in the store-
book.

24. They should examine the books which are kept by
the master, chaplain, medical officer, and porter, and ascertain that they are duly kept ; and they should inquire as
to the due execution of contracts for food, clothing, and
other articles of use or consumption.

25. They should note the entries in the punishment-
book, and ascertain whether the punishments are legal and
proper. They should also satisfy themselves that all punishments are duly recorded by the master, and that the
punishment cells are fit for use.

26. They should ascertain whether due classification of
the inmates is observed, and whether suitable employment
is found for all who can perform any kind of work.

27. As certain details of management cannot be seen at

all hours, it is desirable that the visiting committee should depute one of its members to occasionally inspect the dormitories and vagrant wards at night when the inmates are in bed, and some of them should attend at meal times to observe the mode of cutting up, weighing, and serving the food, as well as the fitness and cooking of the food, and the dislike of the inmates to any kind of food, as shown by the quantity which may be uneaten and wasted.

28. A strict system of inquiry will be a check upon the conduct of the officers, and an incitement to the due discharge of their duties. It will also be a proper protection to the inmates; whilst a kind word to the deserving and a caution to the undeserving inmates will aid the officers in the discharge of their duties.

29. Care should be taken not to interfere with the duties of the officers. The committee should not remark unfavourably on the officers in the presence of the inmates, but, on the contrary, should uphold their authority.

30. They have not power to give any directions as to the management of the workhouse, or to order the expenditure of any money; but their advice would doubtless be received by the officers with respect, and would lead to the speedy removal of minor defects or to the improvement of the administration.

31. They are not required to report to the guardians after every visit, but "from time to time;" yet it is scarcely possible that any properly-conducted visitation should not produce matter for consideration, and a report to every ordinary meeting of the guardians is desirable.

32. The report should be the act of the committee, and not of individual members, and it should be signed by the *quorum*, if one have been appointed, or by all the members who have visited since the last preceding report.

33. The practice which prevails in many workhouses of omitting to report, or of making a general instead of a particular report, is very undesirable.

34. The following are the questions to which the committee are required to give answers in the visitors'-book [*C. O. Art.* 149]:—

1. Is the workhouse, with its wards, offices, yards, and appurtenances, clean and well ventilated in every part? and is the bedding in proper order? and, if not, state the defect or omission.

2. Do the inmates of the workhouse of all classes appear clean in their persons and decent and orderly in their behaviour? and is their clothing regularly changed?

3. Are the inmates of each sex employed and kept at work, as directed by the guardians, and is such work objectionable in its nature? If any improvement can be suggested in their employment, state the same.

4. Are the infirm of each sex properly attended to according to their several conditions?

5. Are the boys and girls in the school properly instructed, as required by the regulations of the commissioners? and is their industrial training properly attended to?

6. Are the young children properly nursed and taken care of, and do they appear in a clean and healthy state? Is there any child not vaccinated?

7. Is regular attendance given by the medical officer? Are the inmates of the sick ward tended properly? Are the nurses efficient? Is there any infectious disease in the workhouse?

8. Is there any dangerous lunatic or idiot in the workhouse?

9. Is Divine service regularly performed? Are prayers regularly read?

10. Is the established dietary duly observed? and are the prescribed hours of meals regularly adhered to?

11. Are the provisions and other supplies of the qualities contracted for?

12. Is the classification properly observed according to Arts. 98 and 99?

13. Is any complaint made by any pauper against any officer, or in respect of the provisions or accommodation? If so, state the name of the complainant and the subject of the complaint.

14. Does the present number of inmates in the workhouse exceed that fixed by the Poor Law Commissioners?

35. Hence the report is a very comprehensive one, and cannot be conscientiously signed by one who has not well satisfied himself by personal observation and inquiry.

36. There is no penalty or other punishment provided for those who carelessly inspect or incorrectly report; but a due sense of the impropriety of misleading the guardians by an erroneous report should be an inducement to make a diligent and careful inquiry.

37. The report of the visiting committee should be read *in extenso*, and not merely in abstract, at the first ordinary meeting of the guardians after its presentation, and action taken thereon immediately if necessary.

38. Having regard to the extent and variety of the duties imposed upon the visiting committee, and the short time which guardians generally can devote to the discharge of them, it is worthy of consideration whether two such committees should not be appointed, or one committee be subdivided into two sub-committees, who would divide the duties between them. One might report upon the fabric and premises generally, as to their state of repair and cleanliness, and upon the furniture and fittings, whilst the other might undertake the inspection of all that refers to management, food, clothing, medical attendance, nursing, and general supervision, including the duties of all the officers.

39. The first might be known as the Property Sub-Committee, and the second as the Management Sub-Committee,

and on every board of guardians there are persons technically or practically fitted to act upon one or other of them.

VISITING COMMITTEE OF LUNATICS.

40. The guardians also appoint a visiting committee of lunatics (who may be the same as the visiting committee) to visit the inmates of unsound mind within the workhouse or in asylums, and to report to the guardians, at least once in each quarter, in a book provided for the purpose and kept by the master [25 & 26 *Vict. c.* 111, *s.* 37]. This committee may enter any observations on the state and treatment of such inmates, including the dietary and accommodation provided for them. The inspection of this helpless class should be made with greater care than that of the ordinary inmates.

41. It is needful that the committee should see and converse with each of these inmates, and that they should satisfy themselves that the latter are suitably fed and clad, kindly treated, and in general properly cared for, and suitably employed, and if they observe any defects to point them out to the guardians, and suggest remedies. Should any of this class of inmates be capable of education, or of acquiring some knowledge which might be useful to them or to others, the committee should recommend that they may be taught; and if it should be ascertained that they are not well treated by certain of the ordinary inmates, they should be removed to other wards. If the master, nurse, or other officials should treat them with harshness, the committee should ascertain the facts and report to the guardians.

Chapter V.

REPORTS OF OFFICERS AND POOR LAW INSPECTOR.

1. The master, matron, chaplain, and medical officer, are also required to report to the guardians; and their report should be read to the board of guardians at the first meeting after they may have been presented, and such action taken thereupon as the guardians may think fit.

2. The guardians are not bound to adopt any of the recommendations which may be contained in those reports, but it is reasonable that they should give to them careful consideration, and that they should not refuse to adopt them except on grounds which would satisfy an independent observer, and particularly the paramount authority of the Poor Law Board and Parliament.

3. The responsibility of the management of the workhouse is with the guardians, and is independent of that of their officers, but it is obviously greatly increased when they decline to adopt the recommendation of their officers on matters affecting their several departments.

4. In reference to technical questions, the guardians have the aid of their medical officer in matters appertaining to sanitary and medical arrangements, but the law has not required them to seek periodically the aid of a technical person in reference to the state of the fabric and the property in general.

5. The guardians are required, once in every year at least, to have all the premises whitewashed, and they are to keep the building, furniture, and fittings in good order and repair. They must also remedy without delay defects in drainage, warmth, and ventilation, and other sanitary appliances [*C. O. Art.* 150 & 151].

6. It is desirable that they should cause an Inspection to be made once a year of the buildings, drains, water supply, and the property generally, by a surveyor.

7. They should also have a plan of the buildings prepared, and corrected from time to time, which would show the various rooms, with their destinations, and the positions of all the offices and drains, and be accessible to every guardian.

POOR LAW INSPECTOR'S REPORTS.

8. The Poor Law Board cause their Inspector to visit each workhouse in his district, and to report upon its state at least twice in the year.

9. His report is sent to the Poor Law Board, and if it should be requisite to take action upon it, the Poor Law Board communicate with the guardians.

10. He is not required to report to the guardians, but usually he makes an entry in the visitors'-book, by which he records the date of his visit and remarks upon the state of the workhouse, and this entry is laid before the guardians at their next meeting.

11. His inspection is made directly for the information of the Poor Law Board, and only indirectly for the guidance of the guardians.

REPORT OF POOR LAW INSPECTOR.

12. He is required to report to the Poor Law Board in answer to the following questions :—

Date of last previous visit.

Is the workhouse generally adequate to the wants of the Union, in respect of size and internal arrangement?

Is the provision for the sick and for infectious cases sufficient ?

Are the receiving wards in a proper state?

Is the workhouse school well managed? Insert a copy of any entry in the visiting committee's or other book, made since your last visit, by an inspector of schools.

What is the number of inmates in the workhouse not in communion with the Church of England, and what arrangements, if any, exist for affording them the religious consolation and instruction of ministers of their own separate persuasion ?

Are the provisions of the 19th Section of the Act of the 4 and 5 Wm. IV. c. 76, duly and systematically observed in the management of the workhouse ?

Are there vagrant wards in the workhouse, and are they sufficient ? Are the arrangements for setting the vagrants to work effective, and is the resolution of the guardians under 5 and 6 Vict. c. 57, sec. 5, duly observed ?

Does the visiting committee regularly inspect the workhouse ? Do any of their answers to the queries in the workhouse regulations suggest the propriety of any interference on the part of the commissioners ?

Insert a copy of any entry made since your last visit in the visiting committee's book, or other report book, by a commissioner in lunacy.

Has the maximum number of inmates of the workhouse, fixed by the commissioners, been constantly observed since your last visit ?

Are the proper extracts from the Poor Law Amendment Act, and the regulations of the commissioners, hung up in the workhouse ?

Have all appointments of new officers, and changes in salaries and districts, since your last visit, been reported to the commissioners ?

Is there any officer whose appointment has been sanctioned provisionally ? If so, state your opinion of his fitness.

Have you any reason to believe that any of the books or accounts prescribed by the commissioners are not properly kept ?

Have you observed any illegal practice, or any departure from the regulations of the commissioners ?

State whether the terms of the contracts for vaccination are generally fulfilled, and whether there is any defect in the vaccination arrangements, upon which you think it desirable that the Board should communicate with the guardians.

Has any marked change taken place in the state of the workhouse, the number of the inmates, or the general condition of the Union since your last visit ?

Observations not falling under any of the preceding heads, and points (if any) upon which it is suggested that the Board should write to the guardians.

13. Hence the inspection by the Poor Law Inspector is similar to that of the visiting committee of the guardians, and when the latter body have done their duty, and the board of guardians have taken due action thereupon, the two sets of reports should agree.

14. In not a few instances, however, these two sets of

reports do not agree, and it is the duty of the Inspector to inform the Poor Law Board of defects and requirements which had not been pointed out to the guardians, or which, if pointed out, had not been remedied at the period of the Inspector's visit.

ACTION OF GUARDIANS UPON REPORTS.

15. In some instances the guardians defer action until they have received the report of the Poor Law Inspector, and thus they in fact regard the Inspector as their own officer, whilst in others they resent the remarks made by him and consider both the Inspector and the Poor Law Board as intruders.

16. Both of these views are incorrect and undesirable. The guardians holding themselves responsible for the proper management of the workhouse, should qualify themselves for the efficient discharge of their duties, and should require that their visiting committees should faithfully discharge theirs, in anticipation of the inspection by the Poor Law Board.

17. On the other hand, the extended sphere of observation which belongs to the Poor Law Inspectors, and through them to the Poor Law Board, may be fairly allowed to exceed that of the guardians of a particular Union, and to lead to improved methods of observations, and to an extended knowledge as to the best modes of management, and should be allowed and even welcomed by the guardians.

18. Whilst any gross defects which may be pointed out by the Poor Law Inspector clearly imply neglect or want of knowledge on the part of guardians, there are numerous questions upon which any board of guardians may well receive observations and information from the Poor Law Board and their Inspectors without regarding it as an injurious reflection upon themselves.

19. In a well managed and adequately constructed workhouse there will be harmony of action between both the

local and the central authority, and it should be the aim of all boards of guardians to conform their mode of management to the requirements of the Union, and to the views of the Legislature as represented by the Poor Law Board.

20. It is also the duty of the Poor Law Inspector to attend at least one meeting of the guardians in each year, and it is the practice of many Inspectors to confer with the guardians, as occasion may require, upon defects in accommodation or management.

21. The guardians generally receive the visits of the Inspector with pleasure, and confer with him frankly and readily; and although the Inspector has not power of himself to issue any order, the expression of his wish, supported by his arguments, has always great weight, and not unfrequently induces guardians to effect improvements more readily than a letter of greater authority from the Poor Law Board could effect.

22. It is not the practice of the Inspector to invite the guardians to accompany him at his inspection, since he does not wish the officers to know when he is about to pay his visit; but when he is at liberty to invite them, the guardians always respond readily, and the personal observations and mutual discussion of both parties often lead to the recognition of defects, and to the removal of them.

23. Hence it is desirable that one inspection in the year should be made by the Poor Law Inspector with the visiting committee of the guardians.

Chapter VI.

ADMISSION AND DISCHARGE.

—•—

ADMISSION.

1. The board of guardians [*C. O. Art.* 88] may give an order for the admission into the workhouse of any applicants for relief, but cannot compel them to enter; and it is not usual, except in cases of sickness or desertion, to admit a part and not the whole of a family seeking relief.

2. The guardians are influenced in the discharge of this duty by two principles of conduct, viz.: to offer the workhouse to those who are known to be really destitute, and particularly to orphan and deserted children, to the aged and the sick when destitute, and to test the alleged destitution of an applicant, whether in reference to his own means or to those of his relatives and friends. Hence, for the first, the workhouse should have the repute of providing necessaries and reasonable comforts, with good medical skill, so as not to deter suitable applicants from entering it; whilst for the second, it should be known to supply only bare necessaries, and be not fitted to entice any to enter it who might gain their living by even the least remunerative kind of labour.

3. When the guardians have ordered relief to be given in the workhouse, the clerk forthwith signs a written or printed order of admission [*C. O. Art.* 42] to be given to the applicant, or to some one on his behalf, for presentation at the workhouse within six days from its date [*C. O. Art.* 89].

4. It would be quite correct to say that applicants are

admitted into the workhouse by the order of the board of guardians only, for although the relieving officer, overseer, churchwarden, master, matron, or porter [*C. O. Art.* 88] may provisionally admit, or give orders of admission, they act only until the next ordinary meeting of the board of guardians, when the person so admitted may be retained or discharged by the order of the board.

5. The order of the relieving officer is the most frequent mode of admission.

6. Overseers, and churchwardens who by virtue of their office are overseers, the master, or, he being absent or incapable, the matron, or both the master and the matron being absent or incapable, the porter, may cause an applicant to be admitted only when the necessity is urgent, as from destitution with or without illness [*C. O. Art.* 88 & 214]. The master also admits paupers on receiving orders of removal.

7. Two justices or a stipendiary or police magistrate may order that a child found begging, &c., apparently under fourteen years of age, shall be admitted temporarily into the workhouse whilst inquiry is being made respecting it or the industrial school to which it is about to be sent [29 & 30 *Vict. c.* 118, *s.* 14 & 19, 1866].

8. The sheriff or two justices in Scotland may order the removal of English paupers from Scotland to a workhouse in England [25 & 26 *Vict. c.* 113].

9. Within the metropolitan district, justices may cause a constable or other peace officer to remove the inmates from dangerous structures, and if such inmates have no other abode, to remove them to the workhouse [18 & 19 *Vict. c.* 122, *s.* 80].

10. The visitors of asylums may apply to the board of guardians of a workhouse having proper accommodation to receive chronic cases of lunacy, with the consent of the Commissioners in Lunacy [25 & 26 *Vict. c.* 111, *s.* 8]. This, however, applies only to cases where there is not sufficient accommodation in asylums for the reception of recent and

probably curable cases, and where there is proper accommodation for the care of chronic cases in certain workhouses— such accommodation to include a liberal dietary, ample means of out-door exercise, medical visitation, paid assistants and proper nurses, besides 500 cubic feet of space in dormitories, 400 cubic feet in day rooms, and 600 cubic feet in separate rooms for each inmate.

11. A greater number of the several classes may not be admitted than that fixed by the Poor Law Board, and the clerk is to report any excess to the Poor Law Board [*C. O. Art.* 100]. This regulation is not unfrequently broken in the winter season, when there is an unusual number of applicants, and the fact is not always reported by the clerk.

12. In numerous workhouses the maximum number of the several classes which should be received has not been fixed by the Poor Law Board, and generally the former mode of estimating the numbers was so defective that proper accommodation cannot be found for the number allowed.

DISCHARGE.

13. The guardians may order the discharge of any inmates whom they believe to be able to obtain their own means of living, except persons afflicted with contagious or infectious diseases, which the medical officer certifies to be dangerous to themselves or others.

14. No dangerous lunatic, dangerous idiot, or dangerous imbecile, who may be so reported by the medical officer [25 & 26 *Vic. c.* 3, *s.* 20], nor any pauper of unsound mind, requiring frequent restraint, may be retained in the workhouse, but should be removed to an asylum or licensed house [*C. O. Art.* 101]. Owing, however, to the want of accommodation in the county lunatic asylums, this regulation cannot be always observed.

15. The Commissioners in Lunacy may, at their visitation, order any lunatic to be received into any borough or county asylum, or into any registered hospital or licensed house,

D

who appears to them to be not a proper person to be kept in the workhouse [25 & 26 *Vic. c.* 3, *s.* 31], and the appeal of the guardians against such an order is not to the Poor Law Board, but to the Secretary of State for the Home Department.

16. When lunatics are placed in the workhouse temporarily with a view to their removal to an asylum, no unnecessary delay should occur in taking the necessary steps for their removal, since it is a maxim of law that there are not in workhouses proper conveniences for the detention and cure of dangerous lunatics.

17. The Poor Law Board, in their Instructional Letter of 1842, remark that it must be remembered that with lunatics the first object ought to be their cure by means of proper medical treatment. This can only be obtained in a well-regulated asylum, and therefore the detention of a curable lunatic in a workhouse is highly objectionable, on the score both of humanity and economy.

18. The guardians should direct their medical officer to inform them of any lunatic who is an unfit person to be allowed to remain in the workhouse.

19. The guardians may not open or detain letters addressed to the inmates which contain money, but they may take the money and appropriate it to the maintenance of the pauper during the preceding twelve months [12 & 13 *Vict. c.* 103, *s.* 16].

20. They may reimburse themselves the cost of the burial of a deceased pauper from the effects of such pauper [12 & 13 *Vict. c.* 103, *s.* 16], but otherwise the personal property of deceased paupers belongs to their personal representatives.

Chapter VII.

CLASSIFICATION OF INMATES.

1. The inmates are divided into seven classes, which may be subdivided according to moral conduct and mental or bodily health ; but a man and his wife, above sixty years of age, may not be separated at night if they desire to be together [10 & 11 *Vic. c.* 109, *s.* 23], and the guardians, for special reasons to be entered on their minutes, may direct a boy or girl above ten years of age to be placed with the adults of their own sex.

2. The seven classes are as follows [*C. O. Art.* 98 ; *Instr. Let., Feb.* 5, 1842] :—

MALES.

1. Infirm men.
2. Able-bodied men, and boys above fifteen years of age.
3. Boys between seven and fifteen years of age.

FEMALES.

4. Infirm women.
5. Able-bodied women, and girls above fifteen years of age.
6. Girls between seven and fifteen years of age.
7. Children of both sexes under seven years of age.

3. The guardians are required to provide proper accommodation for these classes, and for any subdivision of them, on moral and medical grounds, which they may see fit [*Instr. Letter*], and also for vagrants of both sexes [*C. O. Art.* 99].

4. There is no legal definition of the term aged and infirm, but in practice it is usual to term those aged and infirm who are sixty years of age and upwards, although there may be some in good health and enjoying vigour of body and mind ; but nearly all are feeble and unable to perform a day's work.

5. When they are much enfeebled, and require the attention of the medical officer, they are classed amongst the sick.

6. The definition of the term able-bodied is left to the discretion of the guardians, and is not by law restricted to any age above fourteen to sixteen years; but in practice all are termed able-bodied who are between fifteen and sixty years of age, and not suffering from disease. The class is avowedly a very ill-defined and mixed one, since it comprehends the labourer and the servant girl out of work, pregnant women awaiting their confinement, suckling women, and such imbeciles as may be able to work, as well as many inmates who are not able to perform a day's work.

7. In the large workhouses it is sometimes subdivided, as regards the women, into single women of good character, and of bad character; married women, and women with children. There is less reason for subdividing the men; but when any inmates of good character, and approaching sixty years of age, have been long in the workhouse, they are sometimes separated from their class and placed with the aged and infirm.

8. Infants and very young children are retained in the women's ward, where the mothers have free access to them, and usually they do not mix with the older children until they are about five years of age; and until they are seven years of age their mothers have access to them at reasonable times.

9. All children who are above that age are placed together, unless there should be so many in the workhouse as to render it desirable to separate the young children, and to keep them in an infants' ward.

10. All the inmates have the right to claim the privileges of their class, but in some of the smaller workhouses there is not separate accommodation for so many as seven classes, and the aged and infirm men are placed with the able-bodied, whilst women of all ages, and even the children, live together. Such an arrangement is very unsatisfactory.

11. The inmates of the several classes should have sepa-

rate dormitories, day rooms, and yards, and be separated, except when in chapel or at meals, and, when at work or taking exercise, the classes should not be able to communicate with each other.

12. Each class should have a separate dietary. The children are, for this purpose, usually divided into four classes, viz. : under two years of age, between two and five years, between five and nine years, and between nine and sixteen years ; the children in the last division commonly have the dietary allotted to able-bodied women, but it is desirable that a special dietary should be provided for them.

13. Casual wayfarers, or vagrants, of all ages and of both sexes, are admitted into separate wards.

14. The sick are all those inmates whose names are entered in the books of the medical officer, for any reason whatever.

15. They are usually divided into the following classes of both sexes, viz. :—Ordinary sick, infectious (as cases of itch and venereal disease), contagious and infectious (as cases of fever of several kinds, and small-pox).

16. The ordinary sick occupy wards in the body of the workhouse, or in a separate building, and the latter arrangement prevails and ought to be universal.

17. Where there is a large proportion of cases which are simply infirm from age, it is sometimes found convenient to place them in wards separate from the sick, either in the infirmary or in the body of the workhouse.

18. The dirty and offensive cases are usually separated from the others and placed in separate wards, either alone or with the foul cases.

19. Lying-in cases are almost universally placed in rooms apart from the general sick wards, but in many workhouses pregnant women awaiting their confinement occupy the same room, and in a few workhouses ordinary cases of sickness are placed in the same ward. They should be entirely separated from any other inmates.

20. Cases of venereal disease are separated from the ordi-

nary sick where they are numerous, not on sanitary, but on moral grounds ; but in the smaller workhouses they are very few in number, and are placed in the ordinary sick wards.

21. Cases of itch are very generally separated from the ordinary sick, but sometimes they are placed with other separation cases, as venereal and dirty cases.

22. Fever and small-pox cases are generally placed in wards apart from the ordinary sick, either in the body of the workhouse, in the ordinary infirmary, or in a separate building termed infectious.

23. The two classes are usually separated from each other, but in a few instances they are placed in the same room. Fever cases are sometimes placed in the wards with the ordinary cases, and increased space is devoted to them.

24. Inmates of unsound mind are separated from the other inmates in the larger workhouses only, whilst in the smaller workhouses they mix with the ordinary inmates.

25. In some workhouses all the imbeciles are regarded as sick, and placed in the infirmary, but usually only such are so classified as are ill from bodily disease, and those only occupy the infirmary wards.

26. The classification and separation of the sick, and the wards which they should occupy, are not formally prescribed by the Poor Law Board, but depend upon the views of the guardians as to the accommodation to be provided, and upon those of the medical officer as to the particular ward into which individual cases may be sent.

27. Every sick person is entitled to such a dietary as may be directed by the medical officer, without the interference of the guardians, or of any other authority, so long as it is a reasonable one [*C. O. Art.* 207, *No.* 4].

Chapter VIII.

TREATMENT AND EMPLOYMENT OF INMATES.

PRINCIPLES OF TREATMENT.

1. The principles which should guide the guardians in the treatment of the several classes of inmates are somewhat varied.

2. The leading principle is that the treatment should not be such as to encourage pauperism or entice the working classes into the workhouse, whilst at the same time the destitute should be supplied with the necessaries of life.

3. The treatment of the able-bodied should be reasonably deterrent, by enjoining daily labour, a spare and non-luxurious, yet sufficient, dietary, and in general strict discipline.

4. Exception must be made in favour of lying-in women from motives of humanity, notwithstanding the tendency which kind treatment has to increase illegitimacy.

5. Exception must also be made in favour of imbeciles, who may fairly claim considerate and kind treatment.

6. The treatment of the aged and infirm must also be humane, notwithstanding the fact that a large proportion of them have become inmates of workhouses by their own fault, since they have ceased to be able to earn their living, and must be dependent upon the aid of others. Some consideration in their dietary may be reasonably given to the extent which age would require in other circumstances ; but undue sympathy will produce evil results, both in their own minds and in that of the labouring classes, and will tend to the increase of pauperism.

7. The treatment of children may reasonably be kind as well as strict, since they have not become inmates by their own fault, and the State performs some of the duties of a parent towards them.

8. To supply them with such food as shall enable them to grow up into strong and healthy men and women, to give them such an education as shall enable them to earn a living, and to train them morally and religiously, is good public policy, since it may remove many of them in after-life from the rank of paupers and produce useful citizens.

9. To neglect their moral training, to allow them to associate with immoral persons, and to rear them in habits of indulgence or indolence, are to be deprecated.

10. The treatment of the sick should be kind, and when the disease is of a curable nature it is sound public policy to afford them every facility for cure.

11. When the disease is incurable, or when the inmates are afflicted with the infirmities of age only, the treatment should be humane and the food appropriate. These constitute the greater part of the sick in workhouses.

12. It is difficult, if not impossible, in the treatment of any class in the workhouse, to pursue at the present day a course which, if pursued alone, might not tend to increase pauperism.

13. The rule that the pauper inmate of a workhouse should not be better treated than the working man who earns his living cannot be adopted without reservation. Whenever a man receives sufficient food, clothing, and shelter, without making an adequate return by his labour, he is in better circumstances than a large portion of working men, and no inmate of a workhouse can have less advantages than these.

14. The aged and the sick receive aid and comforts which they could not have enjoyed at their own homes, and in many instances are much more highly favoured than the men who are taxed to maintain them.

15. Whilst not admitting mere sentimentality as a guide,

the guardians should provide such and only such comforts as are strictly necessary for the wants of the several classes, and the restriction of pauperism must rather be left to the supply of remunerative labour, the spread of thrifty habits, and the effects of religious teaching and of moral influences.

16. The following were the views of the Poor Law Commissioners in 1839, and should still receive due attention; but it may be doubted whether any institution which provides a dry and warm home, good clothing, and sufficient food, with medical advice, medicines, nursing, and other comforts in case of sickness, does not offer advantages which cannot be obtained by a large proportion of the labouring classes in their old age; and whether the only distinction between a workhouse for the aged and an almshouse is not the further restraint of liberty of the inmate of the former than of the latter :—

17. "By means of the workhouse, however, and its regulations, it is in the power of the guardians and the commissioners to place the condition of the pauper accurately at its level, to provide for all his wants effectually—and yet so as to make the relief thus afforded desirable to those only who are *bonâ fide* in need of it. Throughout all the Unions where we have established workhouses, the principle of the workhouse system is very well understood as respects the able-bodied labourers, and with very few exceptions the benefits which arise from its application are admitted and appreciated. With regard to the aged and infirm, however, there is a strong disposition on the part of a portion of the public so to modify the arrangements of these establishments as to place them on the footing of *almshouses*. The consequences which would flow from this change have only to be pointed out to show its inexpediency and danger. If the condition of the inmates of a workhouse were to be so regulated as to invite the aged and infirm of the labouring classes to take refuge in it, it would immediately be useless as a test between indigence and indolence or fraud; it would no longer operate as an inducement to the young and healthy

to provide support for their later years, or as a stimulus to them whilst they have the means to support their aged parents and relatives. The frugality and forethought of a young labourer would be useless if he foresaw the certainty of a better asylum for his old age than he could possibly provide by his own exertions, and the industrious efforts of a son to provide a maintenance for his parents in his own dwelling would be thrown away, and would cease to be called forth, if the almshouse of the district afforded a refuge for their declining years, in which they might obtain comforts and indulgences which even the most successful of the labouring classes cannot always obtain by their own exertions" [*Report on the further amendment of the Poor Law,* 1839, *p.* 47].

EMPLOYMENT OF INMATES.

18. The guardians are to require all the inmates to labour according to their power, and to provide suitable employment for all classes, without affording any remuneration [*C. O. Art.* 112], but no pauper can be required to pound, grind, or break bones, or to prepare bone dust [*C. O. Art.* 113].

19. Able-bodied women, and girls over seven years of age, may be employed in the female sick wards, in household work, or in the care of the infants [*C. O. Art.* 99].

20. Aged women may be employed as nurses, or as the matron's assistants, and aged men may take care of boys above seven years of age, or be employed in the male sick wards [*C. O. Art.* 99].

21. Able-bodied women, and girls above seven years of age, are not allowed to communicate with able-bodied men and boys when at work, but the aged women may be employed in the men's wards.

22. Women may be employed in washing and getting up the linen, in cleaning, and household work generally, and in repairing or making clothes, whilst men are employed in oakum picking, wood chopping, or out-door labour [*C. O. Art.* 99]. But few men are employed in industrial occupa-

tions, and fewer still in grinding corn. Some are occupied in pumping water by a wheel, whilst others are engaged in household work, in going errands, in assisting the porter in the discharge of his general duties, or in the charge of the vagrants and others in the sick wards.

23. Whilst there is usually work enough to be done in a workhouse, the inmates are not always so fully employed as is desirable ; but in the winter, when there are more able-bodied inmates, and in a few workhouses where there are many able-bodied women with children at all periods of the year, it is difficult to provide a sufficient amount of useful employment.

24. Where an inmate is acquainted with some trade, he may be required to work at it in the workhouse, and in numerous workhouses the inmates make the clothes and the shoes used in the workhouse, and do the ordinary cleaning and repairing of the building or fittings, and are very useful [5 & 6 *Vict. c.* 57, *s.* 5].

25. The guardians should consider whether they cannot train some of the female inmates as nurses, and thus enable them to gain a livelihood, whilst at the same time they supply an urgent want in workhouses and other public institutions.

In most workhouses there are women who have been deserted by their husbands, or widows who, having children which they could not maintain, have been compelled to enter the workhouse, and have become a charge upon the rates to the amount of a pound a week or upwards. Some of them are in middle life, able and willing to work, and, from their previous habits might be readily trained to become efficient nurses, and thus be enabled to leave the workhouse and remove their children. There are also in the school a proportion of girls who would prefer that mode of gaining a living, and who, after proper instruction, might be removed from the rank of paupers and employed as servants in the workhouse or elsewhere.

Chapter IX.

REGULATION OF THE WORKHOUSE AND OF VAGRANTS.

———◆———

GENERAL REGULATIONS.

1. The guardians determine the hour of rising and of going to bed of the different classes of inmates, subject to the approval of the Poor Law Board as to the able-bodied and children of both sexes above seven years of age, or adopt the hours which have been suggested by the Poor Law Board for workhouses generally [*Form N., Art.* 102].

2. They should determine the material of which the clothing of the paupers is to be made [*C. O. Art.* 110].

3. They should provide the paupers' complaint-book, and the notices in reference to complaints by the inmates, to be suspended in each ward or room [*Cir. Sept.* 27, 1866], and permit the inmates to attend the board when they desire to make complaints in person.

4. The guardians of the poor have the like control over orphans and deserted children under sixteen years of age as parents and guardians have, and may detain them in the workhouse until that age, if they have reasonable grounds for believing that it would be injurious to the child to allow him to leave the workhouse.

5. They cannot detain any inmate over sixteen years of age against his or her will, unless of unsound mind, or certified by the medical officer to be afflicted with infectious disease which might be injurious to others [30 & 31 *Vic. c.* 106, *s.* 22], or a wife whose husband is in the workhouse,

and who does not refuse to allow her to leave [*Instr. Letter, Feb.*, 1842], or one who is subpœnaed to attend at a court of justice.

6. They cannot punish any inmate who absconds, unless he has taken or damaged the clothes or other property belonging to the guardians; neither may they capture him and bring him back to the workhouse unless he be a person of unsound mind.

7. They have power to give or withhold leave of absence, as for the purposes of exercise or for private business; and with reference to the latter, it is desirable they should consider each case separately as application may be made to them.

8. They may authorise the master to allow inmates who are not members of the Church of England to attend their place of worship on Sunday, Good Friday, and Christmas Day, if it be not at an inconvenient distance; and they may regulate the use of this privilege [*C. O. Art.* 126].

9. They may make regulations as to the admission of Dissenting ministers to visit such of the inmates as desire their attendance and children who are not members of the Church of England.

VAGRANTS.

10. The guardians should provide wards for vagrants apart from those of the other inmates, of a capacity corresponding to the wants of the Union.

11. Where there is an unusual number of applicants at a particular time of the year, as in certain Unions during the hop-picking season, the guardians should provide additional temporary accommodation, corresponding to the requirements of the Union, and not overcrowd the existing wards.

12. The vagrants should be locked in their wards or yards at night, but have means of communicating with some officer in case of emergency; and the water-closet accommodation should be in a place accessible during the night.

13. They may limit the hours of admission, except to cases

of emergency, but it is not desirable that the wards should be closed before nine o'clock at night.

14. They may detain vagrants in the morning, for any period not exceeding four hours from the breakfast of the ordinary inmates; but usually they allow them to leave as soon as the task of work shall have been completed.

15. A task of work is recommended for vagrants by the Poor Law Board [*Circular, 28th Nov.*, 1868], and whenever a task of work has been adopted by boards of guardians and approved by the Poor Law Board, it becomes compulsory; but a limitation of the duration of labour is provided to meet the case of those who are unable to perform the task in the allotted time.

16. The following is the recommendation referred to :—

Circular, 28th Nov., 1868.

PROPOSED TASK OF WORK FOR VAGRANTS.

The master of the workhouse shall set every adult person not suffering under any temporary or permanent infirmity of body, being an occasional poor person, who shall be relieved in the said workhouse, in return for the food and lodging afforded to such person, to perform the following task of work, that is to say :—

Males—

The breaking of $1\frac{1}{2}$ to 3 cwt. of stones, according to the hardness of the stone.

or

The picking of $1\frac{1}{2}$ pound of oakum.

Females—

The picking of half a pound of oakum,

[or such other task of work as the guardians may deem more suitable and as may be sanctioned by the Poor Law Board.]*

Provided that no such person shall be detained against his or her will for the performance of such task or work, for any time exceeding four hours from the hour of breakfast of the ordinary inmates of the workhouse.

And provided also that such amount of work shall not be required from any person to whose age, strength, and capacity it shall appear not to be suited.

* This alternative to apply to males as well as females.

17. Should the vagrant refuse or neglect to perform the

task of work suited to his strength, age, and capacity, or should he injure or destroy his own clothes, or the property of the guardians, he may be taken before justices as an idle and disorderly person [*5 Geo. IV. c. 83, s. 3*], but where there is no justice residing within several miles of the workhouse, it is scarcely possible that this power can be uniformly exercised.

18. The following circular on vagrancy has recently been issued by the Poor Law Board (28th Nov., 1868), but the subject is now receiving further consideration, with a view to the establishment of a uniform system of treatment of this class of persons :—

" The Poor Law Board, having received from various Unions representations on the subject of the increase of vagrancy, and a request for such information and advice as they may be able to supply, think it desirable to issue the following circular.

So long ago as the year 1848 the difficulties attending the administration of relief to the casual poor were brought prominently under the notice of the Poor Law Board, and a minute on the subject, prepared and signed by the late Mr. Charles Buller, was in consequence circulated among the different Unions in England and Wales. The Board have reason to believe that in the Unions in which the suggestions of that minute have been steadily acted upon, those difficulties have been to some extent diminished.

It appears to the Board, however, that the time has arrived when it is necessary to bring again under the consideration of guardians the main principles embodied in that circular, with a view to their more general and systematic adoption.

A sound and vigilant discrimination as regards those who apply for relief as casual poor, with a view to distinguish between those whose destitution gives them a claim to such relief, and those who, not being destitute, throw themselves habitually on the public rates or on private charity, is of primary importance ; and the guardians will best secure the proper exercise of this discrimination by placing the relief of the casual poor in the hands of officers who, while they relieve the destitute, will, at the same time, have sufficient firmness to repel the impostor. The employment, where practicable, of some member of the police force, or of some person clothed with the authority of a constable, as an assistant relieving officer for this purpose, is shown by general experience to be the most expedient course.

The professional tramp will be comparatively unwilling to confront such an officer, while to the honest but destitute wayfarer his inquiries will occasion no alarm.

By whatever agency, however, relief is administered, the following measures should, as the Board think, be uniformly adopted : —

1. The name and occupation of the applicant, with the place from which he comes and that to which he is going, should be recorded in a book, so as to admit of reference.

2. The applicant for relief should be searched, and if adequate means of support are found upon him, refused relief.

3. If relieved in the workhouse, he should in every case (except when ill) be put in a bath ; and,

4. A certain task should be required and enforced (unless where exceptional circumstances appear to justify exemption) from all who have received a night's relief in the workhouse or in the vagrant ward.

It appears to the Board of great importance that, as far as possible, the diet of the casual paupers in different work-houses should (except in the case of sickness or infirmity) be uniform, and that a task of work similar in kind and quantity should be required wherever relief is given, and enforced under vigilant superintendence.

In all cases of persons refusing to perform the task of work required from them, the person refusing should be taken before a magistrate, to be dealt with according to law.

With a view to the attainment of such uniformity, the

Board append to this circular suggestions as to food and work, to which they request the early consideration of the guardians, and which, after receiving and considering any observations that may be offered, they propose, so far as may be necessary and expedient, to embody in an order.

With regard to the mode of lodging applicants at night, if ascertained to be destitute, the Board are of opinion that, where practicable, the most advisable course is to provide separate accommodation for each individual who is relieved in the workhouse or vagrant ward.

Such a plan seems, though on different grounds, properly applicable to both the classes of casual applicants with which guardians have to deal. The deserving but destitute way-farer, such, for instance, as, in the words of Mr. Buller's circular, "the widow or orphan deprived at a distance from home of their natural supporter, or the honest artisan or labourer who is seeking the employment of which accidental circumstances have suddenly deprived him," should, for obvious reasons, be exempted from the necessity of associa-tion with the idle and the profligate who are to be found in the vagrant ward.

On the other hand, it is very important to deprive the professional tramp of the opportunity of that free and unrestrained companionship which unavoidably takes place in a vagrant ward, and which is especially agreeable to him. With this double object in view, guardians in some Unions have, with the sanction of the Board, adopted the system of placing all casual poor who apply for relief, and who are ascertained to be destitute, in small rooms or cells, each holding (except in the case of a mother and a young child or children) only one person. If accompanied with due pre-cautions, as regards inspection and the power of obtain-ing assistance in case of illness, this system appears to the Board well worthy of adoption.

The Board think it right to advert to a system which has been adopted more or less generally in several counties in England, with the view to effect a discrimination between the deserving wayfarer and the professional tramp.

E

Under this plan a ticket is given at the Union workhouse at which the applicant has first been relieved, setting forth the name, occupation, and cause of seeking relief, and place from which he comes, and marked so as to be available at certain workhouses along the particular route which the holder has previously notified his wish to take.   When the ticket is presented at any of such workhouses, provided that the condition of walking a certain defined number of miles from the last place of receiving relief has been fulfilled, the holder is allowed the relief suited to his condition without the necessity of performing the task of work which would be required in the case of persons not possessing such ticket, or who, if possessed of it, had failed to fulfil the prescribed condition.

The Board are not in possession as yet of sufficient experience to justify them in pronouncing any opinion as to the results of this system, but they think it desirable that it should be brought under the notice of the guardians, as its success must depend to a great extent on its more or less general adoption by neighbouring Unions.

In conclusion, the Board, in the words of the former circular, desire again to " impress upon boards of guardians the absolute necessity of discriminating by careful investigation between real and simulated destitution.   It is to be always borne in mind that, while the law requires that relief should be given to those who really need it, it equally prohibits the misapplication of the public funds to those who are not destitute."   Such a misapplication is unjust to the ratepayers, and leads to public evils of a serious character ; and while it is incumbent on the guardians to exercise the greatest care in the expenditure of all the funds entrusted to them, in no part of the administration of the Poor Law is such care at the present moment so urgently required as in that which relates to the relief of the vagrant population of the country."

Chapter X.

CONSTRUCTION OF WORKHOUSES.

1. Each of the seven classes of inmates before referred to requires separate accommodation, and a suitable number of married couples' sleeping wards should be provided, but the precise nature and extent of the accommodation required for the inmates varies in a degree with the public opinion of the day, and has not been rigidly fixed by the Poor Law Board.

2. The leading principles are convenience of administration and the requirements, in a sanitary point of view, of the several classes, and both are based upon experience and technical knowledge.

3. The Legislature has not entered into details upon this subject, neither have the Poor Law Board prescribed complete plans for adoption by guardians, but they have very recently issued " Instructions " as to accommodation, modes of construction, fittings and appliances, which merit the attention of the guardians, and will be guides to them and to their architects and other officers.

4. The following are the " Instructions " in reference to the construction of workhouses .—

Points to be attended to in the construction of workhouses.

    1. Accommodation, including separate dormitories, day rooms, and yards, should be provided for the following classes :—

        The aged of each sex.
        The able-bodied   do.
        The children   do.
        The sick   do.

2. Provision should also be made, so far as practicable, for the subdivision of the able-bodied women into two or three classes, with reference to moral character or behaviour, the previous habits of the inmates, or such other grounds as may seem expedient.

3. The sick should occupy a separate building, and in the larger workhouses be divided into the following classes :—

> Ordinary sick of both sexes.
> Lying-in women, with a separate labour room adjoining the lying-in ward.
> Itch cases of both sexes.
> Dirty and offensive cases of both sexes.
> Venereal cases of both sexes.
> Fever and small-pox cases of both sexes.
> Children.

4. The accommodation for imbeciles, if they are retained in the workhouse, should be in general accordance with the regulations of the Commissioners in Lunacy.

5. A detached building should be provided, with separate rooms, for fever and small-pox cases of both sexes.

6. The infectious wards should not be inconveniently distant from the paid nurse's apartments, and there should be bells communicating from one to the other.

7. A detached wash-house should, under ordinary circumstances, be provided for washing infected linen, &c.

8. The length of wards should be calculated according to the following minimum wall space for each bed :—

> For dormitories only, four feet.
> For ordinary sick wards, six feet.
> For lying-in, fever, and small-pox wards, seven to eight feet.

9. Day rooms for the sick should afford accommodation for at least one-half of those who occupy the day and night rooms, and those for the inmates in health should be large enough to receive nearly the whole number of their respective classes. Fifteen to twenty feet as a minimum floor space should be allowed to each person in the day rooms.

Day rooms, both for children and adults, should be upon the ground floor, unless in the case of aged inmates another arrangement be deemed desirable. On the other hand, it may sometimes be desirable to provide sleeping accommodation on the ground floor for inmates who are too infirm to go up and down stairs.

10. Ordinary wards should be not less than eighteen feet in width, and ten feet in height.

11. When there is a corridor at the side of ordinary wards, or between two sets of them, there should be windows in the corridor walls.

12. No wards should be placed side by side, without a corridor between them.

13. No corridor in any new building should be less than six feet in width.

14. Sick wards to hold two rows of beds should be at least twenty feet in width, and ten to twelve feet in height, and have windows on opposite sides.

15. The gangway through all wards of the above dimensions should be down the centre, so that two complete rows of beds may be placed in each ward.

16. In the infirmary, one room, or a suite of rooms communicating by a gangway, should rarely exceed ninety feet in length.

17. Such a room, or suite of rooms, may be connected with a similar suite in the same line by the central part of the building, in which would be placed the apartments of the nurses and other offices, or they may be placed in blocks parallel, or otherwise, connected by a corridor.

18. When there are two or more of such blocks of building they should be placed so far apart as to allow free access to air and light; and also have, where possible, such an aspect that the direct rays of the sun may pass between them during several hours of each day.

19. Blocks of buildings directly connected at a right angle or at an acute angle should as far as possible be avoided.

20. No buildings occupied by inmates as sleeping-rooms should be erected upon the boundary line of the workhouse site.

21. Sick wards to hold one row of beds only are not re-commended, but, if adopted, they should be at least twelve feet in width, and have the gangway and fire-place on the side opposite to the beds.

22. When two rows of beds are placed in a day and night ward of sixteen feet or less in width they should be placed with their sides to the walls.

23. Arrangements should be made for the distribution of hot and cold water to bath rooms and sick wards.

24. It will often be desirable to provide a lift for raising heavy articles from floor to floor.

25. In the cases in which hot water is not laid on, or very near, to sick wards, the stoves should be provided with a small self-feeding boiler.

26. Suitable kitchen and sculleries should be provided in connection with infirmary wards.

27. One general dining-hall should be provided for all the inmates who may be able to leave their wards.

28. Suitable work-rooms should be provided in the respective yards of the adult inmates.

29. Suitable store-rooms for the linen and clothing of the several classes of inmates, and for dry and other goods, should be provided in convenient situations.

30. In workhouses having a large number of children

there should be, in addition to the school-rooms, day rooms, covered play sheds in their yards, and industrial work-rooms.

31. The general wash-house and laundry should be a detached one-story building, as should also be the wash-house and laundry for the training of female children, and those for the sick and infectious wards, where such are required. In no case should they be ceiled, and in all cases they should have Louvre ventilators in the ridge of the roof.

32. Where practicable, the water for the boilers and wash-tubs in the general wash-house should be heated by steam.

33. The ventilation should be effected by special means, apart from the usual means of doors, windows, and fire-places, and so arranged that each ward may be brought into constant communication with the outer air. No plan is recommended for universal adoption. One of the simplest methods is the use of air bricks, 9 by 3, or 9 by 6 inches, covered on the inside with finely perforated metal (the perforations being about $\frac{1}{10}$th of an inch in diameter), inserted in the upper and lower parts of the external walls (that is, near the floor level, and immediately under the wall plate), by which only a small body of air would be admitted in one place, and it would be so diffused as to prevent much draught. No permanent means of closing these ventilators should be provided. The internal and external openings may be on the same plane, or the one may be one or two feet above the other, and both be connected by a short shaft. Ventilating fireplaces, whether placed in the middle of the ward, or elsewhere, are found to be very useful. It is very desirable that where hot water pipes are used they should run round the wards, and be so arranged that a portion of the fresh air admitted

into the room should pass over them, and thus be warmed.

34. No external aperture, other than a window, above the bed should be less than from six to seven feet above the pillow.

35. External windows should be filled in with double-hung wooden sashes, and should extend to within 1 foot of the ceiling, and to 3 or 3½ feet from the floor of the ward.

36. When windows or fanlights look into internal spaces they should not be fixed, but hung and stopped so that they may be used as ventilators, and always remain open not less than one inch.

37. The windows are not to be glazed with opaque glass except for special reasons to be approved by the Poor Law Board.

38. Privies are not recommended, but if provided, they should be so constructed as that they can be readily cleared at short intervals, and left as clean as possible. Water-closets, with pans, traps, and a constant supply of water, or suitable earth or other closets, may be advantageously used instead, in many cases.

39. Water-closets should be placed in projections from the building to which they are attached, and have in them, and in the passage leading to them, external windows on opposite sides to ensure a cross draught.

40. Glazed stone pottery-ware, or enamelled iron slop and waste water shoots, should be supplied on the bedroom floors in all the larger workhouses.

41. Soil drains should be constructed of glazed stone-ware pipes, not less than 6 inches in diameter.

42. No soil drains should pass under an inhabited building, and if any other drains pass under such building they should be so placed as to be conveniently accessible for repairs.

43. All drains, and connections therewith, should be properly trapped ; and means provided for flushing them. A plan of the drains should be made and hung up in a convenient place, in each workhouse.

44. In cases in which the sewage from the workhouse premises cannot be conveyed into public sewers, it should be collected in closed tanks, placed at such a distance from the inhabited parts of the work-house as to preclude any nuisance to the inmates ; and the tanks should be so constructed that the contents may be available, by means of a pump or otherwise, for agricultural purposes.

45. In addition to the ordinary means of water supply to the workhouse, the rain water from the build-ings should be collected in covered tanks, conve-niently placed for the purposes of the wash-houses, and be cleansed from time to time.

46. Airing yards for the inmates should be of sufficient size ; if partially or wholly paved with stone or brick, or asphalted or gas-tarred, they are often better than if covered with gravel.

47. All yards to be so formed as that the water may readily pass off into drains.

48. Yards for the sick, aged, and children, to be enclosed with dwarf walls and palisades where practicable.

49. The porter's lodge, receiving and vagrant wards, should, when practicable, occupy a separate position at the front of the workhouse.

50. The receiving and vagrant wards should be provided with water-closets, baths, and lavatories, and with means of supplying warmth, and of drying the wet clothes of the vagrants.

51. A bell should be connected with the porter's room from each of these wards.

52. Small yards, and a work-room, and a covered shed for working in in bad weather, should be attached to the vagrant wards.

53. A disinfecting stove should be provided in the entrance building, and a room for storing the paupers' own clothes.

54. The external walls of all buildings of two or more stories high, and of school-rooms, should, if of brick, be not less than 14 inches thick; and if of stone, not less than 18 inches thick.

55. The staircases should be constructed of stone, and be " Return staircases," not less than 7 feet in width. The steps supported on iron strings, or properly tailed into the walls, and the landings supported on iron girders. All the steps should be " flyers," none exceeding 7 inches rise, and those to the sick wards not exceeding $6\frac{1}{2}$ inches rise. Steps of the former rise should be 10 inches tread, and of the latter rise 11 inches tread.

56. The floors of dormitories, day rooms, school-rooms, and also of the water-closets, bath rooms, and lavatories for the sick, should be boarded; and the boards grooved and tongued.

57. No roof of any sleeping room should be open, or ceiled higher than two feet above the wall plate.

58. The walls of all sick wards should be plastered internally.

59. The timber used in the construction of workhouses should be Baltic fir and English oak.

60. There should be a fire escape in each workhouse.

61. The plans, sections (longitudinal and transverse), and elevations for new workhouses, or for alterations and additions to existing workhouses, are to be drawn to a scale of not less than $\frac{1}{8}$ of an inch to a foot, and should show, in addition to the usual details, the proposed number and position of the beds in the several wards. These plans should be accompanied with a general plan, drawn to a scale of $\frac{1}{16}$ of an inch to a foot, of the workhouse premises (exclusive of the intended agricultural

land), showing the position of the proposed drains, soil and water tanks. Further, the specification of works, and also a description of the general system of heating and ventilation proposed, should accompany the plans.

62. A dead-house should be provided.

63. Refractory wards should be provided.

5. These Instructions will lead to a considerable degree of uniformity in the erection of the same class of buildings, and tend to prevent waste of expenditure in inefficient erections, whilst they will exactly adapt the space to the number of beds required, and prevent loss of space by the improper position of doors, fire-places, and passages, and afford a ready mode of determining the number of beds which should be placed in a ward. They will also save much needless expense and trouble to architects, and through them to the guardians in the preparation of unsuitable plans.

6. The absence of such Instructions has led, during the past thirty years, to the erection of many narrow, low, and inconvenient rooms in workhouses, and to great waste in the bed-holding capacity of rooms by the inconvenient position of doors and gangways, and as such buildings cannot be adapted to the requirements of the present day, great expenditure in the erection of new buildings has become necessary.

7. The principal clauses in these instructions refer to the width and height of wards, the character of sick wards, the amount of wall space for each bed, the height and position of the windows, the most simple means of ventilation, lavatory and water-closet accommodation, and the mode of construction of floors, walls, and yards.

8. The width of ordinary wards has been adopted, not only for present convenience, but to enable the guardians to appropriate them to other purposes, should the future requirements of the Union demand it, without inducing the necessity for material alterations or new erections.

9. The width of sick wards is to be greater than that of ordinary wards, since with their habitation by day and night, and the presence of nurses, greater space is required between the feet of the beds.

10. The height of both has been so apportioned that proper ventilation may be effected without injury to the inmates from the entrance or exit of air at the top of the ward, and to afford the requisite cubical space at the least cost ; and as all these requirements are greater in sick than in ordinary wards, the former should have the greater height.

11. The limitation of the height to which the ceiling may be carried into the roof is to protect the ward from great changes of temperature, and to allow the windows in the side walls to be sufficiently high.

12. The width between the beds has been fixed at the smallest space in which a man may conveniently stand between them, whilst that of the sick wards has been extended so that a nurse may move about between them with facility, and that the breath of a sick person, which is sometimes foul, should not be offensive to the occupant of an adjoining bed.

13. The requirements of the ordinary sick have been based upon the fact that the ward is in a degree occupied by the patients both day and night, and for convenience of administration, but not upon supposed injurious emanations which require to be diluted lest the respiring of them by others should be injurious. In reference to the respiration, the sick for the most part taint the air as little, or even less, than healthy persons.

14. The increased space which is required between the beds of lying-in, fever, and small-pox cases, affords a larger amount of cubic space to each inmate, and enables injurious or offensive emanations or discharges to be diluted.

15. With wards of the above dimensions, it is easy to calculate the number of beds which may be placed in them. The wall space is the guide, and it amounts to four feet for an ordinary inmate, six feet for an ordinary case of sickness,

and seven to eight feet for offensive and infectious cases, the difference consisting chiefly in the width of the interval between the beds.

16. Such infectious cases as itch and venereal disease do not demand a larger wall space than that for the ordinary sick, since the infection is not carried by the air.

17. The space for children has not been fixed in the Instructions, but five feet are required for a double bed, and three feet nine inches for a single bed. Single beds should be provided for one-third of the children, seeing that about that proportion of children are over eleven or twelve years.

18. Economy, therefore, demands that the length of new wards should be multiples of these several amounts of wall space.

19. The height and position of the windows have been fixed so that the inmates, even when very young, or when lying in bed, may look through them at the lower part, and that when opened a little at the upper part for ventilation, the draught will be distant from the occupant of a bed.

20. The system of providing air bricks as ventilators has the advantage of economy and simplicity, and by each admitting only a small quantity of air, they may be numerous, and renew the air in many parts of the room without very perceptible draught. Other systems may be adopted with it if desired by the architect or guardians.

21. Lavatory and water-closet accommodation should be sufficient, but not in excess, since they are sources of uncleanliness. Cross draughts are essential in order to remove foul smells, and prevent them from entering the wards.

22. Earth-closets are used as night stools in country places with advantage, but when night stools are selected the pan should be sealed in the manner patented by Mr. Weare of Wolverhampton, Mr. Jennings of Lambeth, and other sanitary engineers.

23. Boarding of floors is now less expensive than formerly, and such floors are drier and warmer than stone or brick, and are fitted for the sick, the aged, and children. The

mode of construction is to prevent the opening of the joints when the wood becomes dry, and thus prevent the dirty water from passing under the flooring.

24. Bare and uneven walls have a cheerless aspect, and cause dirt to accumulate. To plaster them saves a portion of the expense which would be required to give the finish to the bare brick wall.

25. To cover the walls with an impervious cement is costly, but useful.

26. Rough, dirty, or wet yards are expensive from the wear of boots and clothes, and from the dirt within the wards which they cause. It is in the end much more economical to flag, brick, or gas-tar them.

27. The necessity for day rooms for the ordinary inmates is not denied, although the able-bodied and the aged sometimes occupy the same room, but it is not so generally allowed for the sick. They are necessary for the sick in order to allow the dormitory to be partially emptied and well ventilated during the day, whilst they are convenient to the convalescent in connection with the yards, and of advantage to those who are obliged to keep their beds, by allowing the absence of others to render the wards more quiet.

28. It is desirable that there should be one, rather than several, dining-rooms for such of the inmates as are able to leave their rooms, and that the several day rooms should not be used as dining-rooms.

29. Dimensions for school-rooms and children's day rooms are not given in the Instructions, but it is desirable that they should be 18 to 20 feet wide, and have external windows on both sides. The height of the school-room should be 12 to 16 feet.

30. There is no advantage in having windows in one side only in a school-room, or in placing the windows so high that the children cannot see the ground through them, but, on the contrary, there are disadvantages of a sanitary nature.

31. The floor space for each child in a school-room should be 8 feet to 12 feet. That of the separate day room should be

6 to 8 feet, since it will rarely occur that all the children will occupy it at the same time ; and if the school-room and day room be in one, the space should be 12 feet.

32. The present construction, ventilation, and space of school-rooms are unsatisfactory, and tend to induce feeble health in the children.

33. Separate cells for vagrants, or at least for a portion of them, are desirable. The size of each room should not be less than 5 feet wide by 9 feet long, and 9 to 10 feet high, and the space required is greater than is necessary for one person in an associated room. Care will be required to sufficiently ventilate wards which are so small, and yet to avoid direct draught.

SITE OF THE WORKHOUSE.

34. The following suggestions in reference to the site and the preparation of plans for the construction of workhouses may be of use both to architects and guardians.

35. The site must necessarily be smaller in a large town than in the country, and in the latter it should be sufficiently large to provide employment and means of exercise and re-creation for the inmates.

36. It should not be inconveniently distant from a town, or from railway communication, for the convenience both of the guardians and the friends of the inmates. Neither should it be placed on one side of a Union having a large area ; but it need not be precisely in the centre of the Union, if to do so would interfere with convenience of access.

37. It should not be placed upon a high hill, on account of undue exposure of the sick and aged to cold winds, and the difficulty of access of aged and feeble persons seeking relief; neither should it be enclosed in a valley ; a gentle slope facing the south and west is the most suitable.

38. The soil should, if possible, be porous, but with a good slope for drainage, the subsoil may be of clay.

WATER SUPPLY AND DRAINAGE.

39. A sufficient supply of good water upon the ground or from public water works, with means of good surface and subsoil drainage, are necessary.

40. Cesspools, reservoirs, or tanks for the reception of sewage, should not be permitted, if it be possible at a moderate cost to carry the sewage matters off the premises by a private or public system of sewage.

41. When they are necessary, they should be so constructed, that the fluid parts will drain off at an elevation of about three feet, and the tank for the more solid matters may have an outlet through which the latter may be removed from time to time.

42. They should be covered, so as to lessen the effect of heat in promoting fermentation, but the effect should be sought rather by the plan recommended in the preceding paragraph.

43. Layers of charcoal in the coverings of the tanks are of little value, for after a short period they become saturated with the gases produced by the fermentation of the sewage, and it is not the practice to renew them.

44. All such tanks should be far removed from the inhabited part of the building, and from wells, and care should be taken so to construct the pipes leading to them that they may not leak and saturate the soil around them.

45. Stables are necessary in country Unions, and should be provided even where the workhouse may be near a town, as they increase the facilities for the attendance of the guardians.

46. Piggeries are usually advantageous in country Unions, since there is much refuse food and garden produce in a workhouse, which cannot be otherwise so profitably employed; and as the bacon should be eaten by the inmates, it is not needful that the pigs should be long fed on expensive food.

47. Wherever cows can be conveniently kept, it is very desirable that they should be obtained in order to regularly provide the requisite supply of milk to the children, the sick, and other inmates.

48. Piggeries, cow sheds, and stables should not be placed near to the inhabited part of the buildings and the wells.

49. It is frequently desirable that the quality of drinking water and other foods should be tested chemically, and for that purpose the analysis of Mr. F. Manning, 3, Leadenhall Street, London, E.C., may be relied upon.

50. On the subject of ventilation, Mr. Dewsbury has made a communication to the Poor Law Board which proves that he is fully alive to its importance in saving space, and consequently cost, in the building of workhouses and infirmaries.

Mr. Potts has arranged a ventilating cornice which is both useful and ornamental. It is divided into two horizontal chambers for the ingress and egress of air, one of which is in communication with the outer air and the other with the chimney flue.

Mr. Barber, architect of the Basford Union, has arranged a blower by which the draught of open fireplaces may be regulated. The metal plate is counterpoised by weights, so so that it may be easily moved, and will remain in any position.

51. Mr. Finch has exhibited at the offices of the Poor Law Board a number of useful sanitary inventions.

Chapter II.

ARRANGEMENT OF THE BUILDINGS.

1. The buildings must vary in character somewhat with the number of inmates, and particularly as to the necessity for several detached buildings. But as new workhouses of very small size will probably not be built in future, and as public opinion is in favour of detached buildings, the necessity for variation in character is not great.

2. There is some increase in the cost of detached over combined buildings, but that consideration should not have undue weight.

3. There should be four or five distinct blocks of buildings, but all so situate with respect to the centre, that the administration by the officers, and the supply of cooked food, may not be inconvenient.

FIRST BLOCK.

4. The first block should contain the offices of the porter, relieving officer, and clerk, the board-room, the waiting-room, and the receiving wards and vagrant wards, with store-rooms for inmates' own clothes, and the fumigating stove.

5. It should be of one story only, so as not to throw much shade upon the yards behind, and not to seriously impede the view of the next block of buildings.

6. The vagrant wards for both sexes, and the receiving wards for both sexes, may each occupy one end of the block; or the males of each class, and the females of each class, may severally occupy the ends; but the first plan is the more convenient for administration.

7. Male vagrant wards should be fitted up with an inclined

wooden frame divided into berths of 2 feet 3 inches in width, by boards 10 inches high. The length of the wooden bed should be 6½ to 7 feet, and if the platform occupy one side of the room, the gangway should be 4 feet to 6 feet in width.

8. There should be fires or other sources of warmth in the winter, and means of drying wet clothes, with lavatories, water-closet or earth-closet, and bath, with water laid on, for each sex.

9. Each should be enclosed in a small yard for isolation, and to permit of work being supplied to the men.

10. The receiving wards should not be large, except in the largest workhouses, since no applicant should remain longer than one night in them, and usually there is no need for a day room, or for more than one room for each sex. They should be fitted up with iron bedsteads and proper bedding, with lavatory, water or earth closets, and baths connected with them, and be properly warmed by an open fire.

SECOND BLOCK.

11. The second block of buildings should be the main building, and provision should be made in it for the master, matron, and assistant matron, where one is appointed, and for all the adult inmates except the sick.

12. An entrance hall with the officers' apartments and offices should occupy the centre part, and in the rear of them the dining-hall, kitchen, scullery, stores, wash-houses, and laundry should be placed.

13. The master's office should be close to the entrance hall. The dining-room should be approached from the back of the entrance hall, either with or without any intervening lobby. The kitchens, stores, &c., should be placed in one of the sides of the dining-hall, with a wide glass-covered gangway between them, so as to allow of free ventilation. The wash-house and laundry should be further in the rear in connection with the able-bodied women's yard.

14. A good larder, well ventilated and cool, should be pro-

vided for the meat ; and well drained cellars, partly or wholly underground, are most useful.

15. The dining-hall should be ample in size (providing 6 to 8 feet of floor space for each inmate), and have windows on both sides, which should be opened after every meal, to supply good ventilation and to maintain a proper temperature.

16. The officers' apartments need not have a larger area than 12 by 14 or 14 by 14 feet each, and where two rooms are provided for the master and matron, such space is afforded for their children, should they be married.

17. The smaller workhouses should have the main building of only one room in depth, and thus allow external windows in both sides, but in the larger ones there should be two rooms separated by a wide corridor which should be well lighted and ventilated by openings through the floor, and by large windows at the end.

18. The different staircases should lead to or from this corridor, and the entrance to the wards should be from it, or from the staircases. In all cases there should be windows in the corridor walls into every ward, to give light and air, but they may be placed high up in the wall, and each filled in with one sash swinging from the centre.

19. The whole of the ground floor should be devoted to day rooms and offices, except one or two wards on each side for the use of very infirm men and women, in which they may sleep.

20. This building may be of two or three stories, according to the number of inmates.

21. The yards for the aged and infirm should, where practicable, be placed upon the southern side of the main building, and therefore between the first and second blocks, whilst those for the able-bodied should be at the back of the second block and near to the kitchens, wash-houses, and workshops.

22. They should be of ample size, so as to separate the blocks of buildings, and allow free exposure to the sun and air.

THIRD BLOCK.

23. The third block should be the schools, in those Unions where children are retained and educated in the workhouse. It should provide a school-room and a day room for each sex, with class-rooms and infants' rooms, according to the number of the children, with two rooms for each teacher, and a sufficient number of dormitories for the children.

24. Lavatories, baths, swimming baths for boys in the larger schools, urinals, and water or earth closets, should be placed in positions not inconveniently distant from the day rooms.

25. Play sheds, and a pole for gymnastics, should be erected in the yards, and proper workshops should be provided for the industrial training of the boys, and wash-house and laundry for the training of the girls.

26. The schools should be so situate that the yard may not be exposed to the north and east, and not so distant from the matron's apartments and the kitchen as to render it inconvenient in wet weather for the children to go to work in the wash-house.

27. All the rooms should have external windows in both sides.

28. In small workhouses where the number of children is too few to render it desirable that they should occupy a separate building, they may be placed at either end of the main building, and the above-mentioned accommodation divided between them. In all cases there should be a day room, separate from the school-room. Their yards should be on the southern side of the second block, and by the side of those for the aged.

FOURTH BLOCK.

29. The fourth block of buildings is the infirmary. It should be so placed that neither of the yards connected with it shall be in the shade of the main building, and there

should be a southern and western aspect. It should consist of two stories.

30. The administrative department should occupy the centre, either with or without a central hall, according to the size of the building; to include the nurses' sitting-room and kitchen on the ground floor, with the nurses' bed-room and surgery, or store-room, on the upper floor, the passage between the two sides of the infirmary being through the kitchen below and surgery above.

31. These rooms need not be larger than 10 feet by 12 feet.

32. At either hand the staircases and entrance to the wards should be placed, and the wards for the two sexes should be placed at either hand of the centre, and not one over the other. The staircases should communicate with the wards on their own side, and, by the passage through the kitchen and surgery, with the master's apartments and wards on the other side of the infirmary.

33. The entrance into the wards should be in the centre of the ward.

34. The first ward from the staircases should be the day room, and beyond it wards for the very infirm inmates, or for surgical cases, communicating with each other by the centre of the ward.

35. The upper floor should be entirely devoted to dormitories for the sick. The lying-in cases should have a ward at the end of the series most distant from the staircases. If they need a day or convalescent room, it should be the first of their series, whilst the labour-rooms, if required, should be the last.

36. The lavatories, water or earth closets, bath, and water shoots, should be placed in a projecting building at the back of each staircase, with a short lobby, to allow of the admission of light and air to the staircase.

37. When the ground is so inclined that a basement story is required to obtain the proper level, it would be convenient to place there the warming apparatus to heat

water and to charge the bath, and to raise the charged baths (constructed to have wheels), at the centre of the building, to each floor.

38. All the rooms, except those at the centre, should have external windows on both sides.

39. Where it is desired to isolate itch and venereal cases, two wards should be provided on the ground floor of the infirmary, at either end, which should be enclosed in a separate yard, and be approached by the officers through the central yard. Separate day rooms are not required for them, and therefore as these rooms would be used by day and night, ample space should be allowed.

FIFTH BLOCK.

40. The fifth block is the fever and small-pox building, and should consist of two stories.

41. These buildings are usually small and intended to accommodate a very few persons only at one time.

42. It should offer not less than two wards on each side, one of which would ordinarily be used as a day or convalescent ward, but would be available for the separation of classes of cases when required—as, for example, two kinds of fever, or small-pox and fever.

43. Where it is intended that small-pox cases should be admitted as well as fever cases, it is convenient to erect one or two rooms for each sex, at either end of the fever building, to be enclosed in a separate yard, and the upper one (if any) approached by a separate staircase at the end.

44. The general plan of construction of this block should be that of the fourth block, but as in most country Unions cases of fever are rarely admitted, and a paid nurse is not appointed to the separate charge of them, one nurse's room will suffice, and the room behind it will be both a kitchen and a place in which the movable bath will be placed whilst the room which is over both of them may be used for a special case of either sex, or for children.

Chapter III.

FURNITURE AND FITTINGS.

—♦—

1. The following are the suggestions which the Poor Law Board have issued in reference to the fittings of workhouse wards:

POINTS TO BE ATTENDED TO AS REGARDS FITTINGS AND MEDICAL APPLIANCES.

A.—*For the Ordinary Dormitories.*

1. The bedsteads are to be 2 feet 6 inches wide, and made of iron, with flexible laths.
2. A piece of cocoa fibre matting or other material, or a mattress, is to be placed between the bedstead and the bed to protect the tick from rust.
3. Beds of cocoa fibre, cut straw, chaff, or flock, are to be kept full, and in good condition, such beds to be of the full length of the bedstead.
4. Two sheets, a sufficient number of blankets, according to the time of year, a counterpane, and pillow, are to be supplied to each bed.
5. A pottery urinal to each bed.
6. Night-stools, unless where (as is the better course) a water-closet is easily accessible.
7. Chairs to be placed between the beds upon which to place the inmates' clothes.
8. Bells.
9. Gas where practicable.

B.—*Lavatories and Baths.*

10. Lavatories with fixed metal or pottery basins with plug, tap, and waste pipe ending in a properly trapped drain.
11. Roller towels on rollers should be supplied at least twice a week, and in the proportion of not less than one to six inmates. The towels should be dried after the morning's use, and the lavatory kept dry and clean.
12. The baths should be 5 feet 6 inches long, and not less than 2 feet wide at the top.

C.—*Day Rooms.*

13. An open fireplace.
14. Benches; those for the aged and infirm should have backs, and be of sufficient width for reasonable comfort.
15. A proportion of chairs for the aged and infirm.
16. Cupboards or open shelves (which are better) for the utensils.
17. Tables.
18. Gas, where practicable.
19. Combs and hair-brushes for all classes.

D.—*Dining Room.*

20. Benches.
21. Tables.
22. Knife, fork, and spoon for each inmate.
23. Salt-cellars in sufficient numbers.
24. Plates, mugs, and basins : those made of pottery are to be preferred.
25. Correct balances.
26. Gas where practicable.
27. An open fireplace, if possible.

E.—*Sick Wards.*

The fittings should be such as are usually provided in the wards of general hospitals, and amongst them the following :—

28. The bedsteads should be of iron, with iron laths, of modern make and in good order. The length should be 6 feet 2 inches, and the width 2 feet 8 inches, except for the bedridden, the lying-in cases, and women with children, for whom the width should be 3 to 4 feet.

29. A paliasse of straw or other material, or a layer of cocoa fibre matting, to lie upon the laths.

30. The beds, whether of feathers, carded flock, cut straw or chaff, to be properly made, kept in good order, and sufficiently full. In some Unions, however, hair or wool mattresses are found to be better.

31. Two sheets, two or three blankets, and a cheerful-looking rug.

32. One-half the number of bedsteads to have a raising rack.

33. Separate bed rests.

34. Spittoons.

35. A pottery urinal to each bed and special pottery urinary bottles for the use of bed-ridden men.

36. Medicine glasses and feeding bottles.

37. Stone or metallic feet and chest warmers.

38. Air or water beds.

39. Mackintosh sheeting to be used to all lying-in beds.

40. The same with funnels for dirty cases.

41. Square and round mackintosh cushions with depression in the centre to prevent bed sores.

42. Mackintosh urinals to be worn by men who pass their urine involuntarily.

43. A locker with shelves for the use of two inmates, or a bed-table similar to that recommended by Dr.

Acland of Oxford, an example of which may be seen at the office of the Poor Law Board.

44. Arm and other chairs for two-thirds of the number of sick.

45. Short benches with backs and (for special cases) cushions.

46. Rocking chairs for the lying-in wards.

47. Little arm-chairs and rocking chairs for children's sick wards.

48. Tables.

49. Pottery wash-hand basins for those who are washed in bed.

50. Fixed lavatory basins for others, or wash-stands with fittings.

51. A sufficient number of roller towels, and one small towel to each person who is usually washed in bed.

52. A proper supply of both combs and hair-brushes, to be kept clean and in good order, in each ward.

53. Sealed night stools.

54. Gas, where practicable, to remain lit during the night.

55. Bells to the nurses' room.

56. Jackets with long sleeves, for lunatics.

57. It may be desirable that an inventory of the furniture, fittings, and medical appliances supplied should be fixed in some conspicuous place in each ward.

2 The guiding principles in selecting fittings and furniture for workhouses are utility and rigid economy, but care should be taken that in form and structure all the fittings and furniture are durable and not uncomfortable.

3. Medical appliances should be suggested by the medical officer, and could not be described in detail by the Poor Law Board in such a list of requirements.

4. Mr. Hooper, of Pall Mall, supplies medical appliances of the most durable kind, and has arranged a water-bed with

depressed centre and a tube by which excrement may be at once washed away from bedridden patients.

5. Messrs. Atkinson and Co. are the largest general furnishers to workhouses, and supply every article of their class of trade required by guardians.

6. Warm and cheerful-looking woollen counterpanes, (as made by Messrs. Early, of Witney,) comfortable beds and bedding and pillows, window blinds, a few easy chairs, screens, plenty of linen and towels, and a proper supply of utensils, are especially required in sick wards.

7. Common listing slippers for use in the sick wards, prevent noise from wearing thick boots, and the wear of stocking feet from walking about without boots, whilst they are cheap and economical

8. A common rocking-chair for the lying-in ward, and little chairs for young and sick children, are desirable, as also a warm flannel garment in each ward for the use of the sick who leave their beds in cold weather, or at night to go to the water-closet.

9. The use of night shirts, as well as day shirts, conduces to cleanliness and economy.

10. Sheets should not be worn by the ordinary inmates longer than two weeks without washing, and the upper may be used as the under one during the second week. Clean sheets weekly are requisite for sick cases of an ordinary class.

11. Sheets and shirts should be allowed to cases of itch.

12. It is not needful to burn the linen or beds which have been used by fever or small-pox cases, but they should be well-boiled, or exposed to a dry heat of 250° F. They should not be mixed or washed with other linen, but having been properly washed separately, they may be got up with the other linen in the common laundry.

13. Infected linen should not be kept in a close place, or be needlessly handled, but thrown at once into the boiler with boiling water, and stirred with a stick.

14. The following articles will, however, be needful in

every workhouse, viz.:—Air or water bed and cushions, waterproof sheeting, with and without a funnel, for the use of dirty cases, macintosh and pottery male urinals, spitting pots, bedpans, chest warmers, feet warmers, thermometers, graduated medicine glasses, enema apparatus, vapour bath for use in bed, bed pulleys, rack bedsteads (as made by Mr. Chrispin, of Huddersfield), bed rests and leg rests. Bed tables, to be temporarily placed across the bed for the use of those who take their food in bed, are convenient, and prevent the soiling of the bedding by food.

15 It is not desirable that the beds for any class except lying-in women or women with children, or young children, should be double beds, or hold more than one person.

16. Chrispin's washing, wringing and mangling machines are very valuable and economical in the use of labour, soap, and linen, and where there is a steam-engine they may be worked by steam power.

17. E. Deane's cooking stove is well adapted for use in workhouses on account of the saving of fuel which is effected, and its simplicity and ease of management.

Chapter XIII.

DIETARIES FOR THE ORDINARY INMATES.

———◆———

1. The Dietary for all classes of inmates except the sick, suckling women, and infants under two years of age, should be a fixed one and approved by the Poor Law Board, and it may not be changed (without the consent of the Poor Law Board) except on Christmas Day, or on "the occasion of any public festival or thanksgiving," or under the certificate of the medical officer, when he deems a temporary change of diet to be necessary for an individual, or for one or more classes on urgent sanitary grounds [*C. O. Art.* 107, *and present form of Order*].

2. The following are the Instructions which have been recently issued by the Poor Law Board respecting workhouse dietaries, and in the letter which accompanied them the Board called the attention of the guardians to my report on Uniformity of Dietaries in Workhouses, dated Feb. 1867, with which the "Instructions" were to be considered.

SUGGESTIONS FOR THE PREPARATION OF DIETARIES.

1.—AS TO CLASSES OF INMATES.

In addition to the other classes for whom separate dietaries are sanctioned by the Board, it is desirable that the following should be provided :—

    1. A separate dietary for all aged and infirm inmates who are not placed upon the medical officer's book.

    2. A separate dietary, to be prescribed by the medical officer, for such inmates as are at present placed

upon the books of the medical officer for diet alone. The names of such persons should be entered in a special book, and not in the list of sick in the medical officer's book ; and being once entered, they should not be repeated until they cease to require that dietary.

This book to be laid before the guardians at each meeting.

3. The names of those inmates to whom, under Article 108, Fourthly, of the General Consolidated Order, such an allowance of food as appeared to the guardians necessary has been made on account of the nature of their employment, and of those to whom, on the like account, fermented or spirituous liquors have, in pursuance of a written recommendation of the medical officer, been allowed by the guardians, should be read out at each meeting. The master is not permitted to allow extras without the authority of the guardians previously obtained, or, in case of urgent necessity, without obtaining the sanction of the guardians at their next meeting after such extras have been given. It is not necessary in order to such extra allowance that the medical officer should enter the names of such persons in the sick list.

4. Should the guardians deem it desirable, they may submit to the Poor Law Board a dietary for children from nine to sixteen years of age, instead of allowing to that class the dietary of able-bodied women.

5. The sick dietaries will, as heretofore, be framed by the medical officer ; but the Board deem it desirable that the meat to be allowed to the sick shoul be calculated as cooked meat without bone, and not as raw meat, except in the case of chops ; and they request that the medical officer will so arrange the quantity of food in the sick diets that it may

not be greater than the sick of the particular class can ordinarily eat, and also that he will give his attention to the cooking, conveying, and serving of the sick diets.

6. The dietary of imbeciles and of suckling women should be that of the aged an infirm inmates, with or without the substitution of milk-porridge and bread, at breakfast or supper, or at both meals.

2.—DETAILS OF DIETARIES.

7. Tea or coffee are not to be ordinarily supplied to children, except for supper on Sunday.

8. It is desirable that milk should be supplied to all children under five years of age, and where practicable, to children above that age, at breakfast and supper, and that 2 ozs. or 3 ozs. of bread should be given to each child at 10 a.m.

9. It is suggested that tea, coffee, or cocoa, with milk and sugar, and accompanied by bread and butter or bread and cheese, should be allowed to all the aged and infirm women at breakfast and supper, and the same to the aged and infirm men, or milk-porridge with bread may be given at one of those meals.

10. It is not desirable that more than two soup or broth dinners should be supplied weekly to any class of inmates.

11. Soup is to contain 3 ozs. of raw, or 2 ozs. of cooked meat to the pint, and, when practicable, to be made with meat liquor. From 1 pint to 1½ pints to be the usual ration for an adult.

12. Broth without the meat left in it should not be given with bread alone for dinner; but when it contains the quantity of meat which is required in soup, it may be substituted for soup during the summer months.

13. Broth made without the meat being left in it may be given thrice a week with a sufficient quantity of

bread for supper to the able-bodied, and, in the absence of a sufficient supply of milk, to children from 9 to 16 years of age.

14. It is not desirable that more than two bread and cheese dinners should be supplied weekly, except to the able-bodied adults; and ½ pint of broth, without meat left in it, is to be added in the dietaries for the aged and infirm children.

15. Bread and cheese should not be given alone for breakfast and supper to children under five years of age.

16. Boiled rice is not to be given alone as a substitute for potato and green vegetables. When it is considered desirable to supply it, it should be given with a portion of fresh vegetables or bread.

17. Rice-pudding is not to be given as a dinner, except to children under nine years of age, and then not more frequently than twice a week; and a portion of bread is to be given with it.

18. Suet-pudding is not to be given for dinner more frequently than twice a week, and is to be accompanied by a portion of potato or bread and broth (without meat being left in it), or bread and cheese, except to the able-bodied adults. Where given twice a week it should be baked once. It is to contain 1½ oz. of suet to 8 oz. flour.

19. Meat should be roasted or baked or made into a pudding or pie at least once a week.

20. 4 oz. of cooked meat without bone when given separately should usually be the ration for men, and 3 oz. for women.

21. A ration of meat-pudding or meat-pie to contain 4 oz. of raw meat for men and 3 oz. for women.

22. A portion of bread is to be given at every meal to all classes, except when potato is supplied with meat-pudding or meat-pie.

23. The *usual* quantity of bread to be given at breakfast

G

and supper to children from two to five years, is 3 oz. ; to those from five to nine, 4 oz. ; to those from nine to sixteen, 5 oz. ; to able-bodied men 6 oz. ; to able-bodied women, 5 oz. ; and to the aged of both sexes, 5 oz.

24. Fresh vegetables should, if possible, be given separately or in combination at dinner at least five times weekly.

4. In the selection of dietaries for each workhouse three courses are open to adoption. Thus :—the guardians may frame them, the Poor Law Board may frame them, or they may be framed by the guardians on " Instructions " issued by the Poor Law Board and submitted for the sanction of the Poor Law Board.

5. The first course is that which until recently has been practised, but the Poor Law Board have had the power to give or withhold their sanction, without which the tables could not be used. The Poor Law Board have caused them to be investigated in some degree, but practically they have sanctioned them upon the authority and responsibility of the guardians and their medical officer.

6. The second course is practicable only by the preparation of several model dietaries for different parts of the kingdom, since it is generally admitted that the dietary in each workhouse should correspond in character with that of the labourers in the same locality, and it is well known that the food of labourers differs materially in kind and quantity in different parts of the kingdom.

7. There is, however, no difficulty in preparing a number, say six schemes, of dietaries which would be fitted for so many divisions of the kingdom, and if it were effected it would save the guardians much trouble, would greatly lessen the correspondence of the Poor Law Board, would ensure a nearer approach to fitness as well as uniformity over wide areas of the country.

8. The third course is that which is contemplated by the

recently-issued "Instructions." It is proposed that the guardians everywhere, when framing the dietaries, shall be guided by certain principles now laid down by the Poor Law Board, whilst much liberty is left to them to select the foods which are commonly eaten in their several localities. As the responsibility is thus divided between the local and the central executive, guardians should adopt these suggestions in good faith.

9. It is intended by these Instructions to define the quantities of particular foods to be given when such have been selected by the guardians, and to determine the frequency of their supply, and both are based upon the necessities of the body, economy, and fitness to maintain health.

10. Repulsive food, as pea-soup to certain persons, whether supplied at a small or large cost, is not economical and cannot maintain health ; so also, more of a fitting food, as meat, may be supplied at one time than the body can digest or use at the time, and whether costing little or much is not economical.

11. A food which may be fitting at a particular period, as cheese and suet-pudding, may become unfitted by too frequent repetition, and is therefore wasted.

12. A fitting food, as meat, may be given at too long intervals to maintain health, and a more frequent supply of a smaller quantity would be more economical and useful.

13. As the wants of the body are nearly the same every day and recur at regular periods in each day, a proper and somewhat uniform distribution of food is desirable.

14. Variety in the flavour of food promotes its usefulness and is therefore economical.

15. The cost of dietaries depends upon the following considerations, viz. :—the local prices of foods, the judgment with which the articles are selected and combined, the skill exercised in cooking, the proper apportionment of quantities of food at each meal, and the amount of waste in preparing and cooking food ; and it varies, therefore, in different Unions.

16. The following forms for the composition of foods may be properly adopted in every workhouse :—

FORMULÆ.

17. Pea-soup, to make a pint—Meat (as shin of beef), 3 oz.; bones, 1 oz.; peas, 2 oz.; potato and other fresh vegetables, 2 oz.; dried herb and seasoning; meat liquor.

18. Barley-soup or meat-broth, to make a pint—Meat, 3 oz.; bones, 1 oz.; Scotch barley, 2 oz.; carrots, 1 oz.; seasoning and meat liquor.

19. Broth, to make a pint—Meat liquor, 1 pint; barley, 2 oz.; leeks or onions, 1 oz.; parsley and seasoning.

20. Suet-pudding (baked or boiled), to make one pound—Flour (good seconds), 7 oz. to 8 oz. (according to the quality of the flour and the thickness desired); suet, $1\frac{1}{4}$ to $1\frac{1}{2}$ oz.; skimmed milk, 2 oz.; salt.   To be served with gravy or sweet dip.

21. Rice-pudding, to make one pound—Rice, 3 oz.; suet, $\frac{1}{4}$ oz.; sugar, $\frac{1}{2}$ oz.; skimmed milk, $\frac{1}{4}$ pint; spice and salt.

22. Rice-milk, to make one pint—Rice, 2 oz.; new milk, $\frac{1}{4}$ pint; sugar $\frac{1}{2}$ oz.; allspice and salt.

23. Meat-pudding, to make one pound—Flour, 6 oz.; suet, 1 oz.; uncooked meat, 4 oz.; meat liquor and seasoning.

24. Meat and potato-pie, to make one pound—Flour, $3\frac{1}{2}$ oz.; suet or other fat, $\frac{1}{2}$ oz.; uncooked meat, 3 oz.; potato, 7 oz.; onions, seasoning, and meat liquor.

25. Potato hash or Irish stew, to make one pint—Uncooked meat, 3 oz.; potatoes, 12 oz.; onions, $1\frac{1}{2}$ oz.; meat liquor and seasoning.

26. Gruel, to make one pint—Oatmeal, 2 oz.; treacle, $\frac{1}{4}$ oz.; salt and sometimes allspice; water.

27. Oatmeal-porridge, to make one pint—Oatmeal, 5 oz.; water and seasoning.   To be eaten with milk.

28. Milk-porridge to make one pint—Oatmeal, 2 oz.; milk, $\frac{1}{4}$ pint; water, salt.

29. Tea, to make ten pints—Tea, 1 oz.; sugar, 5 oz.; milk, 1 pint.

30. The following observations will be found useful in preparing schemes of dietaries in all localities in the kingdom according to the habits of the working-classes.

SCHEMES OF DIETARY FOR ALL LOCALITIES.

BREAKFAST AND SUPPER.

For the Aged and Infirm.

31. Tea, with bread and butter or bread and cheese, should be given at both meals to the aged women, and at both or at one meal only to the aged men ; and in the latter case the other meal should consist of milk-porridge or gruel, or, in part, of bread and cheese or bread and broth.

Able-bodied.

32. Bread and gruel, or, in part, bread and cheese or bread and broth, should be given.

Children.

33. Bread and milk should be given to children up to five years of age. Bread and milk should be given to those from five to nine years of age at both meals or at one meal only, and in the latter event bread and gruel, or, in part, bread and cheese or bread and broth, should be supplied. Bread and milk or bread and gruel at one or both meals, or, in part, bread and cheese or bread and broth, should be given to children aged nine to sixteen. Skimmed milk or buttermilk are valuable additions. ' Tea and bread and butter may be given at supper on Sundays to all classes.

DINNER.

Aged and Infirm and Children.

34. Meat with fresh vegetables should be given. separately or cooked in puddings, pies, or hash, three or four times a week. Pea-soup or barley-soup containing meat should be given once a week. Suet-pudding, baked or boiled, should

be given with broth or potato once a week, and bread and cheese and broth should be given once a week.

Able-bodied.

35. Meat with fresh vegetables should be given separately or cooked in puddings, pies, or hash, twice a week. Pea-soup and bread should be given once or twice a week, bread and cheese should be given once or twice a week, and suet-pudding with broth and potato once or twice a week.

36. There is much difference in the selection of foods and the composition and preparation of foods in different counties, so that in using the above scheme it is necessary to select such alternatives as may be specially applicable to each locality.

37. The chief differences in the selection of food in different localities have reference to milk, cheese, bacon, fish, and pudding, so that where milk cannot be procured plentifully, gruel or cheese is used; where cheese is much used, but little meat is obtained; where meat-puddings are common, cooked meat with vegetables as a separate food is rare, and where bacon, pork, or fish is supplied, other meat is rarely eaten. Cheese and pudding are especially supplied in the southern and south-western counties; meat and milk in the midland and part of the northern; oatmeal in the northern; buttermilk and skim milk in Wales and the northern counties; broth and barley-bread in Wales; pork in Cambridgeshire and adjoining counties; bacon in Berkshire and the southern and south-western and south-eastern counties, and fish in certain parts of Wales and other coast districts.

38. Bacon and pork, although supplying more fat than lean, must be regarded as meat.

39. It is a false notion of economy to feed children insufficiently on the ground that their parents were of the poorest class and that they must themselves become the same in after-life.

40. True economy in feeding children consists in giving them plenty of bread and similar common, but nutritious foods, so that they may grow up healthy and fit to earn their living.

41. The younger children require more than three meals daily.

42. Infants under two years of age are often much neglected and ill-fed. They should be fed with milk and bread or milk-puddings with bread and butter, and be supplied with food five to six times during the twenty-four hours.

43. It is a good plan to give 2 oz. of bread to all children at ten o'clock A.M.

44. In constructing dietaries for the aged, regard should be had to the failing powers of taste, mastication, and digestion of that class.

45. Alternative foods at the discretion of the officers, as pea-soup or suet-pudding. Gruel or bread and cheese are agreeable to the inmates, but they render the keeping of accounts difficult and a satisfactory audit impossible, whilst at the same time there is not an efficient check upon the master; but alternative dietaries for specified months, as for example, pea-soup from November to March, and other food for the summer months, are not open to that objection.

46. An uniform dietary for vagrants has been issued by the Poor Law Board for the metropolitan district as follows [*Order, March 3rd,* 1866] :—

DIETARY FOR VAGRANTS.

47. "We, the Poor Law Board, in pursuance of the powers given in and by the statutes in that behalf, hereby order and direct, that, notwithstanding any provision contained in any general or other order heretofore issued by the Poor Law Commissioners or the Poor Law Board to the guardians of the poor of the respective Unions and parishes named in

the schedule hereunto annexed, the destitute wayfarers, wanderers, and foundlings admitted into the vagrant wards of the workhouses belonging to the said several Unions and parishes shall henceforth be dieted with the food and in the manner described and set forth herein, namely :—

SUPPER.

For all persons above nine years of age, 6 oz. of bread and a pint of gruel, and for children under nine years of age, 4 oz. of bread and half a pint of gruel.

BREAKFAST.

For all persons above nine years of age, 6 oz. of bread and a pint of gruel, and for children under nine years of age, 4 oz. of bread and half a pint of gruel.

The pint of gruel for supper for all persons above nine years of age to be withdrawn from the 25th of March to the 29th of September in each year.   And we hereby order and direct that, as regards each of the said Unions and parishes, the master of the workhouse, or, where the vagrant wards are detached from the workhouse, the superintendent of the vagrant wards, shall cause two or more copies of this our order, legibly written or printed in large type, to be hung up in the vagrant wards of the workhouse, and renewed from time to time, so that such copies may be always kept fair and legible.

48. The following is the dietary recommended by the Poor Law Board for the same class in the provincial districts, but its adoption is not at present compulsory [*Cir. Nov. 28th,* 1868] :—

SUPPER.

For males above fifteen years of age—8 oz. of bread, or (at the discretion of the guardians) 6 oz. of bread and 1 pint of gruel.

For females above fifteen years of age, and for children of both sexes from seven to fifteen years of age—6 oz. of bread and a pint of gruel.

For children under seven years of age—4 oz. of bread and ½ pint of gruel.

Breakfast, the same as supper.

Half the quantity of the bread for breakfast to be given to the men and women before commencing the task of work, and the other half of the bread (with the gruel for the women) at its completion.

49. It is very desirable that there should be an uniform dietary (as a part of a uniform scheme of treatment) for vagrants throughout the country, and the foregoing, with the substitution of oatmeal-porridge for bread in the north of England, and of cheese for gruel in the south and south-western counties, and perhaps of coffee for gruel to women generally, would be suitable.

50. No scheme of dietary for ordinary inmates has been issued by the Poor Law Board for compulsory use in work-houses generally, but one for adults has been brought before the attention of the guardians in the metropolitan districts [*Cir. April 23rd*, 1868], and another has recently been commended to the consideration of the guardians in the Midland districts [*Uniformity of Workhouse Dietaries, Feb.* 1, 1867, *and Circular, 25th April*, 1867].

51. The following is the scheme for the inmates of the metropolitan workhouses :—

ORDINARY DIETARY—METROPOLIS.

Able-bodied.

BREAKFAST (daily).

Men   5 oz. bread, 1½ pint oatmeal-porridge.
Women 5 oz. do. 1 pint   do.

DINNER.

Men   3 oz. bread, 1½ pint pea-soup   .   . twice weekly.

Men	5 oz. cooked meat, 12 oz. potatoes or other vegetables . . .	twice weekly.
,,	16 oz. suet-pudding	twice ,,
,,	24 oz. Irish stew . . .	once ,,
Women	3 oz. bread, 1½ pint pea-soup . .	twice ,,
,,	4½ oz. cooked meat, 12 oz. potatoes or other vegetables	twice ,,
,,	16 oz. of suet-pudding . .	twice ,,
,,	20 oz. Irish stew	once ,,

SUPPER.

Men	5 oz. bread, 1½ pint meat-broth .	twice weekly.
,,	5 oz. bread, 1½ pint oatmeal-porridge .	five ,,
Women	5 oz. bread, 1½ pint meat-broth .	twice ,,
,,	5 oz. bread, 1 pint oatmeal-porridge .	five ,,

Infirm Inmates of all ages.

BREAKFAST (both sexes, daily).

5 oz. bread, 1 pint tea, ½ oz. butter.
4 oz. bread, 1 pint tea, ½ oz. butter.

DINNER.

Men	3 oz. bread, 1 pint pea-soup . .	once weekly.
,,	4½ oz. cooked mutton, 12 oz. potatoes or other vegetables . . .	twice ,,
,,	4½ oz. beef, 12 oz. potatoes or other vegetables	once ,,
,,	16 oz. meat-pie or pudding . .	once ,,
,,	14 oz. baked suet-pudding, or 16 oz. baked rice-pudding . . .	once ,,
,,	24 oz. Irish stew	once ,,
Women	3 oz. bread, 1 pint pea-soup .	once ,,
,,	4 oz. cooked mutton, 12 oz. potatoes or other vegetables . . .	twice ,,

Women 4 oz. beef, 2 oz. potatoes or other

     vegetables . . . . once weekly.

 ,,   16 oz. meat-pie or pudding . . once ,,

 ,,   14 oz. baked suet-pudding, or 14 oz.

     baked rice-pudding . . . once ,,

 ,,   20 oz. Irish stew . . . . once ,,

SUPPER.

Men   5 oz. bread, 1 pint tea, ⅓ oz. butter.

Women 4 oz. bread, 1 pint tea, ⅓ oz. butter.

Inmates Employed on Extra Labour.

BREAKFAST (both sexes daily).

6 oz. bread, 1 pint tea, ⅓ oz. butter.

DINNER (both sexes).

5 oz. cooked meat, 12 oz. potatoes or

  other vegetables . . . five weekly.

24 oz. Irish stew . . . once ,,

18 oz. meat-pie . . . . once ,,

SUPPER (both sexes daily).

6 oz. bread, 1 pint tea, ½ oz. butter.

52. The following is the scheme of dietary which I recommended for the use of the ordinary aged and infirm inmates of the metropolitan workhouses, and also for such special or medical cases among them as had been usually placed upon the books of the medical officer for dietary alone. [*Report, 29th September,* 1866, *and Return on Workhouse Dietaries H. C.* 435, 11*th July,* 1867].

DR. SMITH'S DIETARY FOR THE AGED AND INFIRM—METROPOLIS.

1.—*Ordinary.*

BREAKFAST AND SUPPER.

1 pint of tea or coffee, with ⅓ oz. of sugar, and 1 or 2 oz. of milk, 5 oz. of bread, and ⅓ oz. of butter.

DINNER.

Four days weekly—4 oz. of cooked meat, 10 oz. of potatoes, and 3 oz. of bread.

One day weekly — 14 oz. of meat and potato-pie, and 3 oz. of bread.

One day weekly—1¼ pint of soup, with 4 oz. bread, and 1 oz. of cheese.

One day weekly—12 oz. of suet-pudding, with 3 oz. of bread, and 1 pint of broth.

2.—*Special or Medical.*

BREAKFAST AND SUPPER.

One pint of tea or cocoa, with ½ oz. of sugar, and 1 oz. or 2 oz. milk, 5 oz. of bread, and ½ oz. of butter.

DINNER.

Six days weekly—4 oz. of cooked meat, 10 oz. of potatoes; 3 oz. of bread to be added on five days, and 4 oz. of suet-pudding, with vinegar-and-treacle sauce, or 8 oz. of rice, on the other two days.

One day weekly—14 oz. of meat and potato-pie, or meat-pudding, and 3 oz. of bread.

Daily—½ pint of beer if specially directed by the medical officer.

53. The following is the scheme which I prepared for the inmates of workhouses in the Midland and neighbouring counties.

DR. SMITH'S DIETARY FOR THE MIDLAND COUNTIES.

Able-bodied.

BREAKFAST.

Men   6 oz. bread, 1½ pint gruel.
Women   6 oz. bread, 1 pint gruel.

DINNER.

Men	8 oz. bread, 1 pint broth, 1½ oz. cheese twice weekly.	
,,	4 oz. bread, 16 oz. meat-pie . . once ,,	
,,	6 oz. bread, 1 pint soup . . . twice ,,	
,,	4 oz. bread, 10 oz. suet-pudding, 1 pint broth . . . . . twice ,,	
Women	6 oz. bread, 1 pint broth, 1½ oz. cheese twice ,,	
,,	4 oz. bread, 3 oz. meat, 10 oz. potatoes twice ,,	
,,	5 oz. bread, 1 pint soup . . . twice ,,	
,,	4 oz. bread, 8 oz. suet-pudding, 1 pint broth . . . . . once ,,	

SUPPER.

Men	6 oz. bread, 1½ pint gruel . . . four weekly.	
,,	8 oz. bread, 1 pint broth, 1½oz. cheese thrice ,,	
Women	6 oz. bread, 1 pint gruel . . . six ,,	
,,	6 oz. bread, 2 oz. milk, 1 pint tea ½ oz. sugar, ½ oz. butter . . . once ,,	

Aged and Infirm.

BREAKFAST.

Men	6 oz. bread, 1⅓ pint milk-gruel.
Women	6 oz. bread, 1 pint milk-gruel.

DINNER.

Men	4 oz. bread, 3 oz. meat, 10 oz. potatoes, four weekly.
,,	3 oz. bread, 16 oz. meat-pie, ½ oz. cheese, once ,,
,,	5 oz. bread, 1 pint of soup, 1 oz. cheese, once ,,
,,	4 oz. bread, 10 oz. suet-pudding, 1 oz. cheese . . . . . once ,,
Women	3 oz. bread, 3 oz. meat, 10 oz. potatoes four ,,
,,	2 oz. bread, 16 oz. meat-pie, ½ oz. cheese once ,,
,,	4 oz. bread, 1 pint of soup, 1 oz. cheese once ,,
,,	4 oz. bread, 10 oz. suet-pudding, 1 oz. cheese . . . . . once ,,

The guardians may, if they prefer it, substitute 4 oz. of meat instead of 3 oz., at dinner for adults.

SUPPER.

Men   6 oz. bread, 2 oz. milk, 1 pint tea, ⅓ oz.
         sugar, ½ oz. butter   .   .   . thrice weekly.
  ,,   6 oz. bread, 1½ pint milk-gruel . twice   ,,
  ,,   6 oz. bread, ¾ pint broth, 1½ oz. cheese twice   ,,
Women 6 oz. bread, 2 oz. milk, 1 pint tea,
         ½ oz. sugar, ½ oz. butter   .   . daily.

When on the ground of age not being sufficiently advanced it is not deemed proper to give tea for supper, the supper will consist of the same food as is prepared for breakfast.

Children aged 9 to 15 Years.

BREAKFAST AND SUPPER.

6 oz. bread, 1 pint milk-gruel.

DINNER.

4 oz. bread, 3 oz. meat, 8 oz. potatoes .   . thrice weekly.
5 oz. bread, 12 oz. meat-pie .   .   .   . once   ,,
5 oz. bread, 1 pint soup   .   .   .   . twice   ,,
4 oz. bread, 10 oz. suet-pudding, 1 oz. cheese, once   ,,

Children aged 5 to 9 Years.

BREAKFAST.

6 oz. bread, ¾ pint milk-porridge.

DINNER.

3 oz. bread, 2 oz. meat, 8 oz. potatoes .   . twice weekly.
2 oz. bread, 12 oz. meat-pie .   .   .   . once   ,,
3 oz. bread, 1 pint soup   .   .   .   . twice   ,,
3 oz. bread, 8 oz. suet-pudding, ½ pint broth . once   ,,
5 oz. bread, ¼ pint rice-pudding .   .   . once   ,,

SUPPER.

5 oz. bread, ¾ pint milk-porridge.

Children aged 3 to 5 Years.

BREAKFAST AND SUPPER.

4 oz. bread, ¾ pint milk-porridge.

AT 10 A.M.

2 oz. bread.

DINNER.

2 oz. bread, 2 oz. meat, 6 oz. potatoes . . once weekly.
2 oz. bread, 8 oz. meat-pie . . . . once „
4 oz. bread, ¾ pint broth . . . . twice „
3 oz. bread, ½ pint rice-pudding . . . twice „
2 oz. bread, 6 oz. suet-pudding . . . once „

Children aged 1 to 3 Years.

BREAKFAST AND SUPPER.

3 oz. bread, ½ pint milk-porridge,

AT 10 A.M.

2 oz. bread.

DINNER.

3 oz. bread, ¼ pint rice-pudding . . . thrice weekly.
3 oz. bread, 4 oz. suet-pudding, ¼ oz. butter . twice „
4 oz. bread, ½ pint broth, ¼ oz. butter. . twice „

54. It is very desirable, with the present high price of meat, to ascertain whether Australian meat cannot be economically used in workhouses. It is already cooked, and is sent, without bone, in sealed cans. Both mutton and beef, but particularly the former, may be made into Irish stew or meat-pie.

PART II.

THE OFFICERS.

THE MASTER.

Chapter XIV.

APPOINTMENT AND QUALIFICATIONS.

1. The master must be twenty-one years of age, and be able to keep accounts, unless the guardians, with the consent of the Poor Law Board expressly obtained, dispense with those requirements. He must also agree to give one month's notice of his intention to resign his office, or forfeit one month's salary [*C. O. Arts.* 162, 163, 167].

2. He must enter into a bond for the due performance of his duties with two sufficient sureties, who are not officers of the same Union ; and when required by the guardians must prove by a certificate, signed by two householders, that his sureties are alive and solvent, and must supply a new surety as often as either of his sureties may die or become bankrupt or insolvent [*C. O. Art.* 184]. In lieu of his sureties he may offer the security of the European Assurance Society in the sum approved by the Poor Law Board, and deposit with the guardians the certificate and the annual premium with the policy.

3. The following is a copy of the document which he is

required to sign on his election, and which is forwarded to the Poor Law Board for their information :—

—————Union.

APPOINTMENT OF MASTER.

1. State the Christian name and surname of the person appointed as master of the workhouse, in full.
2. His place of residence immediately previous to his appointment.
3. His age.
4. Whether he is married or single.
5. Whether he has any children ; and, if so, whether they are dependent on him, and where it is proposed that they shall reside.

   If it is proposed that any of the children shall reside in the workhouse, the ages and sexes of the children, and what sum per week is to be paid to the guardians by the master for the maintenance of each child.
6. His religious persuasion.
7. His previous occupations or callings.
8. Whether he has been in the army, navy, excise, police, or other public service ; and, if so, which service ; the cause of his leaving the same ; and the date when he left.

   If he has been in the police service whether he produced to the guardians a certificate of good conduct from the police authorities.
9. Whether he has before held any paid office in any Union or parish ; and, if so, what office, and in what Union or parish.

   The cause of his leaving the same.

   And the date when he left.
10. Whether he has ever been bankrupt or insolvent, or executed an assignment for the benefit of, or entered into a composition with his creditors ; and, if so, when.

    If a bankrupt, whether he has obtained his certificate, and what was the class thereof.
11. Whether he has a competent knowledge of accounts.
12. Whether his whole time is given up to the service of the Union.
13. The day on which he was elected by the guardians.
14. The date from which his duties commence.
15. Whether he is to reside in the workhouse.
16. The amount of salary proposed.
17. Whether any rations or other emoluments are allowed ; and, if so, what.

18. Whether he agrees to give the guardians one month's notice previous to resigning his office, or to forfeit one month's amount of salary, to be deducted from the amount of salary due at the time of resignation, pursuant to Article 167 of the General Consolidated Order.

19. The nature and amount of the security
        and
    The names and addresses of the sureties, and their occupations.

20. What testimonials the guardians have received ; and whether they are satisfied thereby, or otherwise, that the person appointed is competent to perform efficiently all the duties of the office of master.

21. The cause of the vacancy on account of which the appointment is made : if a resignation, the cause thereof, the date on which it took effect, and the name of the former officer.

———*Signature of the Clerk.*
——— *Signature of the Officer appointed.*
[The Christian name and surname being written in full.]

Reported to the Poor Law Board
    for their approval.   ——— day of——— 186

4. The position of the master is the most responsible of any of the resident officers, since he is required to enforce the observance of all regulations for the government of the workhouse by the paupers, servants, and officers [*C. O. Art.* 208], and, subject to the provisions of the law and the directions of the guardians, the immediate management of the workhouse rests upon him.

5. He is directly responsible to the Poor Law Board for the right discharge of such of his duties as are prescribed by them, and it would not avail him to plead even that he had the authority of the Board of Guardians for any omission of them. At the same time, he is subject to the authority of the Board of Guardians, as to the mode in which he should discharge his duties when such duties are not prescribed by the Poor Law Board.

6. He is the chief officer and the proper adviser of the Board, on the practical part of the management of the workhouse, subject to the cases in which other officers have special responsibility.

7. He is, at the same time, by the proper discharge of his duty, to be a friend and protector of the inmates.

8. Hence, he should be a person of sufficient education, strength of will, and firmness of purpose, whilst he is considerate and gentle in his bearing, without servility or disrespect to the guardians and the higher officers, and without intolerance or laxity to the other officers and the inmates.

9. He should be of quick intelligence and good judgment to decide upon disputes which will arise amongst the officers and inmates, and of strict integrity in the care and use of the stores entrusted to his care.

10. He should have due control over himself, and never exhibit, or allow others to exhibit, violence of temper, or use, or allow to be used, profane or irritating language.

DURATION OF OFFICE.

11. He holds his office until he dies, or resigns, or is incapable of discharging the duties, or is removed by the Poor Law Board [*C. O. Art.* 187], and when so removed he must not remain upon the premises or enter them, in order to interfere with the management of the workhouse, unless duly appointed to some other office [*C. O. Art.* 190].

12. When the master and matron are husband and wife, and the wife dies, resigns, or is dismissed by order of the Poor Law Board, the master vacates his office at the expiration of the current quarter, but may be reappointed if the guardians and the Poor Law Board should think fit [*C. O. Art.* 189.]

13. Should he be suspended from performing the duties of his office, he remains within the workhouse until the decision of the Poor Law Board shall have been given, when, if he is not required to resign his appointment or is not dismissed, his suspension is removed, and he again performs the duties of his office. His salary ceases from the date of his suspension, only in the event of his being dismissed, or called upon to resign by the Poor Law Board.

GENERAL OBSERVATIONS ON DUTIES.

14. He must personally discharge the duties of his office except with the special permission of the Poor Law Board obtained by the guardians [*C. O. Art.* 198], but in the event of incapability from illness the guardians may appoint a temporary substitute [*C. O. Art.* 193].

15. He must stay in the workhouse during the night unless he have received the permission of the Board of Guardians to be absent therefrom [*Instr. Let., Feb.* 5, 1842].

16. He should be well versed in the duties of his office, and not only conduct the establishment in the most efficient manner, but observe and point out to the guardians any improved methods by which efficiency may be further increased. He should clearly understand that his duty consists not only in conducting the affairs of the workhouse in the manner prescribed to him, but in improving the administration by increasing efficiency and reducing waste as far as possible, and by adapting the management to requisite changes.

17. He should devote the whole of his time to the discharge of his duties, and he cannot be an efficient officer if he devote himself to pleasures or even to duties away from the workhouse.

18. Hence it is not desirable that he should at the same time hold the office of relieving officer or registrar of births, deaths, and marriages, or that he should frequent places of entertainment or amusement.

19. In some workhouses the master and the medical officer do not act together harmoniously, and the one complains of undue interference by the other. Mutual forbearance should prevent this.

20. It is the duty of the master to exercise a general superintendence over every department of the workhouse, and over all classes of inmates; but the medical officer has exclusive control over the diets and medicines for the sick,

and the selection of the wards in which the sick should be placed, and his opinion should be sought by the master before requiring a sick person to perform any labour.

21. The master should defer to the opinion of the medical officer in reference to the ventilation of the wards, the amount and kind of bedding to be supplied to the sick, and so far as he may be able, should supply from his stock, the requisites required by the medical officer for the use of the sick, and, in general, whilst affording aid, should allow the responsibility to devolve upon the medical officer in all matters directly affecting the care and treatment of the sick.

22. In like manner he should abstain as far as possible from interfering with the duties of the matron and nurse in the care of the sick, whilst he should maintain a general supervision over them.

Chapter XV.

ADMISSIONS AND DISCHARGES.

——◆——

1. He is required to admit all destitute persons who apply for admission at any hour of the day or night, except during the hours of divine service on Sundays [*C. O. Art.* 208, *No.* 1], so far as there may be vacant room in the workhouse, but he must not admit a larger number than has been authorised by the Poor Law Board. The authority for admission, which he may not question, is the printed or written order of the board of guardians, duly drawn up and signed by the clerk, and presented within six days of its date ; the order of the relieving officer ; the order of two justices, or of a magistrate acting under the Industrial Schools Act ; the order of removal made by the sheriff or two justices in Scotland, or the proper parish authorities in England, and the order by justices in the metropolitan districts for the removal of the inhabitants of dangerous structures.

2. An overseers' or churchwardens' order is valid only when the case presenting it is urgent. Should the master be satisfied that the case is not urgent, he is not bound to admit the applicant ; but, having in view his own responsibility, should his decision be wrong, he should admit all such applicants.

3. He should admit any case of urgency without an order, if he is satisfied as to the urgency—as, for example, a person who is manifestly very ill, or a woman in labour, or a person in immediate need of food from extreme destitution.

4. He must admit such cases on his own judgment and responsibility, and must determine whether the urgency of

the illness, the weakness or want of food, or the imminence of childbirth, would render it dangerous to the applicant to go, or at least make it undesirable that the applicant should go to the relieving officer to obtain an order of admission; and generally his own sense of responsibility should induce him to lean towards the admission of such a person.

5. He is not bound to admit, upon his own responsibility only, a person who is incapable through drunkenness, or in charge of the police for theft, or any other crime; but when an applicant is brought to the workhouse by the police on the ground of alleged destitution he should admit him; and, in reference to the case of supposed drunkenness, he should be quite satisfied that the applicant is not suffering from apoplexy or other disease which produces effects similar to drunkenness.

6. He is not bound to admit the corpse of a person who has died outside the workhouse unless such person were an inmate at the time of his death; but in some cases it may be desirable that he should do so, and particularly if the guardians have not provided mortuaries.

7. He is not bound to admit a person, except under legal authority, who has money in his possession, or who has property which might be immediately converted into money or food. But if the applicant have property which he cannot immediately sell, and is without money and food and the means of immediately obtaining them whilst he is suffering from destitution, he should admit him.

8. He must admit the following persons who are not paupers, viz. :—

> The guardians, on board days, and on such other days as the board of guardians may direct.
>
> Any person specially authorised by the board of guardians.
>
> The members of the visiting committee.
>
> A Poor Law Inspector, whether attached to the district in which the Union is placed or otherwise.
>
> The Commissioners in Lunacy [16 & 17 *Vic. c.* 96].

The Auditor of the district.

Inspectors of Vaccination.

Justices of the peace for the county.

The chaplain, the medical officer, and other officers.

Servants and others employed by the guardians within the workhouse.

Visitors of paupers at the periods directed by the guardians, or in case of illness.

Ministers of religion (not being the chaplain) to see those paupers who request their attendance, at periods prescribed by the guardians, or in case of illness.

The parents of children in the workhouse, and others who have the right to examine the creed register of the children, to the room in which such register is kept.

The coroner and the inquest, when there is a dead body in the workhouse on which an inquest is to be held.

9. Those only who have a right to inspect the whole workhouse are the visiting committee, justices of the peace for the county, Poor Law Inspectors, and the medical officer of the workhouse.

10. The chaplain may enter any room where there are pauper inmates.

11. All other persons are admitted for specific purposes, to special cases, and to see particular inmates.

12. He reports to the guardians at their next ordinary meeting the names of all paupers who have been admitted since the previous meeting, and makes an inventory in duplicate of the clothes and other property found upon them; and he causes the names of all visitors to be entered in the porter's book, and laid before the guardians at each meeting.

13. He causes the applicants to be examined by the medical officer on the day of admission or on the following day [*C. O. Art.* 208], after which he directs the pauper to

be properly bathed and cleansed, dressed in the workhouse clothes, and placed in the proper ward. He causes the clothes of the pauper to be properly cleansed and placed in a dry store room, and the pauper, if over seven years of age, to be searched [*C. O. Art.* 208], and he takes possession of any money or other valuables which may be found upon him.

14. He cannot detain letters not of an improper tendency, nor prevent the pauper from receiving money, but in the latter event he reports the fact to the guardians.

15. If the applicant present the order of admission in the early part of the day, after the visit of the medical officer, he sends for that officer on the same day or defers the examination until the following morning, according to the distance of the residence of the medical officer from the workhouse and the urgency of the case, and if the medical officer should not visit the workhouse on the following morning, he sends for him.

16. He is not justified in admitting an applicant without previous medical inspection, except in cases of urgency from illness, or in allowing him to remain in the receiving ward more than one night. He has not, however, power to compel any person to submit to such an examination.

17. He makes the proper entry in the admission book, and in the register of creed book [*Letter with G. O. Nov.* 26, 1868].

" Where any *child* under the age of 12 years is in the workhouse, (whether either of its parents be in the workhouse or not, or whether it be an orphan or deserted child,) the master shall enter in such register as the religious creed of such child the religious creed of the *father*, if he know or can ascertain the same by reasonable inquiry,—or, if the same cannot be ascertained, the creed of the *mother*, if the same be known to him, or can be ascertained in like manner.

The creed of an *illegitimate* child under the said age shall be deemed to be that of its *mother*, when that can be ascertained."

18. He will keep the book in a room to be provided by the guardians, and allow every *minister* of any denomination officiating in the church, chapel, or other registered place of worship of such denomination which shall be nearest to the workhouse, or any *ratepayer* of any parish in the Union, to inspect it at any time of the day, except Sunday, between the hours of 10 before noon, and 4 after noon [*Letter with G. O. Nov.* 26, 1868.]

19. The following is the prescribed form—

Religious Creed Register.

——————————Union [*or* Parish].　——————————*Master* [*or Matron*]
of the Workhouse at——————————.

Date of Entry.	Date of Admission.	NAME. —— Christian and Surname.	From whence Admitted.	Religious Creed.	Name of Informant	Discharged or Dead.

20. Mr. White, the master of the Newington workhouse, has added to the creed register four columns from the "index of admissions and discharges," whereby the latter is rendered unnecessary, and the creed register and index are as follows :—

Date of Entry.	No. in Relief List.	Date of Admission.	NAME: Christian and Surname.	When born.	From whence Admitted.	Religious Creed.	Name and Address of Informant.	Discharged or Dead.	Date of Discharge or Death.	Remarks.

21. He permits any person to visit a pauper inmate on the days and at the hours prescribed by the guardians, and

with the exception of visits to sick paupers, the interview should be held in a room separate from the other inmates, but in the presence of himself, matron, or porter [*C. O. Art.* 118].

22. He takes care that the visitor does not give to the pauper spirits, food, or papers of an improper tendency, or permit any improper conversation, but he should not needlessly watch the visitor and pauper, or prevent proper intercourse [*Instruct. Letter, Feb.* 1842].

23. He allows any licensed minister of religion to visit any inmate of the same religious persuasion [*C. O. Art.* 122], as shown by the creed register, who may desire to see him, but not to converse with other inmates, except in cases where the guardians may lawfully allow it, or to interfere with the good order of the workhouse. Such visits to sick inmates may be repeated at reasonable times, as long as the said inmates may desire.

24. In numerous workhouses, the guardians, with the consent of the chaplain, permit the town or city missionaries to hold divine service in the workhouse at stated periods, and to visit and distribute tracts to the inmates generally ; and in workhouses where there is not a chaplain, the guardians permit the Wesleyans or dissenting ministers to do the same.

25. He allows, under the directions of the guardians, any inmates who are members of the Church of England to attend the services at the parish church on every Sunday, Good Friday, and Christmas Day, under the charge of some officer [*C. O. Art.* 125]. In London and other large towns, the well-conducted inmates who are over sixty years of age, are allowed to leave the workhouse until night, in order that they may attend any place of worship.

26. He allows all inmates, for whom a religious service is not provided in the workhouse, to attend a place of worship of their own denomination, if there be such within a convenient distance [*C. O. Art.* 126], subject to the regulations and approval of the Poor Law Board, unless the guardians

have refused this permission to any inmate from his having abused it, and have entered the ground of their refusal in their minutes [31 & 32 *Vic. c.* 122, *s.* 21].

27. He does not require any inmates above twelve years of age to attend at prayers, or at the religious services in the workhouse, or elsewhere, who may object to do so on account of their religious principles differing from those of the Established Church [*C. O. Art.* 124].

28. He does not allow any child under twelve years of age, who may be regularly visited by a minister of the same religious denomination as the child, to be instructed in any other religion than that indicated by the creed register; if the parents or surviving parent of the child, or in the case of orphan and deserted children, such minister, makes a request in writing to that effect. He allows any child above twelve years of age to receive instruction in any religious creed that the child desires, if the Poor Law Board consider the child competent to exercise a judgment thereon [31 & 32 *Vic. c.* 122, *s.* 22].

DISCHARGE OF PAUPERS.

29. He is required, at their request, after reasonable notice, to discharge all inmates of sound mind who are not suffering from infectious disease [30 & 31 *Vic. c.* 106, *s.* 22], the discharge of whom, on the certificate of the medical officer, would be injurious to themselves or to others, and who are 16 years of age, and also all inmates ordered to be discharged by the Board of Guardians, at any time of the day (but not usually during the night), except during divine service on Sunday. In the event of an able-bodied pauper with a family in the workhouse wishing to leave, the master must discharge the family also, unless the guardians have directed him to allow them to remain [*C. O. Art.* 115].

30. He may not detain in the workhouse a lunatic, idiot, or imbecile who is reported by the medical officer to be dangerous to himself or to others [*C. O. Art.* 101]; and in

the event of any inmate of unsound mind becoming violent or dangerous, he should request the attendance of the medical officer, and on his certificate the relieving officer should remove such inmate to the county asylum, or to an asylum which may have been indicated by the guardians for that purpose, and report to the guardians [16 & 17 *Vic.* c. 97, s. 67, and C. O. Art. 208].

31. Undesirable delay often occurs in the removal of these cases from want of diligence on the part of the relieving officer, the difficulty of obtaining the certificate of a magistrate, and the want of accommodation in the county asylum or in neighbouring private asylums.

Chapter XVI.

INSPECTION AND GENERAL ARRANGEMENTS
OF THE WORKHOUSE.

——◆——

1. He visits every part of the workhouse occupied by male paupers once daily, and their sleeping-wards twice a day, viz : at or before 11 a.m., and before 9 p.m. in winter, or 10 p.m. in summer, to see that all the inmates are in bed and the fires and lights extinguished, except such as may be necessary for the sick [*C. O.* 208, *Nos. 7 and 10*].

2. He does not allow more than two persons to occupy the same bed unless all are under seven years of age, or they are a mother and her infant children [*C. O. Art.* 111]. It is desirable that he should not allow more than one person above ten years of age to sleep together, except a mother and infant.

3. In his visits to the wards occupied by females, he should be accompanied by the matron or other officer, and he should not enter such wards at night alone.

4. He is responsible for the cleanliness of the wards, and in his visits should everywhere notice the degree of cleanliness and tidiness, and give such directions as may be necessary.

5. He should notice the state of repair of the furniture and buildings, and call the attention of the visiting committee or guardians to any defects.

6. He should ascertain that all furniture, vessels, appliances, and goods generally which have been ordered by the guardians, are supplied correctly and in good order.

7. He should ascertain whether any inmates wish to

make complaints and give them a proper opportunity to do so, and if he cannot remedy the evils complained of, and if the complainant wishes to make his complaint to the guardians, he shall take him to the next ordinary meeting of the board.

8. He should ascertain that the inmates do not accumulate food or other prohibited articles, and that they have the means of properly placing their clothes aside at night. He should, however, allow such of the sick as cannot eat their food at once to retain it for a reasonable time.

9. He should not allow the inmates to keep combustible matters, playing-cards, or written or printed papers of an improper tendency, or to play at cards or any game of hazard; but it is usual to allow the aged and the sick to play at dominoes, draughts, fox and goose, and similar games, and to read periodicals of a proper character [*C. O. Art.* 119, 120, 121].

10. He should not allow the inmates to smoke tobacco in any room of the workhouse, except by the special permission of the guardians or the medical officer; and the guardians may forbid smoking even in the yards [*C. O. Art.* 121].

11. He should ascertain that the drains, water-closets, privies, urinals, taps and sinks, water-supply, and all sanitary apparatus, are in good repair and efficient.

12. Where there is only one porter, the master receives the keys of the workhouse from him at 9 p.m., and delivers them to the same officer at 6 a.m. daily, or at other hours at the discretion of the guardians [*C. O. Art.* 208], but where there is both a night and a day porter the keys are usually transferred from one to the other without the intervention of the master.

13. He reads, or in the event of absence, indisposition, or religious objection, causes to be read, prayers to the paupers daily, before breakfast and after supper, and says, or causes to be said, grace before each meal [*C. O. Art.* 208, *Nos.* 4 and 9].

14. He inspects the paupers, or causes them to be in-

spected, daily, and observes their clothing and state of cleanliness, and calls over their names, or causes them to be called over, in their respective wards half-an-hour after the bell shall have been rung for rising [*C. O. Art.* 208, *No.* 5].

15. He causes the able-bodied and children between the ages of seven and fifteen years, of both sexes, to rise, take meals, begin work, leave off work, and go to bed at the following hours, subject to any change which may be made by the guardians with the consent of the Poor Law Board, and also subject to the hours to be devoted to the education of the children in schools.

Form N, C. O. Art. 102.

	Rise.	Breakfast.	Work.	Dinner.	Work.	Supper.	Go to Bed.
	A.M.	A.M.	A.M.	P.M.	P.M.	P.M.	P.M.
March 25th to Sep. 29th	5¾	6½ to 7	7 to 12	12 to 1	1 to 6	6 to 7	8
Sep. 29th to March 25th	6¾	7¾ to 8	8 to 12	12 to 1	1 to 6	6 to 7	8

16. He, with the matron, acting under the direction of the guardians, and after consultation with the medical officer [*C. O. Art.* 106, *Inst. Letter, Feb.* 1842], fixes the hour of rising and going to bed of the aged inmates and children, and enforces the directions of the guardians as to time and place; when and where the meals of those classes shall be eaten. He takes care that the meals of the able-bodied inmates, excepting imbeciles and suckling women, shall be always taken in the dining-hall or day room [*C. O. Art.* 104], and the same rule is adopted in reference to all classes except vagrants, the sick, infants, and such of the aged as cannot leave their beds or their wards, who eat their meals in their wards.

17. He does not permit any able-bodied inmate, or any child of either sex, between seven and fifteen years of age, to go into or remain in the sleeping rooms during work hours, without a special reason for so doing [*C. O. Art.* 105].

CLASSIFICATION.

18. He is required to observe the division of the inmates into seven classes [*C. O. Art.* 98], viz. :—
   1. Men infirm through age or other cause.
   2. Able-bodied men and youths above the age of fifteen years.
   3. Boys between seven and fifteen years of age.
   4. Women infirm through age or other cause.
   5. Able-bodied women and girls above fifteen years of age.
   6. Girls between seven and fifteen years of age.
   7. Children under seven years of age.

19. He is to suggest to the guardians and take their instructions as to the most suitable accommodation for these classes, and for any subdivision of them on moral grounds, for the providing a proper number of aged married couples' sleeping-rooms, and wards for vagrants of both sexes.

20. He reports to the guardians when the workhouse is full.

Chapter XVII.

SERVING OF FOOD.

1. He should be present at the serving and distribution of the food [*C. O. Art.* 208, *No.* 8], and notice that the food is properly cooked, cut, and served, and that there is a proper supply of knives, forks, spoons, plates, and other utensils for each inmate, and the means of conveying the food to distant parts of the workhouse whilst warm, without undue delay.

2. He should notice the quality of the food, and particularly of the meat and bread, and the proportion of fat to lean in the former. He should see that there are sufficient scales, and that they are in good order and correct, and in the event of any pauper requiring his food to be weighed, the master or the matron must weigh it in the presence of the complainant and of two other persons [*C. O. Art.* 109].

3. The plates and mugs should be of pottery, and there should be a knife, fork, spoon, plate, and mug or basin, for each inmate.

4. He should not crowd the inmates so as to cause inconvenience, but distribute them conveniently on the benches.

5. He should not occupy an undue portion of the dining-room for the cutting and distribution of the food, so as to place the benches for the inmates too closely together, but allow the benches to be properly distributed about the room, since otherwise the air will become unduly foul.

6. He should take care that the ventilation of the dining-room is sufficient, and particularly in hot weather, but draughts of cold air should not fall directly upon the food or the inmates.

7. He should keep silence and order during the meals.

8. Care should be taken to prevent the inmates, and par-

ticularly the sick, aged, and children, from sitting down with wet clothes or wet feet.

9. All the inmates should be clean and tidy when they arrive at the dining-room, and come and go in a quiet and orderly manner.

10. Several carvers and pairs of scales are required in many workhouses, and proper persons should be told off to carry the food rapidly to the inmates, as soon as it is ready for two or more persons.

11. Whatever can be placed upon the tables before the hot food is served should be done—as, for example, bread, salt, and utensils.

12. In the serving of food the special dislikes of certain inmates should be noted—as, for example, in reference to fat, and thus lessen waste.

13. All uneaten food should be collected in a cleanly manner [*Inst. Let.* 1842], and, if possible, served at a subsequent meal. It should not be carried away by the inmates.

14. Interchanges of food between the inmates should be allowed *within the limits of order*, since with a fixed dietary some will eat less and others more, whilst some would gladly exchange food, as bread for meat, or fat for lean.

15. He should cause printed notices in reference to complaints by inmates, to be placed in every ward [*Cir. Sep.* 27, 1866], and those in reference to the introduction of spirituous and fermented liquors in the entrance-hall and dining-room [4 *& 5 Will. IV. c.* 76, *s.* 94]. Printed copies of the dietaries are to be suspended in the dining-rooms and day rooms.

16. He allows proper facilities to suckling mothers to have access to their infants [*C. O. Art.* 99]. He permits parents and children who are in the workhouse to have interviews daily, and members of the same family who reside in different workhouses to see each other occasionally [*Inst. Let. Feb.* 1842].

17. He should not give tobacco, spirituous or fermented liquors, or extra food, to any inmate without the authority of the guardians or the medical officer [*C. O.* 107 *& 108, and Circular, December* 7, 1868].

Chapter XVIII.

LEAVE OF ABSENCE, EXERCISE, AND EMPLOYMENT.

LEAVE OF ABSENCE.

1. He has power, by the authority of the board of guardians, to allow inmates temporary leave of absence, and must report such allowance to the guardians at their next ordinary meeting [*C. O. Art.* 116]. When leave is given for absence during a part of a day, he should require the pauper to return to the workhouse at a convenient hour.

2. Leave should be given to inmates of intemperate habits, or of bad character, with much discretion; but to the aged of good character liberally, whilst children and imbeciles may be permitted to leave the workhouse for exercise, under the charge of the schoolmistress or other officer.

3. Any inmate may attend a court of law on *subpœna*, and demand his own clothes for that purpose, without being discharged by the master.

4. To deny the privilege of leave of absence during a part of a day, for a lengthened period, as many weeks, to any inmate who seeks it, should be very exceptional, and be based upon the most satisfactory ground. In such exceptional cases, the master should take the instructions of the board of guardians.

5. He should give or allow reasonable permission to all inmates to take exercise in the garden, but so that the sexes may be kept separate, and the several classes be not mixed together. This permission is particularly desirable in the case of children and the aged, but proper supervision should be provided.

6. In reference to the sick, and particularly to infectious cases, as fever and small-pox, he should allow this privilege under the advice of the medical officer, and the latter class of cases should be isolated.

EMPLOYMENT.

7. He should regulate the labour to be performed by all classes of male inmates [*C. O. Art.* 208], subject to the directions of the board of guardians, and also of the medical officer in reference to the sick.

8. He should bear in mind that occupation is desirable for all inmates, subject to the considerations of health and strength [*C. O. Art.* 208 , so that none who are able to work should be idle; and he should particularly enforce labour upon the able-bodied inmates. The kind of employment should, as far as possible, be useful in the management of the workhouse, and, if possible, remunerative. It should not be of a very dirty nature, or performed at inconvenient places and hours; and in reference to the children, it should be such as to fit them to gain their own living in after-life. By a judicious selection of occupation and careful training in habits of industry, many masters have the great pleasure of seeing boys raise themselves in the social scale in after life.

9. He may employ the inmates in domestic work in his own apartments, or in other service for himself, but this should be done with the approval of the guardians.

10. He takes care that the children are not so engaged in labour that they do not have education in school, during at least eighteen hours weekly [*C. O. Art.* 114], and it is very desirable that each child should be in school daily.

11. He may not require the inmates to perform other than necessary work on Christmas Day, Good Friday, general fast days, and Sundays [*C. O. Art.* 123].

12. He should cause proper supervision to be exercised over inmates who are engaged in any kind of labour.

Chapter III.

PUNISHMENTS.

1. He has power to punish the inmates for disorderly and refractory conduct, but it should be exercised discretely and not vindictively, and not overpass in any degree the letter and spirit of the law. This power, in reference to the children, is to be exercised concurrently with that of the schoolmaster [*C. O. Art.* 127, 128].

2. Where the master frequently and severely punishes the inmates, it may raise a presumption of his own unfitness for the task of governing the workhouse.

3. Frequent and severe punishment is likely to arouse vindictive feelings in the inmates, and to render them reckless rather than orderly; and whilst the master should not allow laxity of discipline or tolerate improper conduct on the part of any inmate, he should unite firmness with kindness, and strive to avoid punishment.

4. He should report incorrigible offenders to the board of guardians and take the instructions of the latter thereon; but he has power to take proceedings before the justices of the peace against disorderly paupers, if the case does not admit of delay.

5. He has power to punish specified classes of paupers, who by the Consolidated Order are termed *Disorderly*, by substituting for his dinner on one or two days 8 oz. of bread or 1 lb. of cooked potatoes or boiled rice, and by withholding from such pauper for any period not greater than forty-eight consecutive hours certain specified articles of food which the pauper would otherwise receive, viz., butter, cheese, tea, sugar, and broth [*C. O. Art.* 129].

6. He must carefully bear in mind the exact limitations of his authority, and not restrict the whole dietary of the day to bread and water, if milk porridge, or any other food besides butter, cheese, tea, sugar, and broth would have been otherwise supplied at breakfast or supper.

7. He has power to punish specified classes of paupers who by the Consolidated Order are termed *Refractory, with certain specified circumstances of aggravation*, with confinement in a room for any period not exceeding twelve hours [*C. O. Art.* 131], or he may punish such as *Disorderly* [*C. O. Art.* 132]; but having so elected to punish them, he cannot also punish them as refractory.

8. He may not, even under orders from the guardians, confine any pauper for a longer period than twenty-four consecutive hours, unless it be intended to take such pauper before a magistrate, and that period is not sufficient for the purpose [4 *& 5 Wm. IV. c.* 76, *s.* 93; *C. O. Art.* 130].

9. He should take care that the place of confinement is not cold, ill ventilated, or dark, and that there is a seat and a night stool therein, with the addition of a bed when used by night, viz., from 8 p.m. to 6 a.m. [*C. O. Art.* 135.]

10. The proper place for confinement is the refractory cell, as sanctioned by the Poor Law Board; but he may confine an inmate in an ordinary ward if for special reasons he may deem it desirable so to do.

11. It is desirable to restrict the duration of the confinement to a short period—say from one to three hours, and not to extend it into the night.

12. He may not inflict corporal punishment on any adult pauper [*C. O. Art.* 142], neither may he flog a boy over 14 years of age; but he may cane a boy under 15 years of age over his clothes, or he may use a rod or similar other instrument which had been approved by the guardians [*C. O. Art.* 139], but he should inflict this punishment in the presence of the schoolmaster [*C. O. Art.* 141].

13. He may not punish a boy until two hours after the commission of the offence [*C. O. Art.* 140], a restriction

which is fitted to prevent punishment in a fit of anger, and to render the punishment less vindictive and more deterrent in the estimation of the boy.

14. He has not power to inflict personal chastisement except upon a male child, and should it be necessary to resort to force in order to put the refractory pauper in the place of confinement, he should direct the porter or other officer to exert it.

15. He may not punish by either change of diet or confinement any pauper under twelve years of age, or over sixty years of age, or any pregnant woman, or suckling woman, or any inmates who have been under medical treatment, or on the medical weekly return as sick or infirm, at any time within seven days immediately preceding without the certificate of the medical officer [*C. O. Art.* 134], and he must modify the punishment in such exceptional cases as the medical officer may suggest.

16. He cannot reasonably in every case require the opinion of the medical officer as to the pregnancy of a refractory female before he punishes her; but if he have any reason to believe that the pauper in question is pregnant, he should obtain that opinion or forbear to inflict the punishment.

17. Whenever he punishes any disorderly or refractory pauper he must enter the required particulars in the punishment-book, and lay the book before the guardians at the next ordinary meeting [*C. O. Art.* 143, 144, 145]. He must not inflict punishment for misconduct committed before the last admission of the inmate [*C. O. Art.* 133].

18. The following is the form of punishment-book [*Form O, C. O. Art.* 143].

No. of the Case.	Name.	Offence.	Date of Offence.	Punishment inflicted by Master or other Officer.	Opinion of the Guardians thereon.	Punishment ordered by Board of Guardians.	Date of Punishment.	Initials of Clerk.	Observations.

Chapter XX.

ILLNESS AND DEATH OF INMATES.

1. In the event of the illness or insanity of any inmates, or of an injury befalling them, he is required to take such immediate action for their relief as the case may require [C. O. Art. 208, No. 14], and to direct the attention of the medical officer to it on the next visit of that officer, or request his immediate attendance ; or should the case be urgent and the medical officer absent, he would be justified in calling in any medical practitioner whilst he sent for the medical officer.

2. Whilst taking due care that every sick pauper may obtain the assistance of the medical officer, he should not send for that officer except in cases of urgency, or when he has omitted to make his usual visit.

3. He informs any relative or friend of an inmate living near to the workhouse, or within a reasonable distance therefrom, when such inmate is dangerously ill [C. O. Art. 208, No. 14], and he carefully provides that no person who is dangerously ill, or who may be about to die, is left without a competent attendant by day or night [C. O. Art. 208, No. 15].

4. When medicines are required and are not dispensed at the workhouse, he directs a messenger to fetch them with due speed.

5. He should allow all proper facilities for the visits of friends of the sick, and particularly those of one who is very ill, and he should take care that religious consolation and advice should be offered to the dying.

6. Where there is a chaplain, his duties to the sick will be defined by the board of guardians; but in cases of dangerous illness the master should request the attendance of the chaplain or of some other minister of religion whose attendance may be desired by the inmates [*C. O. Art.* 208, *No.* 14], and in the latter case he should see that the attention of such minister is restricted to that particular inmate or to any other who may wish his advice.

7. In the event of the death of an inmate, he causes the death to be duly registered by the registrar, and the body to be removed with convenient speed to the dead-house [*C. O. Art.* 208, *No.* 17], and informs the medical officer, and the nearest relative of the deceased who may be known to him, or who resides within a reasonable distance [*C. O. Art.* 208, *No.* 16].

8. If the body be not removed by the relatives, and there be not a necessity for a coroner's inquest, he takes such steps for the interment of the body as may have been directed by the guardians in reference to paupers generally.

9. He takes charge of the effects of the deceased and delivers an inventory of them to the guardians at their next ordinary meeting, and enters the occurrence of the death in his journal and in the proper register of deaths [*C. O. Art.* 208, *Nos.* 17 & 18]. He delivers the effects to the next of kin or the executor or administrator; but if money be found amongst the effects, the guardians may reimburse themselves for the cost of maintenance of the pauper for the preceding twelve months and for the cost of burial, and the repayment of any loan which they may have made to him, and then hand over the surplus to the next of kin, executor, or administrator.

10. He may not allow a post-mortem examination of any deceased pauper to be made if the husband or wife or any known relative of such deceased pauper object [2 & 3 *Wm. IV. c.* 75, *s.* 7].

11. If the body of a deceased pauper be unclaimed by any relative, and such body is legally required for the purpose of

anatomical dissection, he may permit the body to be removed for that purpose on fulfilling all the legal requirements, but he should obtain the authority of the board of guardians for such a course where the requirement for dissection is likely to be made, as in a town where there is a medical school.

12. The following is the regulation by which he must be guided, viz. [2 & 3 *Wm. IV. c.* 75, *s.* 9] :—

" In no case shall the body of any person be removed for anatomical examination from any place where such person may have died until after forty-eight hours from the time of such person's decease, nor until after twenty-four hours' notice, to be reckoned from the time of such decease, to the inspector (of anatomy) of the district of the intended removal of the body, or if no such inspector have been appointed, to some physician, surgeon, or apothecary residing at or near the place of death, nor unless a certificate stating in what manner such person came by his death shall previously to the removal of the body have been signed by the physician, surgeon, or apothecary, who shall be called in after the death of such person to view the body, and who shall state the manner or cause of death according to the best of his knowledge and belief, but who shall not be concerned in examining the body after removal ; and that in case of such removal, such certificate shall be delivered, together with the body, to the party receiving the same for anatomical examination."

13. As to the place of burial of a deceased pauper, the Poor Law Commissioners expressed the following opinion as to the requirements of 7 & 8 *Vic. c.* 101, *s.* 31, in a correspondence with the guardians of the West Derby Union [*Official Circular, Oct* 1, 1847] :—

" 1. As a general rule, all bodies buried by guardians are to be buried in the churchyard or in a consecrated burial-ground, and this in the parish or township of the death. 2. But the burial in such churchyard or consecrated burial-ground may be dispensed with by the desire of the deceased, or husband, wife, or next of kin. 3. If the burial in the churchyard or consecrated burial-ground be dispensed with in compliance with such desire, the guardians may apparently authorise the burial anywhere, *i.e.*, in unconsecrated ground, or in ground out of the parish of the death. Also the guardians may authoritatively direct the burial to take place in the parish where the deceased was chargeable. But this is a departure from the general law, and is in this clause made the exception. It is only authorised when the deceased or his relatives have desired it, or the guardians see particular cause for it. This case may arise (as in case 2) when there is an objection of the deceased or his friends to burial in the churchyard or consecrated burial-ground of the parish. And if there be any burial-ground of the parish or township (*i.e.*, belonging to the township) which is not consecrated, the guardians may bury the body in such burial-ground."

Chapter III.

VAGRANTS.

———•———

1. He is responsible for the proper state of the vagrant wards, and should report to the guardians any defect in the amount of accommodation, and in the sanitary arrangements for vagrants.

2. He should not allow a larger number of persons to be admitted into them than the Poor Law Board have directed, and where plank beds are provided, a width of not less than twenty-seven inches should be allowed to each person.

3. If the space provided be insufficient to properly accommodate the number of applicants, he should take the instructions of the guardians with a view to appropriate an additional room.

4. He should take care that each person on admission is observed as to the apparent state of health, and that proper means of communication, as by bells, exist between the vagrant wards and the apartments of the porter or other officer.

5. If a vagrant be sick, the master should call the attention of the medical officer to the case, and if necessary should send for him.

6. Should the vagrant refuse or neglect to perform a proper task of work (even if he at the same time should refuse his breakfast), or injure or destroy his own clothes, or the property of the guardians, the master should take him before the justices for punishment [5 *Geo. IV. c.* 83, *s.* 3, & 5 & 6 *Vic. c.* 57, *s.* 3] if it be possible for him to do so.

7. He should take care that food is given to every

vagrant who is in urgent need of it, and carry out the instructions of the guardians where food is ordered to be given to every vagrant.

8. He is not required to admit applicants who have the means of paying for a lodging, and rarely would he be justified in admitting a drunken person.

9. When the weather is wet and cold, he should cause the inmates, and particularly the women and children, to be properly warmed, and their clothes dried.

10. When it is practicable, he should distinguish between the professional tramp, and the well-conducted person seeking employment, and if there be the means of separating the two classes, he should do so.

11. The vagrants should not be allowed to smoke in the wards, and care should be taken that they do not destroy or set on fire the bedding and furniture.

12. He should cause them to be locked up at night, and supply them with proper conveniences, and, where a bath is provided, cause them to be bathed on their admission, provided the water be not too cold in cold weather. Proper lavatory basins and towels should be supplied.

Chapter XXIII.

REMUNERATION AND WASTE.

———•———

1. His remuneration consists of salary, emoluments, and a superannuation allowance, which may be calculated upon the total amount of both the former, but he is not entitled to any perquisites.

2. The salary is not unfrequently very small in relation to the extent of the duties and the responsibility of the office, and, consequently, the efficiency of the master is in not a few instances equally unsatisfactory. Where the master evinces efficiency, there is, however, a tendency to increase the salary; but deficiency of salary is no excuse for neglect or inefficient performance of duty.

3. The emoluments consist of lodgings, furnished or unfurnished, washing, servants, and rations of food, which are usually specifically prescribed by a minute of the guardians, or computed as double the rations of the highest-class dietary of the inmates, with or without power to exchange a part for some other kind of food. There is usually a provision in the meat contract for the supply of superior joints to the master and other officers.

4. His wife is commonly the matron, with a salary and similar emoluments, and it is usual to allow one or more children to live with them on paying for each child above the age of infancy a sum which equals the cost of the dietary of an inmate.

5. They are not allowed to sell their rations or to give them to their visitors; neither can they legally make a private arrangement with the tradesmen who supply goods to the workhouse to deliver to them food of better quality than that ordered by the guardians.

6. Although the rations of the officers are given for their own use only, it is very usual for the officers to supply food thus obtained to friends who may visit them, and officers very generally consider that, as they are entitled to the food thus allowed, they may consume it in any way which seems good to them. The regulation which forbids the sale of such provisions is intended to remove a motive to fraud, in the appropriation of food to which they might not be entitled, in order to obtain money; and that which forbids the giving of it to visitors has the same object, as well as to discourage the too frequent reception of friends.

7. These regulations are sometimes so greatly disregarded that the master and matron have several children living with them, for whose board and lodging they do not pay, and receive visitors for many weeks at a time.

8. The value of the emoluments to the master frequently equals the amount of his salary, but the relation varies much.

9. The guardians may, with the consent of the Poor Law Board, award him gratuities for extra services [C. O. Art. 172].

10. The superannuation allowance is not obtained by the master as a right, but at the discretion of the guardians with the consent of the Poor Law Board, after he has been in the service of the guardians of some parish or Union for twenty years, and is himself sixty years of age; but the amount cannot exceed two-thirds of the annual value of his salary and emoluments.

11. The dependence of the amount of this allowance upon the will of the guardians is intended to promote efficiency in the discharge of duty, since those who see the result of his labours determine the amount to be allowed to him; but it is not an unmixed good, since it tends to induce a spirit of servility to the whole board, or more frequently to the leading member or members of the board, or the dominant party at the board, and thus to induce him to regard some of the members as his friends and others as his

enemies, and to make him a partisan. Moreover, he is less the servant of the Poor Law Board than is desirable, since he will naturally regard it as his first duty to stand well with the guardians, and particularly on questions of cost of management.

12. It is not desirable that this allowance should be made without the concurrence of the guardians ; but the guardians and the Poor Law Inspector having expressed their satisfaction with the manner in which his duties have been discharged, the allowance should be, as a matter of right, in proportion to length of service.

13. It is most undesirable that the income of the master should be in any degree increased by perquisites.

14. He must not receive a commission upon goods purchased by him for the guardians. He should not appropriate to himself an unauthorised allowance of any stores, nor make any personal gain in cooking and distributing food and other articles [*C. O. Art.* 218].

15. Dripping and other articles of waste should not be used or sold by him for his own benefit, but accounted for to the guardians [*Inst. Letter, Feb.* 5, 1842].

16. When preparing foods, as tea, which are prepared for many persons together, the specific allowance for each person should be given.

17. When butter is allowed it should be apportioned to each person, and not spread upon the bread, so that the inmate cannot have the weight tested. This is now easily effected in many workhouses by the use of a board with depressions each to hold half an ounce of butter, but it is requisite that the butter be kept cool.

18. The allowance for waste in the cooking and distribution of food should not be guessed at but determined with great care, and the amount entered daily or at short intervals.

19. It is not possible to lay down a rule as to the amount of waste which occurs in cooking meat, since it varies with the degree and mode of cooking, the quality of the meat,

K

and the age of the animal, the joint which is cooked, and the relative proportion of lean and fat. Some masters find that 20 per cent., or one-fifth of the weight of raw meat, is lost in the cooking, whilst others charge between 30 and 40 per cent. as loss.

20. The loss in boiling meat without bone, and without much fat, is from 20 to 25 per cent. ; whilst that in roasting meat is from 25 to 30 per cent. ; but there is also a loss in cutting up the meat, so that the loss on boiled meat from both causes is often one-third of the weight of the meat when raw.

21. There must be loss in keeping and cutting up the bread, since, by keeping, the water which it contains evaporates ; and in cutting up, the turn of the scale and the weight of crumbs cannot be estimated. The master should take care that the whole of the bread is weighed when it arrives, and that it is not received until it is required for immediate use, that it is not delivered when new, and that it is not so underbaked as to contain too much moisture.

22. When it is baked in the workhouse it is convenient to bake some of it in loaves of 4 oz., 5 oz., or 6 oz., for the use of each inmate.

23. The loss in keeping and distributing dry goods, except soap and large old potatoes, should be almost inappreciable if the weight on receipt be duly tested.

24. The loss on brandy and other spirits should not be great, if no larger quantity is purchased at one time than will be distributed within a month, and if they are kept in stone, well-corked, or well-stoppered vessels. When kept for a long time in casks, or other wooden vessels, closed by common corks, and frequently opened, there will be considerable loss by evaporation.

25. There should not be any appreciable loss in the distribution, since not more than the allowance should be given, and in filling a measure a slight deficiency must be allowed, in order that no overflow may occur.

26. When the spirit is purchased in casks, the master

should measure it, and put it in stone bottles with sealed corks, and open one at a time only.

27. Wines and spirits should be kept in the charge of the master only, and the store-rooms for dry goods should be at all times locked.

28. The master, or a trustworthy substitute, should always be present at the distribution of such stores as are in his immediate charge.

29. He should keep a rough day book for his own use of the quantity of goods received into and sent out of stock, and of the amount of waste which he has proved to have occurred.

Chapter XXXX.

BOOK-KEEPING AND BOOKS.

—◆—

SUMMARY.

1. The following is a summary of the chief duties which devolve upon the master in reference to the keeping of the books under his care :—

DAILY.

1. Compare and check the rough admission and discharge book, with the admission and discharge tickets, and notices of births and deaths.
2. Copy into the admission and discharge book.
3. Complete the index of admissions and discharges, and the creed register.
4. Issue orders for provisions.
5. Complete daily provision account, and check it with the admission and discharge book.
6. Entries in the master's day book.
7. Entries in the petty-cash portion of the day book, with memoranda of receipts and payments.
8. Complete the various clothing books, and clothing registers.
9. Issue tickets of stores, and enter memoranda made by the matron, as to the disposal of articles for the daily consumption book.
10. Entries in Union medical relief book, and compare the various diets and cards for the sick before each

meal, and accurately charge the various quantities of food.

11. Complete inventory, or stock book.

12. Entries in master's journal.

WEEKLY.

13. Complete the weekly provision book, and check the items with the indoor medical relief book and daily provision book.

14. Complete the weekly provision and consumption book, and compare items with the invoices.

QUARTERLY.

15. Prepare the quarterly summary, and the abstract and balance-sheet.

AT VARIOUS PERIODS.

16. Issue notices to registrar of births and deaths, and orders for burial, funerals, and admission to hospitals, make entries in punishment book, etc.

2. Besides all these, there are numerous clerical duties which need not be particularised, and it is quite evident that so large an amount of clerical duty demands ready assistants, and presses very heavily upon the time and attention of the masters of many workhouses.

3. In the larger workhouses it may be desirable that a steward should be appointed, who would have charge of all matters connected with the stores, and perform much of the clerical work now devolving upon the master. The present arrangement is not consistent with efficient performance of duty, and the proper supervision of large workhouses.

BOOKS.

4. The following are forms of the chief books which the Poor Law Board have prescribed by the General Order of Accounts, 14th January, 1867, and by other orders, to be kept by the master, viz. :—

The Inventory Book.
Admission and Discharge Book.
    Ditto   ditto   for Vagrants.
In-door Relief List.
Abstract of ditto.
Master's Day Book.
Summary of ditto.
Master's Book of Receipts and Payments.
Master's Receipt Check Book.
Daily Provisions Consumption Account.
Weekly ditto   ditto.
Provisions Receipt and Consumption, ditto.
Summary of Provisions Received and Consumed.
Balance of Provisions Account.
Clothing Materials Receipt and Conversion Account.
Clothing Receipt and Expenditure Account.
Clothing Register Book.
Necessaries and Miscellaneous Account.
Quarterly Summary of the Necessaries and Miscellaneous Account.
Balance of ditto.
Punishment Book (see page 120).
Creed Register (see page 106).
Register of Births.
Register of Deaths.

The Inventory Book.

UNION. _____   Master.

Date of Entry.	Fixtures.	Furniture.	Utensils.	Bedding.†	House Linen.†	Other Effects.	Articles transferred, condemned, or disposed of.		
							Date.	Notes of Articles transferred to other Parts of the House.	Notes of Articles condemned or disposed of.
(*)									

* A separate page is to be devoted to each office, room, or apartment, and in this space is to be inserted the name of the office, room, or apartment to which the page is appropriated.

† Under the head "Bedding" are to be entered mattresses, beds, blankets, sheets, and rugs; and under "House Linen" are to be entered tablecloths and towels.

A blank space should be left at the end of the account for each apartment or division for the insertion of new articles.

Notes of articles transferred to other parts of the house, condemned, or disposed of, should be made as soon as the same takes place, and the new purchases should be punctually entered so as to represent the exact state of the house in reference to the articles to be entered in this book at all times.

Admission and Discharge Book for Vagrants.

Master of the Workhouse at _____

UNION. _____

ADMITTED.						Where he slept last night.	DISCHARGED.					Whether searched on Admission, and if so, what, if anything, found.†
Day of the Month.	Day of the Week.	Hour of Admission.	Names of Vagrant, wife, and family.	Age.	Calling or Occupation.		At what hour of the next day discharged.*	Whether set to work.	If not, why?	What work done.	To what place going.	

* _Note._—When a Vagrant has remained in the Vagrant Ward for 24 hours and is not then discharged, or when he is sooner removed into the ordinary wards of the Workhouse, he should be forthwith duly entered in the Workhouse Admission and Discharge Book.

† See the Provision in the Statute 11 & 12 Vict. c. 110. s. 10.

In Unions within the Metropolis, columns must be added for the nature and quantity of food given and the cost.

Admission and Discharge Book.

UNION. _____

Master of the Workhouse at _____

ADMITTED.

Day of the Month.	Day of the Week.	Next Meal after Admission.	Name.	Calling, if any.	Religious Persuasion.	When Born.	Class for Diet.*											Number affixed to the Pauper's Clothes.	Parish from which Admitted.†	By whose Order admitted.	Date of the Order of Admission.	If born in the House, Name of Parent.	Observations on Condition at the Time of Admission, and any other General Remarks.
							1	2	3	4	4a	5	6	7	8	8a	9						

DISCHARGED.

Date.	Day of the Week.	Last Meal before Discharge.	Name.	Class for Diet.*											How Discharged; and if by Order, by whose Order.	In case of Death, say "Dead."	Observations on general Character and Behaviour in the Workhouse.
				1	2	3	4	4a	5	6	7	8	8a	9			

When a Pauper is admitted before breakfast the Master is to enter in the column for "next meal after admission" the letter B: when before dinner the letter D; and when before supper the letter S. And when a Pauper is discharged after breakfast the Master is to enter in the column for "last meal before discharge" the letter B; when after dinner the letter D; and when after supper the letter S.

* The columns "Class for Diet" are to be filled up by the figure 1. The Classes should correspond with the Classes of the Diet Table in use in the Workhouse. The columns 4a and 8a are for the Children.

† Unless the Guardians require the Vagrants to be entered in another book, the word "Vagrant" must be entered in this column against every person admitted as a Vagrant instead of the name of the Parish.

___ UNION. Half-year ending ___ 18__. ___ Master of the Workhouse at ___.

Able-bodied and their Families (exclusive of Vagrants).						Not Able-bodied and their Families (exclusive of Vagrants).										Calling of Pauper.	When born.	Of what Religious Persuasion.	Name of Pauper.	Number of Days in the House in each Week.												
Adults.				Children under 16 of Able-bodied Inmates.		Adults.				Children under 16.			Lunatics, Insane Persons, and Idiots.							1st Week.	2nd Week.	3rd Week.	4th Week.	5th Week.	6th Week.	7th Week.	8th Week.	9th Week.	10th Week.	11th Week.	12th Week to 27th Week.	Totals for the Half-year.
Married Couples.						Married Couples.				Of Parents (not Able-bodied) being Inmates.		Orphans or other Children relieved without their Parents.																				
Males.	Females.	Other Males.	Other Females.	Illegitimate.	Other Children.	Males.	Females.	Other Males.	Other Females.	Illegitimate.	Other Children.		Males	Females.	Children under 16.																		
1	2	3	4	5	6	7	8	9	10	11	12	13	14	15	16																		

Totals of each Class. Total Days for each Week ...

1. The columns for the classification of the Paupers are to be filled by inserting the figure 1 in the proper column opposite each name, and leaving all the rest blank.

2. Whenever, in this Relief List, two or more persons of the same name occur, the Master of the Workhouse shall annex to the name of each of such persons a number in brackets, to distinguish him from other persons of the same name.

3. The number of each class of Paupers actually relieved on the *first of January* and on the *first of July* respectively, in each year, is to be shown at the beginning of this book, a portion of the book being set apart and ruled for this purpose.

* This should be the Parish from which the Pauper, or in case of a child born in the Workhouse from which its mother, was admitted.

Abstract of the In-door Relief Lists for the Half-year
ending _____ 18 .

_____ UNION.　　　　_____ *Master of the Workhouse at* _____

Folio of the In-door Relief List.	Parishes.	Number of Days in each Week.																	Total Days for the Half-year
		1st Week.	2nd Week.	3rd Week.	4th Week.	5th Week.	6th Week.	7th Week.	8th Week.	9th Week.	10th Week.	11th Week.	12th Week.	13th Week.	14th Week.	15th Week.	16th Week. &c., to 27th Week.	
	Vagrants . .																	
	Total Days for each Week																	

The aggregate number of days in each week passed in the Workhouse by the total number of Paupers from each Parish must be taken from the Columns of total days for the several weeks in the In-door Relief Lists. Paupers admitted as Vagrants who remain in the Workhouse are to be enumerated among the paupers admitted from the Parish where the Workhouse is situated.

A few sheets of this Abstract (according to the extent of the Union) are to be bound up at the end of the Book containing the In-door Relief Lists.

The Master's Book of Receipts and Payments.

_____ UNION.　　　　_____ *Master of the Workhouse at* _____

RECEIPTS.			PAYMENTS.		
Date.	Name and Particulars.		Date.	Name and Particulars.	

Balanced this ___ day of _____ .　　(Signed) _____ Master.

Master's Receipt Check Book.

This part to be retained by the Master.

No. ___ .

_____ Union.

___ day of _____ 18 .

Mr. _____

For _____

_____

£ _____

No. ___ .

_____ Union.

_____ day of _____ 18 .

Received of _____

the Sum of _____

on behalf of the above-named Union in respect of _____

£

(Signed) _____

Master of the Workhouse at _____

The Master's Day Book.

_____ UNION.

Master of the Workhouse at _____

					INVOICES.					
Date.	No. of Order.	No. of Invoice or Bill.	Name.	Trade.	Pro-visions.	Clothing.	Furniture and Property.	Ne-cessaries.	Repairs.	
					£ s. d.	£ s. d.	£ s. d.	£ s. d.	£ s. d.	£ s. d.
				Total . .						

The money columns should be added up weekly.

Summary of the Master's Day Book for the Quarter ending _____ 18___.

_____ UNION.

Master of the Workhouse at _____

No. of the Week.	NAMES OR TRADE.			ACCOUNT CHARGED.					
				Pro-visions.	Clothing.	Furniture and Property.	Ne-cessaries.	Repairs.	Total.
	£ s. d.	£ s. d.	£ s. d.	£ s. d.	£ s. d.	£ s. d.	£ s. d.	£ s. d.	£ s. d.
1. &c. to 13. .									
Totals									

Daily Provisions Consumption Account for ——— *the* ——— *day of* ——— 18——.

——— UNION.

——— *Master of the Workhouse at* ———

	BREAKFAST.				Prepared Provisions. (1)					DINNER.					Prepared Provisions.					SUPPER.					Prepared Provisions.			
CLASS.	Total Numbers.	Deduct Sick.	Absent.	Net Numbers.	oz. each.	lb. oz.	Pints each.	each.	each.	CLASS.	Total Numbers.	Sick.*	Absent.	Net Numbers.	oz. each.	lb. oz.	each.	each.	CLASS.	Total Numbers.	Sick.	Absent.	Net Numbers.	oz. each.	lb. oz.	each.	each.
1										1									1								
2										2									2								
3										3									3								
4										4									4								
4a										4a									4a								
5										5									5								
6										6									6								
7										7									7								
8										8									8								
8a										8a									8a								
9										9									9								
Vagrants.										Totals									Totals								
Totals (2)																											
Quantities of the several principal Articles in their unprepared state taken from the stores to supply the above meals. (3)																											
Waste (if any)																											

(1) The names of the articles prescribed in the Dietary are to be inserted.

(2) The total quantities on this line represent the quantities of the several articles of prepared provisions required for each meal.

(3) The quantities of the several principal articles in their unprepared state, necessary to supply the quantities of prepared provisions so required, are to be entered under the quantities of prepared provisions for each meal, and carried to the "*Weekly Provisions Consumption Account.*" Here also the Master may enter the allowance which he claims for *waste*, arising out of the preparation or distribution of the provisions; and in the case of meat, out of the weight of bone.

* Those only of the Sick who have not the ordinary Diet are to be deducted.

† On this line are to be placed such of Class 5 as have larger allowances than the Diet Table gives, on account of their being employed as nurses or in the household work, or such Paupers as receive peculiar allowances under the Medical Officer's advice without being entered on the Sick List.

_____ UNION.

_____ Master of the Workhouse at _____

Date.	Day of the Week.	Meal.	Consumed by the Paupers.		Taken from the Stores for the Officers and Servants of the Workhouse. (1)	Number of Paupers in the House during the Day.	Number of Members of the Establish-ment.
			lb. oz.	lb. oz.	lb. oz.		
		Breakfast .. :: ::					
		Dinner .. :: ::					
		Supper .. :: ::					
		Etc. :: ::					
Sick as per Medical Relief Book .. ::							
Supplied to A.B., Relieving Officer of District							
to C.D., Relieving Officer of District							
Extraordinary Supplies .. :: ::							
TOTALS to be carried to the "*Provisions Receipt and Consumption Account.*"					(2)		

(1) The quantities of the articles taken from the stores for the Officers and Servants of the Workhouse are to be entered at the time when they are taken.

(2) This total should agree with the total number of days in the Abstract of the In-door Relief List for the corresponding week.

Provisions Receipt and Consumption Account for the _____ *Week of the Quarter ending* _____ 18 _____.

_____ UNION.

_____ Master of the Workhouse at _____

ARTICLES.	Stock brought forward.	New Stock.	No. of Invoice.	Totals of Stock brought forward and new Stock.	Consumed.		Totals con-sumed and re-maining in Store.	Remaining in Store.	Required for next Week.
					By the Paupers.	By the Officers and Servants of the Workhouse.			

The "New Stock" of the several Articles, and the quantities "Consumed" "by the Paupers," and "by the Officers and Servants of the Workhouse" respectively, are to be carried to the "*Summary of Provisions Received and Provisions Consumed.*"

Summary of Provisions Received and Provisions Consumed
in the Quarter ending_____18 .

_____UNION.   _____*Master of the Workhouse at*_____

	*		*										
	lb.	oz.	lb.	oz.										
Received 1st week . .														
,, 2nd ,, . .														
,, 3rd ,, . .														
,, 4th ,, . .														
,, 5th ,, . .														
,, 6th ,, . .														
,, 7th ,, . .														
,, 8th ,, . .														
,, 9th ,, . .														
,, 10th ,, . .														
,, 11th ,, . .														
,, 12th ,, . .														
,, 13th ,, . .														
Totals received . .														
Consumed by the Paupers. 1st Week .														
2nd ,, .														
3rd ,, .														
4th ,, .														
5th ,, .														
6th ,, .														
7th ,, .														
8th ,, .														
9th ,, .														
10th ,, .														
11th ,, .														
12th ,, .														
13th ,, .														
Totals consumed by the Paupers . . .														
Consumed by the Officers and Servants of the Workhouse. 1st week .														
2nd ,, .														
3rd ,, .														
4th ,, .														
5th ,, .														
6th ,, .														
7th ,, .														
8th ,, .														
9th ,, .														
10th ,, .														
11th ,, .														
12th ,, .														
13th ,, .														
Totals consumed by the Officers and Servants of the Workhouse . .														

* The names of the Articles are to be placed at the head of the several Columns.
The "Totals received," the "Totals consumed by the Paupers," and the
"Totals consumed by the Officers and Servants of the Workhouse" are to be
carried to the "Balance of the Provisions Account for the Quarter,"

Balance of the Provisions Account for the Quarter ending _____ 18 .

Master of the Workhouse at

UNION.

Articles.	New Stock — Stock brought forward.		New Stock		Total Cost of New Stock, and Stock brought forward.	Consumed.				Stock remaining in Store.		Total Cost of Articles Consumed and In Store.
	Price.	Cost of Stock brought forward.	Price.	Cost of New Stock.		By the Paupers.		By the Officers and Servants of the Workhouse.		Cost of Stock remaining in Store.	Stock remaining in Store. Quantities.	
						Quantities.	Cost.	Quantities.	Cost.			
	s. d.	£ s. d.	s. d.	£ s. d.	£ s. d.		£ s. d.		£ s. d.	£ s. d.		£ s. d.

Submitted to _____ Member of the Visiting Committee this _____ day of _____ 18 , and found to be correct.

(Signed) {

Clothing Materials Receipt and Conversion Account.

Master of the Workhouse at _____

UNION.

RECEIVED.				CONVERTED.			
Date	Of whom.	No. of Invoice.	Quantity.	Date.	Into what.	Quantity used.	Folio of Clothing Receipt and Expenditure Book, or of Inventory Book.

Submitted to _____ Member of the Visiting Committee this _____ day of _____ 18 , and found to be correct.

(Signed) {

* A separate Account is to be kept of each article, and the name of the article is to be entered at the head of the page. The entries are to be made in the true order of time according as the articles are received and converted; and the account is to be made up and balanced every half-year.

Sheets, bedding, and house linen are to be entered in the *Inventory*.

The articles of clothing into which the materials are converted are to be carried to the *Clothing Receipt and Expenditure Account* in their proper columns.

Clothing Receipt and Expenditure Account.

_____ UNION.

Master of the Workhouse at _____

RECEIVED.

Date.	From whom or whence received, and No. of the Invoice.	Men's & Boys' Clothing.								Women's & Girls' Clothing.									
		Coats and Jackets.	Waistcoats.	Trousers.	Shirts.	Shoes.	Stockings.	Hats.	Handkerchiefs.	Gowns and Frocks.	Under Petticoats.	Upper Petticoats.	Shirts.	Aprons.	Handkerchiefs.	Shoes.	Stockings.	Caps.	Bonnets.

GIVEN OUT.

Date.	Number of the Suit.	Size.	Men's & Boys' Clothing.							Number of the Suit.	Size.	Women's & Girls' Clothing.									
			Coats and Jackets.	Waistcoats.	Shirts.	Shoes.	Stockings.	Hats.	Handkerchiefs.			Gowns and Frocks.	Under Petticoats.	Upper Petticoats.	Shirts.	Aprons.	Handkerchiefs.	Shoes.	Stockings.	Caps.	Bonnets.

Submitted to _____ Member _____ of the Visiting Committee this _____ day of _____ 18   , and found to be correct.

(Signed) {

In the several Columns is to be entered, according to the circumstances of the case, the number of the articles received and given out. The entries are to be made in the true order of time, according as the articles are received and converted, and the Account is to be made up and balanced every half-year.

Clothing Register Book.

Master of the Workhouse at _____

_____ UNION.

MALES.

Date of Admission.	Names.	No.*	[Size .]	Date of Discharge.	Date of Admission.	Names.	No. .	[Size .]	Date of Discharge.	Date of Admission.	Names.	No. .	[Size .]	Date of Discharge.

FEMALES.

Date of Admission.	Names.	No. .	[Size .]	Date of Discharge.	Date of Admission.	Names.	No. .	[Size .]	Date of Discharge.	Date of Admission.	Names.	No. .	[Size .]	Date of Discharge.

* By the No. here is intended the Number given by the Master to each Suit. The odd numbers shall be assigned to the Males, and the even numbers to the Females.

Necessaries and Miscellaneous Account for the_____
Week of the Quarter ending_____18 __.

_____UNION. _____*Master of the Workhouse at*_____

ARTICLES.	Stock brought forward.	New Stock.	No. of Invoice.	Totals of Stock brought forward and New Stock.	Consumed			Remaining in Store.	Totals consumed and remaining in Store.	Observations.
					By the Paupers.	By the Officers and Servants of the Workhouse.	On the Workhouse.			

Quarterly Summary of the Necessaries and Miscellaneous
Account for the Quarter ending_____18 __.

_____UNION. _____*Master of the Workhouse at*_____

Week.	*										Week.
Received. { 1st											1st
2nd											2nd
3rd											3rd
4th											4th
5th											5th
6th to											6th to
13th											13th
Totals											Totals.
Consumed by the Paupers. { 1st											1st
2nd											2nd
3rd											3rd
4th											4th
5th											5th
6th to											6th to
13th											13th
Totals.......											Totals.
Consumed by the Officers and Servants and on the Workhouse. { 1st											1st
2nd											2nd
3rd											3rd
4th											4th
5th											5th
6th to											6th to
13th											13th
Totals........											Totals.

* The names of the several articles are to be placed at the head of the several columns.

L

Balance of the Necessaries and Miscellaneous Account for the Quarter ending ———— 18—.

———— UNION.

———— Master of the Workhouse at ————

ARTICLES.	Stock brought forward.	Price.	Cost of Stock brought forward. £ s. d.	New Stock.	Price.	Cost of New Stock. £ s. d.	Total Cost of New Stock and Stock brought forward. £ s. d.	By the Paupers. Quantities.	Cost. £ s. d.	By the Officers and Servants of the Workhouse. Quantities.	Cost. £ s. d.	On the Workhouse. Quantities.	Cost. £ s. d.	Stock remaining in Store. Quantities.	Cost of Stock remaining in Store. £ s. d.	Total Cost of Articles consumed and in Store. £ s. d.

CONSUMED.

Totals..

Submitted to ———— Member of the Visiting Committee, this ———— day of ———— 18—, and found to be correct.

Signed { ————

———— Master of the Workhouse.

Register of Births in the ———— Workhouse.

———— UNION.

———— Master.

Date of Birth.	Whether Male or Female.	Name of Parents, or Mother.	From what Parish Parents admitted.*	When and where baptized.	In what name baptized.	Remarks.

*Note.—In the case of a Vagrant admitted into the Workhouse who becomes a Mother therein, the word *Vagrant* must be inserted.

Register of Deaths in the ———— Workhouse.

———— UNION.

———— Master.

Date of Death.	Name.	Age.	From what Parish admitted	Where buried.

†Note.—In the case of a Vagrant admitted into the Workhouse who dies therein, the words *admitted as a Vagrant* should be inserted.

Chapter XIIV.

NON-OFFICIAL FORMS OF BOOKS.

———◆———

There are numerous books which are useful in the administration of a workhouse, which are not prescribed by the Poor Law Board, and some of the books which are directed by the Poor Law Board to be kept may be prepared in any convenient form. Mr. White, the Master of St. Mary's Workhouse, Newington, has been good enough to supply me with forms of books, some of which are used in that workhouse exclusively, but which at the same time may be conveniently used elsewhere. The following forms are, I think, worthy of attention :—

1. Temporary Admission Paper.
2. Vagrants' Admission Paper.
3. Discharge Paper addressed to the Porter.
4. Admissions and Discharges.
5. Notice of Illness.
6. Notice of Birth to the Registrar.
7. Notice of Death to the Registrar.
8. Order of Burial to Undertaker.
9. Register of Burial, &c.
10. Diets of the Sick for the Kitchen, and Summary for the use of the Cutter-up of the Food.
11. List of Inmates, and Diets in each Ward.
12. Order for Supply of Goods by Tradesmen, as Meat, &c.
13. Application for Clothing from Stores.
14. Nurse's Report.
15. Gas Consumption, weekly.

16. Inventory of Paupers' own Clothing, Male.
17. „ „ „ Female.
18. Inventory of Property in each Ward.
19. The Nurse's List of Clothing sent to the Wash-house.
20. Estimate of Articles required.
21. Abstract of the same.
22. Summary of Articles supplied.

---

1. *Master's Temporary Admission Paper.*

(To be retained by the Master.)

Name

Age

Religion

Trade or Occupation

Residence, where found, }
    or by whom brought. }

---

2. *Vagrants Admitted*

During the Week ended   day of   18 , into   Workhouse.

	Men.	Women.	Boys.	Girls.	Total.
Sunday					
Monday					
Tuesday					
Wednesday ...					
Thursday					
Friday					
Saturday					
Total......					

Master.

3.   *Discharge Paper addressed to the Porter.*

No.   No.

                       To the Porter.

Name

                       Discharge

Age

                         Age

                                  _____ *Master.*

_____   Nature of Discharge

---

4.   *Admissions.*

Date.	Meal.	Name	Age.	By whose Order.	Cause.	Address of Relatives or previous Residence and other Remarks.

Discharges.

Date.	Name.	Age.	What Discharged for and other Remarks.

---

5.   *Notice of Illness.*

_____ WORKHOUSE.   _____ WORKHOUSE.

NOTICE OF ILLNESS.   NOTICE OF ILLNESS.

Mr. _____   I beg to inform you that _____

has been informed of the   is ___ ill in ___ Ward, and desires to see you.

illness of ___   By presenting this at the gate you will be

in _____ Ward.   permitted to visit.

                               _____ *Master.*

_____ *Master.*

           18   _____ 18

                 Mr. _____

6.   *Notice of Birth to the Registrar.*

NOTICE OF BIRTH IN _____ WORKHOUSE.

To the Registrar of Births and Deaths in the District of _____

Take Notice that the following Birth has occurred in the _____ Workhouse, in the Parish of _____, and that you are required to attend there and register the same according to the following particulars :—

Time and Place of Birth.	Name of Child.	Sex.	Name and Surname of Father.	Name, Surname and Maiden Surname of Mother.	Rank or Occupation of Father

Witness my hand this   day of   18

_____ *Master of the Workhouse.*

7.   *Notice of Death to the Registrar.*

NOTICE OF DEATH IN_____ WORKHOUSE.

To the Registrar of Births and Deaths in the District of _____

Take Notice that the following Death has occurred in the _____ Workhouse, in the Parish of _____, and that you are required to attend there and register the same according to the following particulars :—

Time and place of Death.	Name and Surname of the Deceased Person.	Sex	Age	Rank or Occupation.	Cause of Death.

Witness my hand this   day of   186

_____ *Master of the Workhouse.*

8.   *Order of Burial to Undertaker.*

_____WORKHOUSE.   _____WORKHOUSE.

Order to bury the body   18

of_____   Mr._____

_____lying at the above   Be pleased to remove and

Workhouse.   inter the body of_____, belonging

    Dated   18   to the Parish of_____, now lying at the

                      above Workhouse.

_____*Master.*   _____*Master.*

9.   *Register of Burial.*

_____ Workhouse.

Claimed or unclaimed.	Name and address of nearest relative or friend.	Where buried.	If disposed of under 2 & 3 Wm. 4, c. 75, state date when taken.	Remarks.

10.   *Diet Card for the Sick.*

(To be sent to the Kitchen.)

[*A summary of the whole is prepared on one Card, for the use of the Matron or other officer when cutting up.*]

Ward No._____

Date_____

Name of Inmate.	Tea.	Gruel.	Diet. 1.	Diet. 2, &c.	Arrow-root.	Milk. Pints.	Fish.	Eggs.	Beer. Pints.	Wine. oz.	Gin. oz.	Brandy. oz.

11.   *List of Inmates, and Diets in each Ward.*

Day_____ Date_____

Ward No. _____

Number of Inmates who dine } _____
    in the Ward

	Men.	Women.	Children.
On Able-bodied Diet, No.			
On Old and Infirm Diet. No.			
On Extra Diet for Labour, No. ...			
On Medical Officer's Book for Sick Diets, viz. :—			
On Full Diet, No.			
On Low Diet, Milk, No.			
On Fish Diet, No.			
On Eggs			
On Beef Tea			
On Arrowroot			
Totals..................			

12.   *Order for Supply of Goods by Tradesmen.*

ORDER FOR GOODS.

No.

_____ day of _____ 18

Mr. _____

Stone of Beef
    ,,   Mutton
    ,,   Joints for Officers
    ,,   Beef Suet
    ,,   Legs and Shins
_____*Master.*

ORDER FOR GOODS.

No.

_____ day of _____ 18

Mr. _____

Supply for the use of the _____
Workhouse,—

Stone of Beef
    ,,   Mutton
    ,,   Joints for Officers
    ,,   Beef Suet
    ,,   Legs and Shins
_____*Master.*

13.   *Application for Clothing from Stores.*

Date.	Articles Applied for.	No. of Suit.	Name.

_____*Matron.*

14.   *Nurse's Report.*

_____WORKHOUSE.

_____WARD.

Report of _____for the Week ending
the_____day of_____18

I have carefully examined the various Sick Patients under my
charge, and they are_____and to the best of my knowledge
and belief, the Medicines_____and the Patients in every
respect_____

To_____

15.   *Gas Consumption, Weekly.*

State of the Meter week ending Thursday at Noon_____
    day of_____18___ . . . .

State of the Meter last week . . . .

Week's Consumption . . . .

Last Week's ditto . . . .
                     crease . . . . .

16. *Inmates' own Clothing.—Males.*

Name _____   Name _____

Date of Admission _____   Date of Admission _____

_____ 18   _____ 18

   Coat   Coat
   Jacket   Jacket
   Waistcoat   Waistcoat
   Pair of Trousers   Pair of Trousers
   Shirt   Shirt
   Pair of Stockings   Pair of Stockings
   Pair of Shoes   Pair of Shoes
   Handkerchief   Handkerchief
   Hat   Hat
   Drawers   Drawers

The above is a correct List of the Clothing brought in by me.

_____ 18

Received the above Clothing

_____

Date of Discharge _____

_____ 18

17. *Inmates' own Clothing.—Females.*

Name _____   Name _____

Date of Admission _____   Date of Admission _____

_____ 18   _____ 18

   Cloak   Cloak
   Shawl   Shawl
   Gown   Gown
   Frock   Frock
   Petticoats   Petticoats
   Shift   Shift
   Pair of Stockings   Pair of Stockings
   Pair of Shoes   Pair of Shoes
   Cap   Cap
   Bonnet   Bonnet
   Aprons   Aprons
   Pair of Stays   Pair of Stays
   Nightgown   Nightgown
   Handkerchief   Handkerchief

The above is a correct List of the Clothing brought in by me.

_____ 18

Received the above Clothing.

_____

Date of Discharge _____

_____ 18

18.   *Inventory of Property in each Ward.*

_____ UNION WORKHOUSE.

Date,   18

Describe on this line
what part of the house,
and name of person in
charge . . . . .

FIXTURES.	Number.	BEDDING.	In the Ward	In the Ward	Total.
Ranges with Ovens and Boilers . . .		Iron Bedsteads .			
Gas Burners . . .		Bed Rests .			
Grates . . .		Feather Beds . .			
Gas Burners . .		Flock Beds . .			
Fixed Cupboards .		Bolsters . . .			
Stoves . .		Pillows . . .			
Benches fixed to the wall		Sheets (single, not pairs)			
Supply Cisterns for Ranges . . .		Blankets (single, not pairs) . . .			
		Rugs, Woollen . .			
FURNITURE.		Blue Cotton Rugs .			
Arm Chairs . .		Linen Pillow Cases .			
Chairs without Arms .		White Counterpanes .			
Forms . . .		Baize Curtains for Windows . .			
Tables . . .		Ditto for Screens .			
Fire Irons . .		India Rubber Sheets .			
Fender . . .		Air or Water Cushions .			
Fire Guard . .					
Lockers . .		HOUSE LINEN.			
Night Stools (Patent) .		Table Cloths . .			
Night Stools (Ordinary) .		Round Towels. .			
Screens . . .		Square Towels .			
Cupboards, not fixed .		Tea Cloths . .			
Rollers for Blinds .		Window Blinds .			
Pictures or Prints Framed and Glazed . .		Dinner Cloths for Beds .			
Bibles . . .		PERSONAL CLOTHING.			
Prayer Books . .		Bed Gowns . .			
Hymn Books . .		Dressing Gowns .			
		Night Caps . .			
UTENSILS.		Day Caps . .			
Tea Kettles . .		Shawls . . .			
Saucepans . .		Upper Petticoats .			
Large Jugs . .		Flannel Petticoats .			
Wash-hand Basins .		Chemises . .			
Chambers . .		Pocket Handkerchiefs .			
Small Jugs or Mugs .		Stockings . .			
Plates . . .		Neckerchiefs . .			
Basins . . .		Men's Shirts . .			
Saucers . .		OTHER EFFECTS.			
Foot Pans . .		Long Brooms . .			
Wooden Trays . .		Short Hand Brooms .			
Scales and Weights .		Scrubs . .			
Moveable Baths .		Stove Brushes .			
Dirty Clothes Baskets .		Mops . . .			
Patients' Clothes Baskets.		Pails . . .			
Chest Warmers . .		Dust Pans . .			
Feet Warmers . .					

Infirmary.

(To be kept by the Superintendent Nurse.)

No. ———

——— day of ——— 18   .

Counterpanes
Do.　White
Blankets
Sheets
Pillow Cases
Bed Gowns
Do.　White
Shifts
Shirts
Flannel Capes
Shawls
Infants' Flannels
Do.　Gowns
Cotton Rollers

Flannel Rollers
Napkins
Night Caps
Jack Towels
Tea　do.
Bath　do.
Sick　do.
Dusters
Table Cloths
Mackintoshes
Mattress Covers
Comb Bags
Aprons
Gowns

No. ———

——— day of ——— 18   .

TO THE SUPERINTENDENT OF THE LAUNDRY.

Please to receive the Articles named below (1) ——— Nurse.

Counterpanes
Do.　White
Blankets
Sheets
Pillow Cases
Bed Gowns
Do.　White
Shifts
Shirts
Flannel Capes
Shawls
Infants' Flannels
Do.　Gowns
Cotton Rollers

Flannel Rollers
Napkins
Night Caps
Jack Towels
Tea　do.
Bath　do.
Sick　do.
Dusters
Table Cloths
Mackintoshes
Mattress Covers
Comb Bags
Aprons
Gowns

Received the Articles above named (2).

Dated this ——— day of ——— 18 ——— Superintendent.

The Articles above named have all been returned to me (3).

Dated this ——— day of ——— 18 ——— *Nurse.*

1. This paper to be signed by the Nurse and sent with the Clothes.
2. To be signed by the Female Superintendent as correctly received.
3. To be signed by the Nurse as correctly returned, and the paper then sent to the Master's Office.

19.

Estimates.   WORKHOUSE.

20.

Week		Quarter ending	18

Week

FLOUR FACTOR.
Sacks Flour, Households
Do. Do. Cones
YEAST DEALER.
Gallons Yeast
POTATO SALESMAN.
Cwt. Potatoes
Do. do. for Bakers
Bunches Carrots
Do. Leeks
BUTCHER.
Stone of Beef
Do. Mutton
Do. Beef Suet
Do. Legs and Shins
MEALMAN.
Sacks Split Peas
Do. Oatmeal
CHEESEMONGER.
Cwt. Waterford Bacon
Do. Gouda Cheese
Lbs. Cheshire Cheese
Firkins Salt Butter
Lbs. Dorset do.
Dozen Eggs
GROCER.
Cwt. Moist Sugar
Lbs. Loaf do.
Chests Congou Tea
Lbs. Green do.
Do. Best Black do.
Do. Coffee
Do. Rice
Do. Arrowroot

MILKMAN.
Gallons of Milk
BREWER.
Barrels of Porter
FISHMONGER.
Fish Diets for Sick
WINE AND SPIRIT MERCHANT.
Cask of Port Wine
Gallons of Gin
Do Brandy
COAL MERCHANT.
Tons of Stewart's Wallsend Coals
Tons of West Hartleys
OILMAN.
Cwt. Salt
Lbs. Mustard
Do. Pepper
Gallons Vinegar
Cwt. Soap
Do. Soda
Lbs. Candles
Do. Rushlights
Do. Starch
Do. Stone Blue
Do. Black Lead
Cwt. Hearth Stone
Do. Fuller's Earth
Do. Whiting
Do. White Lead
Gallons Linseed Oil
Do. Boiled do.
Do. Sweet do.

Quarter ending

Gallons Pale Seal Oil.
Do. Turpentine
Firkins, Double Size
Gross Lucifer Matches
Dozen Bath Bricks
Ream Emery Paper
Box Blacking
Bags Plaster Paris
WOOLLEN DRAPER.
Pieces Drab Cloth
Do. Fustian
Do. Cotton Cord
HOSIER.
Dozen Men's Speckled Hose
Do. Boys' do.
Do. Women's Grey do.
Do. Girls' do.
Do. Children's Socks, Sizes, No.
LINEN DRAPER.
Pieces Welsh Flannel
Do. 38 inch Blue Cotton
Do. 38 ,, Stout Grey Calico
Do. 38 ,, Striped Do.
Do. 36 ,, White do. for Shrouds
Do. 38 ,, White do. Woods F.
Do. 38 ,, Horrocks Long Cloth, H
Do. 72 ,, Linen Sheeting
Do. 54 ,, Union Check
Do. 38 ,, Forfar
Dozen 36 ,, Square Cotton Handkerchiefs
Pieces Bed Ticking
Do. Huckaback

18

Pieces House Flannel
Shawls
Rugs, Worsted
Blankets, 9-4
,, 10-4
Counterpanes, 8-4
Do. 10-4
SHOEMAKER.
Dozen Pair Men's Shoes
Do. Boys' do.
Do. Women's do.
Do. Girls' do.
Do. Infants' do.
IRONMONGER.

TIMBER MERCHANT.

PLUMBER.

ROPEMAKER.
Chain of Wood Tyers
Lbs. Horse Rope
Balls Lay Cord
SUNDRIES.

} *Visiting Committee.*

21.   *Abstract of Provisions and Necessaries for the Quarter ending* ____ 18____

Week.	Bread.		Flour.		Meat.		Legs and Shins		Suet.		Potatoes.		Vegetables.		Cheese.	
	lbs.	£ s. d.	lbs.	£ s. d.	lbs.	£ s. d.	lbs.	£ s. d.	lbs.	£ s. d.	lbs.	£ s. d.	lbs.	£ s. d.	lbs.	£ s. d.
1.																
2.																

Abstract of Provisions, &c., continued.

Week.	Butter.		Eggs.		Tea.		Coffee.		Sugar.		Arrowroot.		Rice.		Peas.	
	lbs.	£ s. d.		£ s. d.	lbs.	£ s. d.	lbs.	£ s. d.	lbs.	£ s. d.	lbs.	£ s. d.	lbs.	£ s. d.	qts.	£ s. d.
1.																
2.																

Abstract of Provisions, &c., continued.

Week.	Oatmeal.		Milk.		Wine.		Brandy.		Gin.		Porter.		Vinegar.		Pepper.	
	lbs.	£ s. d.	galls.	£ s. d.	pts.	£ s. d.	pts.	£ s. d.	pts.	£ s. d.	galls.	£ s. d.	pts.	£ s. d.	lbs.	£ s. d.
1.																
2.																

Abstract of Provisions, &c., continued.

Week.	Mustard.		Salt.		Coals.		Candles.		Soap.		Starch.		Soda.		Blue, and Black Lead.	
	lbs.	£ s. d.	lbs.	£ s. d.	cwt.	£ s. d.	lbs.	£ s. d.	cwt.	£ s. d.	lbs.	£ s. d.	lbs.	£ s. d.	lbs.	£ s. d.
1.																
2.																

Summary of Provisions and Necessaries for the Quarter ending_____18__.

	1st Week ending	2nd Week ending	3rd Week ending	4th Week ending	5th Week ending	6th Week ending	7th Week ending
	£ s. d.	£ s. d.	£ s. d.	£ s. d.	£ s. d.	£ s. d.	£ s. d.
Bread and Flour..							
Meat							
Potatoes							
Vegetables							
Cheese and Butter							
Oatmeal, &c.							
Grocery							
Milk							
Porter							
Wine, &c.							
Sundries for Sick							
Oilman's goods ..							
Total Provisions							
Soda							
Soap							
Candles							
Coals							
Starch							
Blue							
Black Lead							
Total Necessaries							
Total Provisions and Necessaries							

Chapter XIV.

QUALIFICATION, APPOINTMENT, AND REMOVAL.

QUALIFICATION.

1. The workhouse medical officer is not unfrequently a district medical officer also, but the duties and responsibilities of the two offices are distinct, and he may vacate the one and retain the other. Hence, when they co-exist, they should be held under separate contracts.

2. He must be a registered medical pr actitioner under the Medical Act, and possess a qualification to practise both medicine and surgery, granted by some competent authority in Great Britain and Ireland, which he will produce at his election [*Order, Dec.* 10, 1859].

3. Proof of his having been in medical practice on August 1, 1815, is regarded as equivalent to the production of the certificate of the Apothecaries' Company; and surgeons and assistant surgeons of Her Majesty's Navy and Army, as also apothecaries in Her Majesty's Navy, whose commissions or warrants are dated before August 1, 1826, are qualified to become medical officers under the Poor Law Board [*C. O. Art.* 168].

4. The diplomas of the following authorities (amongst others) are recognised, viz. :—

FOR MEDICINE.

Royal College of Physicians of Edinburgh.
The Society of Apothecaries, London.
The University of Oxford.
The University of Cambridge.

Degree in Medicine and Degree in Surgery.

The University and King's College, Aberdeen.

The Apothecaries' Hall of Dublin.

The King's and Queen's College, Ireland.

FOR SURGERY.

The Royal College of Surgeons of England.

The Royal College of Surgeons of Edinburgh.

The Faculty of Physicians and Surgeons of Glasgow.

The Royal College of Surgeons of Ireland.

FOR MEDICINE AND SURGERY.

The Royal College of Physicians of London.

The University of London.

The University of Durham.

The University of Edinburgh.

The University of Glasgow, Degree in Medicine, Degree or License in Surgery.

The Marischal College and University, Aberdeen.

The University of St. Andrew's.

The University of Dublin.

APPOINTMENT.

5. The medical officer is appointed by the board of guardians in answer to an advertisement issued by the board, and at a salary named previous to his election.

6. He is required to fill up a document containing the following particulars :—

———Union.

APPOINTMENT OF MEDICAL OFFICER TO THE UNION WORKHOUSE.

1. State the Christian name and surname of the person appointed as medical officer to the Union workhouse in full.

2. His place of residence.

3. His age.

4. How long he has been in practice as a medical man.

5. Whether he has before held any similar office ; and, if so, when, and in what Union or parish.

6. Whether he is medical officer of any district in this or any other Union ; and, if so, what district, and in what Union ?

M

7 The day on which he was appointed by the guardians.

8. The date from which his duties commence.

9. The amount of the fee proposed to be paid to the medical officer for vaccination in the workhouse in pursuance of Sec. 6 of the 30 and 31 Vic c. 84.

10. Whether a contract in writing has been entered into with him as medical officer.

11. The amount of salary proposed (exclusive of the fees allowed for cases of midwifery).

12. The cause of the vacancy on account of which the appointment is made ; if a resignation, the cause thereof, the day on which it took effect, and the name of the former officer.

13. With reference to the qualifications prescribed by the Order of the 10th December, 1859, state—

    1. What diplomas, certificates of degrees, licenses, or other instruments granted or issued by competent legal authority in Great Britain or Ireland, testifying to the medical or surgical, or medical and surgical qualification or qualifications of the person appointed, have been produced to the guardians.

    2. Whether he was in practice as an apothecary on the first day of August, one thousand eight hundred and fifteen, and

    3. Whether he possesses a warrant or commission as surgeon or assistant-surgeon in Her Majesty's Navy, or as surgeon or assistant-surgeon in the service of the Honourable East India Company, dated previous to the first day of August, one thousand eight hundred and twenty-six.

14. Whether he is registered pursuant to the 21 & 22 Vic. c. 90, s. 15 ; and, if so, the nature of the proof of such registration which was produced to the guardians.

15. At what distance he will reside from the workhouse.

16. What other medical men residing near to the workhouse, the distances of their residences therefrom, and how they are supposed to be qualified.

—————————————————————————*Signature of the Clerk.*

——————————— { *Signature of the Officer appointed. (The Christian Name and Surname being written in full.)*

Reported to the Poor Law Board   day of   18 .

7. This document, together with a statement from the clerk of the Union that he has been elected by the guardians, is forwarded by the clerk to the Poor Law Board,

with a request that the Poor Law Board will sanction the appointment.

8. Should the document be properly filled up, and the qualification of the medical officer be found sufficient, and should there be no record at the Poor Law Board against the medical officer, the sanction of the Board is given.

9. A contract is then drawn up between the guardians and the medical officer, setting forth his duties and emoluments, and approved by the Poor Law Board.

SUSPENSION AND REMOVAL.

10. Should he have been dismissed by order of the Poor Law Board, he is incapable of holding an appointment under the Poor Law Board.

11. Should he have been called upon by the Poor Law Board to resign, or should there have been complaints made against him, the Poor Law Board would probably inform the guardians of such a circumstance, and give them the opportunity of reconsidering their decision. Should the guardians persist in their wish to appoint him, the Poor Law Board would arrive at a decision after considering all the circumstances of the case.

12. Without the sanction of the Poor Law Board he could not hold office, or, if holding it, he could be removed from it, and the guardians would be unable to pay his salary out of the rates of the Union.

13. His appointment is held for life, subject to good behaviour and competency to discharge the duties of the office, or until he resign or be removed by the Poor Law Board [4 *& 5 Wm. IV. c.* 76, *& G. O. 25th May,* 1857; *Instr. Letter, June,* 1857].

14. The guardians in some places appoint the medical officer with his consent for a term of years, or take power to terminate it on giving notice, but such an arrangement is now illegal [*Instr. Letter,* 1857].

15. Hence he has greater liberty of action than the

guardians who appoint him, since he may quit his office at his pleasure, after having given one month's notice, whilst they cannot remove him without the consent of the Poor Law Board. The guardians have power to suspend him [*C. O. Art.* 192], and should the Poor Law Board call upon him to resign, or should they dismiss him by order, his salary ceases on the day of his suspension; but should he be reinstated by the Poor Law Board, his salary is continued without abatement [*C. O. Art.* 173 & 175].

16. The Poor Law Board is to judge of his fitness to hold office in view of his removal from office, but reasonable grounds for his removal must be alleged and proved to their satisfaction [4 & 5 *Wm. IV. c.* 76].

17. They may remove him for a sufficient cause without any formal process beyond a communication to that effect sent to him and to the guardians, but usually they are moved by a request to that effect from the guardians, to which they may express their assent or dissent, or direct an official inquiry upon oath to be held in the Union by the Poor Law Inspector for their further information.

18. The most frequent causes of removal are neglect of duty or personal misconduct, as drunkenness, but sometimes the medical officer is removed for incompetency or persistent disagreement with the guardians.

19. The two first are readily determined; the third is proved with difficulty, since, being a legally qualified medical practitioner, there is a presumption of competency, and the Poor Law Board would not lightly interfere with his discretion in the treatment of disease; whilst the fourth, although determined with ease, is tolerated to the utmost limits compatible with the proper administration of the affairs of the Union.

20. He has no appeal from their decision, except to the Court of Queen's Bench.

Chapter XXVI.

GENERAL STATEMENT OF DUTIES.

———◆———

1. He is not a member of the board of guardians, and cannot claim to attend the meetings of the board as a matter of right, and should the guardians desire his attendance they must request it on each occasion, and not by a general direction.

2. It is not improbable that it would be of advantage to the Poor Law administration if he had the right to attend the meetings of the guardians, but it would not be agreeable to him to attend and to spend so much time in the middle of the day unless he had the right to speak and to vote—a right which would be incompatible with the position of an officer of the board.

3. It is his duty to attend the meetings of the board of guardians when requested to give information to them respecting any sick pauper who is or has been under his care [C. O. Art. 205], or of any prevalent sickness amongst the paupers ; to certify as to the bodily health of any child whom the guardians purpose to apprentice [C. O. Art. 59] ; to give a certificate of death of a child for whom burial money is claimed if he have attended it, or if no medical practitioner had attended it ; to give a certificate of the state of health of a lunatic discharged from an asylum on trial [21 & 22 Vic. c. 101, s. 2], or of any sick pauper in the workhouse, whether such pauper belonged to a benefit society or not ; and to report to the guardians on any matter affecting his duties.

4. He is not required to attend before justices of the peace to testify to any case of sickness or lunacy unless subpœnaed, and on payment of a fee.

5. He is required to perform the duties of his office personally [*C. O. Art.* 199] as far as may be practicable, and under all circumstances is responsible for the attendance upon the sick paupers.

HIS DEPUTY.

6. He should name to the guardians a deputy to act in his absence [*C. O. Art.* 200], and it is desirable that the deputy should live near to the workhouse.

7. His deputy must be also a registered practitioner, with or without the double qualification, but he is not entitled as such to visit the workhouse except at the request of the medical officer, the master, or other officer of the workhouse.

8. The medical officer cannot devolve his own responsibility upon either his deputy or a legally qualified assistant.

9. The medical officer should not absent himself from his duties without the sanction of the board of guardians except in case of urgent necessity, but he might claim to be allowed a reasonable holiday yearly.

10. When he is absent even for a day, he should previously ascertain that his deputy is able and willing to perform his duties, and when he is likely to be absent for two or more days he should also inform the master of the workhouse of his intention.

11. He should communicate the address of the deputy to the guardians and the master.

12. He should acquaint the deputy with any case which specially requires attention, and the deputy should be conversant with the routine of the duties of the medical officer.

SUMMARY OF DUTIES.

13. His duties consist in visiting the workhouse, in examining all applicants on admission, in vaccinating the children, in attending any inmate requiring his advice from sickness or infirmity, and in prescribing medicines and diet for them ; in performing all requisite surgical operations ; in classifying the sick, and giving directions as to the wards in which they may be placed ; in reporting to the guardians any defects which exist in the accommodation and conveniences for the sick, or in the sanitary arrangements of the workhouse ; in advising the guardians in respect of the dietaries for the inmates ; in keeping the workhouse medical relief book, and in reporting on the sanitary state of the workhouse and the provision for the sick.

14. He is not required to attend professionally upon the officers of the workhouse.

Chapter XXVII.

ATTENDANCE AT WORKHOUSE AND ADMISSION OF PAUPERS.

———•———

1. He is required to attend at the workhouse at periods to be fixed by the guardians, and also when sent for by the master or matron [C. O. Art. 207].

2. It is not usual to insert in the contract between the medical officer and the guardians the frequency with which he shall visit the workhouse, but it is left to his discretion and the requirements of the sick inmates.

3. When the workhouse is situate in a town it is usual for the medical officer to attend daily, and in large workhouses even twice a day, whilst in many country Unions with small workhouses only one visit is paid in two or three days, and the attendance is irregular.

4. Having regard to the facts that there are some sick inmates in every workhouse, and that persons may apply for admission on any day, it is desirable that everywhere the medical officer should attend at the workhouse daily, and that such an arrangement should be entered in the contract.

5. The admission of applicants into the workhouse is irregularly conducted in many Unions, and particularly where the medical officer does not attend daily, or where he lives at such a distance as to render it inconvenient to the master to send for him, or for him to attend.

6. As the application for admission is usually made in the afternoon, it is not expected that the medical officer should always discharge this duty on the first day, and therefore the consolidated order provides for the accommodation of the

applicant in receiving or probationary wards for one night, and it is expected that the medical officer will attend the next morning and conduct the examination.

7. It is, therefore, a neglect of duty when the medical officer omits his visit, and the applicant is required to remain in the receiving ward during another day and night, or the master, in his discretion, admits the applicant without the previous authorisation of the medical officer.

8. The examination of applicants for admission, and particularly that of children, should not be hasty or formal, lest infectious disease should be introduced by them into the ordinary wards.

9. Care should be taken to determine whether fever, incipient small-pox, or other eruptive infectious disease, or itch, be present; and, if so, to direct the proper isolation of the applicant.

10. It is also needful to determine whether the applicant be in good health, or whether he should be at once placed in the ordinary sick wards, and to give directions accordingly.

11. It is desirable, moreover, but not a part of his duty, that the medical officer should occasionally satisfy himself that applicants are properly cleansed before being admitted.

Chapter XXVIII.

CLASSES OF CASES.

———◆———

LUNATICS.

1. He is required to examine all persons of unsound mind who are admitted to the workhouse, and to report to the guardians as to their fitness to remain there, within fourteen days. No such inmate may remain for a longer period without his certificate [25 & 26 Vic. c. 111].

2. He makes a quarterly report to the guardians as to lunatics in the workhouse in the following form [25 & 26 Vic. c. 111, s. 21, & 16 & 17 Vic. c. 97, s. 66]:—

SCHEDULE B.

County of
Union [or parish of]
District of

Quarterly List of Lunatic paupers within the District of the Union of   [or the parish of   ], in the county or borough of   , not in an asylum, registered hospital, or licensed house.

Name	Sex	Age.	Form of mental Disorder	Duration of present attack of insanity, and if idiotic, whether or not from birth.	Resident in work-house.	Non-resident in workhouse, where and with whom resident.	Date of visit.	In what condition, and if ever restrained, why and by what means and how often.

I declare that I have personally examined the several persons whose names are specified in the above list on the days set opposite their names ; and I certify, firstly, with respect to those appearing by the above list to be in the workhouse, that the accommodation in the workhouse is sufficient for their reception, and that they are all [*or* all except A. B. and C.D.] proper patients to be kept in the workhouse ; and, secondly, with respect to those appearing by the above list to be resident elsewhere than in the workhouse, that they are all [*or* all except A. B. and C. D.] properly taken care of, and may properly remain out of an asylum.

I declare that the persons in the above list are to the best of my knowledge the only pauper lunatics in the District of the Union of   [*or* in the parish of   ] who are not in an asylum, registered hospital, or duly licensed house.

(Signed)   A. B.

Medical Officer of the   District

of the Union [or parish] of

Dated the   day of   one thousand eight hundred and

3. He should report to the guardians any pauper of unsound mind in the workhouse whom he deems to be dangerous, or who for that or other cause should be sent to an asylum ; and in reference to the removal of a dangerous lunatic to an asylum he should give notice in writing to the relieving officer of the Union [16 & 17 *Vic. c.* 97, *s.* 67].

4. As the expense of patients at an asylum is greater than at the workhouse, the guardians sometimes prefer to retain them there, even when they are of dirty habits and helpless, and where there are not proper arrangements for their cure ; but the medical officer should not hesitate to report to them when such cases require to be removed, and to reiterate the report if the patient should not be removed.

VACCINATION.

5. He should ascertain whether the children in the workhouse and schools have been effectively vaccinated or not [*C. O. Art.* 207], and if not he should vaccinate them at his earliest convenience. It is also desirable that the same inquiry should be made in respect of adults, and if they have not been vaccinated he should induce them, if possible, to submit to the operation.

6. It is also his duty to vaccinate children who may be born in the workhouse, and who remain there until of sufficient age [*C. O. Art.* 207], but as many infants are removed before they are six weeks old, he cannot discharge this duty in all cases.

7. It would be a neglect of duty not to vaccinate any child so born, which remained until it was three months old.

LYING-IN CASES.

8. It is usual for the medical officer to attend all cases of midwifery occurring within the workhouse, and it is desirable that this practice should be universal; but in some of the larger workhouses the guardians employ a midwife, and the medical officer attends only in cases of difficulty. The medical officer is not allowed to employ a midwife as his substitute.

9. In some instances the medical officer directs the paid nurse to attend ordinary cases, and gives her a pecuniary consideration for so doing; but wherever the medical officer is engaged by the guardians to attend such cases, he should do so personally, or by his deputy or qualified assistant, except in very urgent cases.

10. He should take care that the lying-in room is kept quiet, out of the line of ordinary traffic, not on the ground-floor, with windows on both sides, and properly lighted and ventilated, and kept in a cleanly state.

11. Puerperal fever is a very rare malady in workhouses, but whenever it occurs the lying-in ward should be emptied as soon as possible, and the walls, floors, beds, and bedding cleansed, and, if necessary, disinfected or destroyed.

12. He should see that the ward is of proper temperature, and not liable to draughts, and that the inmates have proper means of cleansing themselves and their children, and are properly clad.

13. A common rocking-chair should be supplied, as also bed-pans, feet and stomach warmers, sealed night-stools with

covers, and an abundant supply of flannel and linen. It is also desirable that mackintosh sheeting should be supplied to all lying-in beds.

14. It is desirable that there should be a separate labour ward, whenever there are several lying-in women in the wards at the same time; and in the small workhouses where this is not practicable, there should be a portion of the room curtained off, so as to separate the patient, medical officer, and nurse, from the other inmates.

15. Care should be taken that the separate labour room be not too small, that it be properly lighted, warmed, and ventilated, and close to the ordinary lying-in ward.

16. In some workhouses the patient is removed from the labour bed to the lying-in ward within two to four hours after her confinement, and injury has very seldom resulted; but it is desirable that she should occupy that bed, or one placed by its side, for two or three days, or for a longer period where the number of cases will admit of such an arrangement. The labour room might have two beds in the larger workhouses.

17. As difficult and dangerous cases of midwifery may at any time occur, the medical officer should have brandy, laudanum, ergot, and other medicines, as well as midwifery forceps and proper instruments at hand.

SURGICAL CASES.

18. Surgical cases of a serious nature are rarely brought into workhouses, and capital operations are but rarely performed, since accidents are commonly taken to the general hospitals, and cases requiring capital operations have often already been under the care of a surgeon to the hospital.

19. There are some exceptions, and particularly where the general hospital is distant, and factories, where accidents occur, are near to the workhouse, and to these must be added the wish of the medical officer for, and his reputation in the performance of, such operations.

20. It is much more usual than was formerly the case, for the general practitioner to perform such capital operations as lithotomy and amputation, and where there is a proper nurse, and surgical ward, which can be made of proper temperature, and kept in quietude, and the medical officer desires to perform them, there is no reason why they should not be performed in a workhouse.

21. At the same time, it is only in the larger workhouses, and not always there, that proper nursing and proper wards may be obtained, whilst the reputation of the county hospitals, and of the surgeons connected with them, will attract such cases thither.

22. The medical officer should secure the assistance of other practitioners when he performs such operations, and if the case require medical attention at night, he should direct his assistant to spend the night there.

23. Whilst proper encouragement should be given for the performance of such operations, the fact that there are rarely the proper conveniences renders the performance of them more difficult, and the responsibility of the medical officer greater.

24. He should take care that every surgical instrument and appliance which may be required is at hand, and in good order.

25. He cannot compel a pauper of sound mind to submit to an operation against his will.

PUNISHMENTS.

26. He may be required [*C. O. Art.* 134] to determine whether a disorderly or refractory female pauper inmate is or is not pregnant, and to certify in writing whether injury to health may be reasonably apprehended from the punishment of a pauper who has been upon the list of sick and infirm paupers within seven days, or of a pregnant or suckling female pauper, and to suggest such modification of the punishment as he may deem to be necessary.

Chapter XXII.

VISITS, SEPARATION, AND DISCHARGE OF CASES.

VISITS.

1. He should visit every room inhabited by the paupers once a week, and it is desirable that he should notice the state of the inmates, and particularly of the aged, as to their health, clothing, cleanliness, and comfort.

VISITS TO THE SCHOOLS.

2. He should see all the children in the workhouse and schools, perhaps once a week, and examine their eyes and skins, and inquire into their general health.

3. At every daily visit he should not merely enter each sick ward where there are patients, and inquire in a general manner whether any inmate wishes to speak to him, but he should walk through each ward and see every inmate, stopping to converse with those who require his attention on that day.

4. As all the sick inmates do not require his attention daily, it will be convenient to him, and lead to regular attendance upon all the sick, to select two or three days in each week on which he will speak to every person upon his medical list.

5. Such days should be known to all the inmates and to the nurses, and on the intervening days the medical officer could specially see such as may require. daily attention, and such others as from increase of disease or for any reason wish to speak to him.

6. In all his visits to the sick inmates, and particularly at night, he should be accompanied by the nurse ; in those to the children, by the schoolmaster and schoolmistress ; and at his weekly inspection of the whole workhouse it is desirable that he should occasionally invite the master or matron to accompany him.

7. He should make notes at the time of observation of such matters as require further action on his part, and preserve them for future reference.

SEPARATION OF CASES.

8. It is desirable for convenience of administration, and for proper isolation, that the sick should be separated from the other inmates either in special wards of the common building or in separate buildings.

9. In the smaller workhouses there is not the opportunity of separating the merely aged and infirm from the sick, or the surgical from the medical cases, and the number of exceptional cases does not demand such a course ; but in the large workhouses where the number of really sick inmates and of surgical cases is large, it is desirable that they should be placed apart from the merely aged and infirm.

10. If there be a choice of sick wards, the best should be devoted to the really sick, and such rooms should be sufficiently spacious, lighted, ventilated, and warmed.

11. Smaller floor space or less width between the beds may be allowed to the aged who are not of dirty habits, whilst in cases which require separation, either from their offensive or infectious nature, it will be proper to enlarge the space, or even to allow an intermediate bed to remain empty.

12. Dirty and offensive cases should be separated, but not placed in close, dark, and ill-ventilated wards.

13. Cases of fever are said by some physicians to do as well in wards with the ordinary sick as in separate wards, and are not usually dangerous to others in properly constructed rooms, provided the space of two beds be allowed to

each; but when the rooms are not perfect in construction and ventilation, or where there is so much movement of persons in the room as to prevent proper quietude, it is better to place them in separate wards.

14. To place cases of fever and small-pox in separate wards of good construction cannot be wrong, but it is not desirable that they should be placed in ill-constructed and ill-ventilated wards in order to separate them.

15. Cases of small-pox should be always separated from others.

16. Cases of measles, scarlet fever, and hooping-cough should not be placed in wards where there are children who have not had these diseases.

17. The classification of the sick, and the warding of individual cases, are subject to the direction of the medical officer [*C. O. Art.* 207, *No.* 4].

18. In too many workhouses the discretion of the medical officer is fettered by want of space for proper classification of the sick, and of good rooms for the more dangerous cases.

DISCHARGE OF SICK.

19. He has power to discharge any inmate from the sick wards who is sufficiently recovered, but he cannot discharge such from the workhouse.

20. He may prevent, by an examination and written report to the guardians, the discharge from the workhouse of an inmate afflicted with any mental, infectious, or contagious disease, if he is of opinion that to permit the discharge would be injurious to the health of the pauper or of others [30 & 31 *Vic. c.* 106, *s.* 22], except in the case of the removal of a lunatic to an asylum, or of any inmate whose parent or next of kin may satisfy the guardians that the pauper will be removed and maintained with due care so long as the malady shall continue.

N

Chapter XXX.

MEDICINES AND DIETARIES.

———◆———

MEDICINES.

1. His prescriptions for medical and other extras should be written in ink upon the bed-card of each patient [*G. O. April* 4, 1868], and it is desirable that he should, as far as possible, give the more important directions to the nurse in writing.

2. The following is a convenient form of bed-card, the size of which should be about eight inches square :—

Ward_____   .   Date of Admission _____

Name_____   Discharge_____

Disease_____

Date.	Diet and Medical Extras.	Medicines.

3. The medical prescriptions may be written upon the bed-card or in a special book. The former will be more convenient when the medicines are dispensed in the workhouse, and the latter when dispensed away from the workhouse.

4. Where he provides the medicine and dispenses it away from the workhouse, he should see that it is sent to the patients with due speed and regularity, and in proper

labelled bottles and boxes, which he is bound to supply; and at the same time he should have a few of the most important medicines, as well as a few of the most ordinary mixtures—as house medicine and cough medicines—with the means of dispensing them, at the workhouse for immediate use.

5. He should in all instances dispense the medicines or see that they are dispensed by a competent assistant.

6. The dose and frequency of administration should be written or printed upon the label of the vessel containing the medicine, as should also be the name of the patient. Such directions should never be verbal.

7. Proper graduated and other measures for preparing and administering the medicines should be provided, the latter at the cost of the guardians.

DIETARIES AND STIMULANTS.

8. The scheme of dietary for the inmates generally is prepared by the guardians and approved by the Poor Law Board, and cannot be changed without the assent of the Poor Law Board; but the medical officer may direct in writing the diet for an individual pauper as he may deem necessary, or if he should consider that a temporary change in the diet of any class of paupers is essential to their health, he may certify the guardians to that effect [*C. O. Art.* 108], and prescribe a new dietary; but both of these powers are temporary in their nature, and should not be exercised except upon urgent necessity.

9. He also advises the matron as to the proper food for suckling mothers and their infants [*C. O. Arts.* 108 *and* 207], and the time when the latter should be weaned; but the Poor Law Board, in their circular of Dec. 7th, 1868, recommend that the dietary of suckling women shall be that of the aged and infirm inmates, with or without the substitution of milk at breakfast or supper, or at both meals.

10. He also prescribes fermented or spirituous liquors to inmates at work, if he deem them to be necessary [*C. O. Art.* 108, *fourthly*], and it is desirable that he should limit

the exercise of this power to the cases where such stimulants are *necessary* to health [*Circular & Instructions on Dietaries, Dec. 7th,* 1868, *at page* 185].

11. He has power given to him by the recent circular of the Poor Law Board (see page 185) to prescribe a dietary for such of the aged inmates as are under his care for dietary only. The names of such inmates need not be entered in his medical relief-book, but a separate book may be provided for that purpose, and the names having been once entered they need not be repeated until a change of dietary is required.

DIETARIES FOR THE SICK.

12. He has power to direct the diet which shall be given to each sick inmate, and it is his duty to prepare a scheme of sick dietaries [*C. O. Art.* 207, No. 4].

13. This power should be highly valued by him, and exercised with the greatest discretion, both as respects the requirements of the sick inmates and the expense to the guardians, and the more so that the guardians cannot control him except on the ground of the unfitness of his directions.

14. The necessity of the sick should be the sole ground of his action. If the case be a curable one, and requires for the cure a particular dietary, it should receive it at whatever reasonable cost.

15. If it be an incurable one, or be simply one of age and infirmity, the same reason does not lie, and only such diet should be prescribed as may suffice to maintain the body and give a reasonable degree of comfort.

16. In the latter cases the medical officer should have due regard to the position in life which those inmates have had and now have, and when the dietary prescribed is with a view to their comfort only, it should be limited in its scope.

17. If the inmate have been a drunkard, and being in the workhouse, feels the want of stimulants, the medical officer is not warranted in ordering ardent spirits or wine on that ground only, even although the inmate be aged and infirm.

18. If there be debility from age, the medical officer is not warranted in supplying spirits or wine as a daily comfort except in urgent cases, since the benefit to be derived from them is questionable, and they could not be obtained by many persons who have to pay for them.

19. If aged persons have some difficulty in passing urine, it is not unusual for them to take gin as a remedy, and not unusual for the medical officer to order one or more glasses of gin daily for months and years together; but he is not warranted in so doing, if the proper effect can be produced by medicines.

20. The wishes of the inmate in this matter should have little or no weight with the medical officer.

21. A grave difficulty arises in the mind of the medical officer in incurable cases in comparatively young persons, as those in consumption, in reference to the extent to which he may order daily supplies of wines and spirits, and he is influenced by a sense of pity in ordering such things as comforts, without waiting to prove that they are necessary. As a general rule it is very doubtful whether they prolong life, and in not a few they disorder the digestion, diminish appetite, and increase cough, and hence are comforts in name only.

22. There is great diversity of action among medical officers in such cases, and a very general belief exists that the exercise of the power which he possesses is not strictly limited to the cases where its exercise may save or prolong life.

23. As a rule, wines and spirits should not be given where food or medicine would be equally useful, and it does not admit of doubt that the consumption of these fluids in workhouses should be materially lessened.

24. The medical officer should make a special report to the guardians monthly upon all the cases in which he may think it necessary to order wine or spirits continuously, for a period exceeeding one month, stating his reasons for so doing.

25. Medical officers differ as to the propriety of ordering

ale daily to the aged and infirm, and many order it, not on the ground of necessity, but of comfort. This is an undesirable course.

26. The construction of sick dietary tables is necessary, in order to avert the great trouble which would ensue if the medical officer were to order a distinct diet for each person.

27. The following is the form prescribed by the Poor Law Board, but the number of diets, as well as the diets themselves, may be prescribed by the medical officer at his discretion.

Form R. (See C. O. Art. 207, No. 9.)

* DIETARY FOR SICK PAUPERS.									
No. 1	House Diet, being the ordinary diet for the Paupers in the House.								
No. 2		BREAKFAST.		DINNER.					SUPPER.
2	Full Diet . .								
		ozs.	pints.	ozs.	pints.	ozs.	ozs.	pints.	ozs.	pints.
2	Males . . .								
2	Females .								
3	Low Diet . .	BREAKFAST.		DINNER.					SUPPER.
		ozs.	pints.	ozs.	pints.	ozs.	ozs.	pints.	ozs.	pints.
3	Males . . .								
3	Females . .								
4	Fever Diet .	BREAKFAST.		DINNER.					SUPPER.
		ozs.	pints.	ozs.	pints.	ozs.	ozs.	pints.	ozs.	pints.
4	Males . . .								
4	Females . .								

N.B.—Sugar, Arrowroot, Sago, Butter, Milk, Wine, Spirits, Porter and Beer, are in all cases to be treated as extras, to be expressly ordered when required, and the quantity is to be then specified in the proper column of this Book.

* If thought proper by the Medical Officer, any additional number of Dietaries may be introduced, and numbered consecutively.

DR. SMITH'S SICK DIETARIES.

28. It is desirable in the preparation of tables to use as far as practicable the ordinary diets of the workhouse.

29. There should be several kinds of low diet, viz, one consisting of tea and bread-and-butter at each meal, and another of pudding, or bread-and-milk, or broth and bread, for the dinner.

30. There should be two medium diets. In both, the breakfast and supper should consist of tea and bread-and-butter. In one, the dinner should be that which is served on the day for the aged and infirm; in the other, the quantity of meat and potatoes which is supplied to the aged and infirm on certain days should be extended to every day in the week.

31. There should be two kinds of full diet, each supplying tea and bread-and-butter for breakfast, but one consisting of 4 or 5 oz. of cooked meat, 12 oz. of potatoes, and 3 oz. of bread daily. The other, substituting a chop or steak weighing 7 to 8 oz. when raw, instead of the meat.

32. On this plan there would be the same breakfast and supper for all the sick, and the only special requirement would be to indicate by a number the particular dinner required.

Thus—No. 1. Tea and bread-and-butter.

2. Milk pudding.
3. Milk and bread.
4. Broth and bread.
5. Ordinary diet for the aged.
6. 4 oz. meat, 12 oz. vegetables, daily.
7. 5 oz. meat, 12 oz. vegetables.
8. Chop and vegetables.

No. 2 might be added to any of the others.

33. The order may be varied at the subsequent visit, and thus, if needful, the dietary may be frequently changed.

34. Each medical officer will doubtless have special views on this subject and may add to this scheme. If he should prescribe milk at breakfast or supper, or at other times, or

milk-pudding in addition to the meat, he might order it specially for the particular case.

35. The meat in diets No. 6 and 7 should be mutton and beef alternately, and when boiled meat is not specially ordered, it should be roasted.

36. The value of beef-tea in the treatment of the sick has been exaggerated, and as the expense of preparing it from minced meat soaked in cold water is very great, its use should be restricted within the narrowest limits.

37. The ordinary beef-tea prepared from shin of beef should be preferred, and the whole or part of the fat may be skimmed off, if the state of the patient demand it. It is a great error to state that the gelatine which thus enters into its composition is not nutritious. Such beef tea is far more nutritious than that above mentioned, and is as stimulating.

38. The beef-tea which is prepared from Liebig's extract of meat must not be regarded as a nutrient. Its true function is that of a restorative, but it is rather valuable to give flavour to soup, or beef-tea, prepared from shin of beef. The Ramornie Extract is of good quality.

DIETARIES FOR ORDINARY INMATES.

39. It is desirable that the medical officer should approve the dietaries which the guardians forward for the sanction of the Poor Law Board, but it is not essential.

40. The preparation of dietaries for persons in health requires knowledge special and apart from that which is needful in the treatment of disease, and as a medical officer should not prepare a table from general observation only, but from chemical and scientific data, such knowledge should not be required of every medical officer.

41. The medical officer will sometimes be exposed to conflicting influences in the performance of this duty, from a wish to meet the views of the guardians in reference to economy, and to know that the inmates will receive enough food.

42. It has, however, been the practice of the Poor Law

Board to require the signature of the medical officer of the guardians to a proposed scheme of dietary, and the signature has been obtained to very faulty and to improved dietaries alike.

43. The necessity for special knowledge has led the Poor Law Board to cause to be prepared and to issue from time to time recommendations and suggestions on the subject, and recently a document on uniformity of workhouse dietaries, and suggestions on the preparation of dietaries, have entered into the discussion more fully.

44. The "Suggestions," which are cited below, together with the "Report on Uniformity of Workhouse Dietaries," should be duly considered by the medical officer when assisting the guardians to prepare a scheme of dietary.

45. SUGGESTIONS FOR THE PREPARATION OF DIETARIES.

1.—*As to Classes of Inmates.*

In addition to the other classes for whom separate dietaries are sanctioned by the Board, it is desirable that the following should be provided :—

1. A separate dietary for all aged and infirm inmates who are not placed upon the medical officer's book.

2. A separate dietary, to be prescribed by the medical officer, for such inmates as are at present placed upon the books of the medical officer for diet alone. The names of such persons should be entered in a special book, and not in the list of sick in the medical officer's book ; and being once entered, they should not be repeated until they cease to require that dietary.

   This book to be laid before the guardians at each meeting.

3. The names of those inmates to whom, under Article 108, Fourthly, of the General Consolidated Order, such an allowance of food as appeared to the guardians necessary has been made on account of

the nature of their employment, and of those to whom, on the like account, fermented or spirituous liquors have, in pursuance of a written recommendation of the medical officer, been allowed by the guardians, should be read out at each meeting. The master is not permitted to allow extras without the authority of the guardians previously obtained, or, in case of urgent necessity, without obtaining the sanction of the guardians at their next meeting after such extras have been given. It is not necessary in order to such extra allowance that the medical officer should enter the names of such persons in his sick list.

4. Should the guardians deem it desirable, they may submit to the Poor Law Board a dietary for children from 9 to 16 years of age, instead of allowing to that class the dietary of able-bodied women.

5. The sick dietaries will, as heretofore, be framed by the medical officer; but the Board deem it desirable that the meat to be allowed to the sick should be calculated as cooked meat without bone, and not as raw meat, except in the case of chops; and they request that the medical officer will so arrange the quantity of food in the sick diets that it may not be greater than the sick of the particular class can ordinarily eat, and also that he will give his attention to the cooking, conveying, and serving of the sick diets.

6. The dietary of imbeciles and of suckling women should be that of the aged and infirm inmates, with or without the substitution of milk-porridge and bread at breakfast or supper, or at both meals.

2.—*Details of Dietaries.*

7. Tea or coffee are not to be ordinarily supplied to children, except for supper on Sunday.

8. It is desirable that milk should be supplied to all

children under five years of age, and, where practicable, to children above that age, at breakfast and
supper, and that 2 oz. or 3 oz. of bread should be
given to each child at 10 a.m.

9. It is suggested that tea, coffee, or cocoa, with milk
and sugar, and accompanied by bread-and-butter
or bread and cheese, should be allowed to all the
aged and infirm women at breakfast and supper,
and the same to the aged and infirm men, or milk-
porridge with bread may be given at one of those
meals.

10. It is not desirable that more than two soup or
broth dinners should be supplied weekly to any
class of inmates.

11. Soup is to contain 3 oz. of raw, or 2 oz. of cooked,
meat to the pint, and, when practicable, to be made
with meat liquor. From 1 pint to 1½ pints to be
the usual ration for an adult.

12. Broth without the meat left in it should not be
given with bread alone for dinner; but when it
contains the quantity of meat which is required in
soup, it may be substituted for soup during the
summer months.

13. Broth made without the meat being left in it
may be given thrice a week with a sufficient
quantity of bread for supper to the able-bodied,
and, in the absence of a sufficient supply of
milk, to children from 9 to 16 years of age.

14. It is not desirable that more than two bread-and-
cheese dinners should be supplied weekly, except
to the able-bodied adults; and half a pint of broth,
without meat left in it, is to be added in the
dietaries for the aged and infirm and children.

15. Bread and cheese should not be given alone for
breakfast and supper to children under 5 years of
age.

16. Boiled rice is not to be given alone as a substitute

for potato and green vegetables. When it is considered desirable to supply it, it should be given
with a portion of fresh vegetables or bread.

17. Rice-pudding is not to be given as a dinner, except
to children under 9 years of age, and to them not
more frequently than twice a week; and a portion
of bread is to be given with it.

18. Suet-pudding is not to be given for dinner more
frequently than twice a week, and is to be accompanied by a portion of potato or bread and broth
(without meat being left in it), or bread and
cheese, except to the able-bodied adults. Where
given twice a week it should be baked once. It is
to contain 1½ oz. of suet to 8 oz. of flour.

19. Meat should be roasted or baked or made into a
pudding or pie at least once a week.

20. 4 oz. of cooked meat without bone, when given
separately, should usually be the ration for men,
and 3 oz. for women.

21. A ration of meat-pudding or meat-pie, to contain
4 oz. of raw meat for men and 3 oz. for women.

22. A portion of bread is to be given at every meal to
all classes, except when potato is supplied with
meat-pudding or meat-pie.

23. The *usual* quantity of bread to be given at breakfast and supper to children from 2 to 5 years of
age is 3 ozs.; to those from 5 to 9 years of age,
4 oz.; to those from 9 to 16 years of age, 5 oz.;
to able-bodied men, 6 oz.; to able-bodied women,
5 oz.; and to the aged of both sexes, 5 oz.

24. Fresh vegetables should, if possible, be given separately or in combination at dinner at least five
times weekly.

46. The medical officer should especially consider the following principles :—

(a) The ordinary foods eaten by the poorer labourers
in the neighbourhood.

(*b*) The ordinary mode of preparing foods, as, for example, whether meat is eaten with vegetables separately or made into puddings, or whether flour-dumplings are a daily food, as in Norfolk and Somerset.

(*c*) The quantity of foods strictly necessary to maintain life, and the amount of strength required by the aged living in a workhouse.

(*d*) The requirements of growth in children.

(*e*) The failure of powers of mastication and digestion in the aged.

47. He should avoid sentimentality on the one hand and niggardly economy on the other; and whilst providing an abundant diet of plain food for children, supply just enough of plain and suitable food for the aged, and not more than enough of plain food for the able-bodied.

48. It cannot be wrong to acknowledge the fact that even paupers have tastes, which must in a degree be gratified by food, and that variety of food is needful to health.

49. Bread being the cheapest and most nutritive food in relation to its cost, and used universally, should form a large part of workhouse dietaries.

50. No dietary for a man should supply less than 4,500 grains of carbon and 200 grains of nitrogen daily, and the materials should be capable of ready digestion.

51. He should occasionally watch the mode of cooking, and notice the state in which the cooked food is when served and the mode of serving the food, and suggest such improvements as may be required.

52. As the food for the sick must be cooked in the general kitchen, except in the largest workhouses, or where the infirmary is far removed from the workhouse, great care should be taken that it is served in a hot state.

53. When practicable, it is desirable in the larger infirmaries that the joint of meat should be covered and carried into each ward, and the inmates served directly from it.

54. Condiments should be supplied.

Chapter XXIX.

REPORTS.

———◆———

SANITARY ARRANGEMENTS.

1. The medical officer is required to report to the guardians any excess in the number of inmates, which in his opinion may be injurious to health [*C. O. Art.* 207, *No.* 6].

2. "He shall keep a book, to be termed *The Workhouse Medical Officer's Report Book* (to be supplied by the guardians), in which he shall enter in writing, duly and punctually and under the correct dates, every report required by the said orders to be made by him to the board of guardians as to the defects in the diet, drainage, ventilation, warmth, and other arrangements of the workhouse; as to any excess in the number of any class of inmates which he may deem to be detrimental to health; as to every defect which he may observe in the arrangements of the infirmary or sick wards, and in the performance of their duties by the nurses of the sick; and, further, a report of any other matter which, in the discharge of the duties of his office, he shall consider to require the attention of the guardians; and also such recommendations relating to any of the matters aforesaid as he may think it right to submit to the said guardians" [*G. O. April* 4, 1868].

3. "He shall cause this book to be delivered to the clerk to the guardians in sufficient time to allow it to be laid before the board of guardians at the ordinary meeting held at or next following the date of the report, and to be produced to the visiting committee, and to the Inspectors of the Poor Law Board, when they shall require to see it" [*G. O. April* 4, 1868].

4. He will take as his guide the suggestions of the Board as to the fittings of wards cited at page 72, and will add to them such others as may be needed. It is also very desirable that he should make himself familiar with recent sanitary investigations, and the requirements of an officer of public health.

5. Whilst discharging this duty with discretion, and in a courteous manner, he should not be deterred from discharging it fully and faithfully.

6. He is by the terms of the Consolidated Order [*C. O. Art.* 207, *Nos.* 6 *and* 7], the adviser of the guardians upon all such questions, and whilst it is desirable that the guardians should seek his aid, he should be at all times ready to afford it.

7. It is of the greatest importance that he should fully satisfy himself as to the state and requirements of the workhouse, and that he should make his entries with care and correctness, since it will render him yet more responsible than heretofore for any defects in the care of the sick in the event of omissions or errors, and might be one of the grounds upon which the Poor Law Board would base their judgment as to his fitness to hold office. At the same time, the proper discharge of this duty, including, as it must, proper suggestions to the guardians on the matters in question, will greatly lessen his responsibility, for having pointed out defects and suggested the remedies, he cannot be held responsible if the guardians do not take proper action thereupon.

8. At the same time, he should make every proper effort to induce the guardians to remedy defects, even beyond presenting his official reports, for the reasons that public bodies are moved with difficulty, and that it will be to his own comfort to obtain such requisites as are really needful for the efficient discharge of his duties.

9. There is in too many workhouses a want of proper harmony of action between the medical officer and the guardians, the former thinking himself slighted by not being consulted, or by his recommendations not being adopted;

and the latter thinking that the medical officer does not treat them with proper respect, or that his recommendations would lead to needless expense.

10. It is most desirable that the medical officer should gain the confidence and esteem of the guardians, and good judgment, with firmness and courtesy, will effect this much more certainly than intemperate haste, neglect, or servility. Gentlemanly independence, combined with attention to duty, intelligence, and courtesy in any office, almost always ensure influence and consideration.

11. The medical officer should, if possible, avoid allying himself with any party on the board of guardians, but regard them all as his employers and friends.

12. He should not consider that inferiority of station on the part of any of them is a reason for not showing them due respect so long as they remain in office.

MEDICAL RELIEF BOOK.

13. The medical relief book which he is required to keep is in the following form :

Consolidated Order.   *Schedule—Form Q.*

Form Q.— Workhouse Medical Relief Book. (C. O. Art. 207, No. 8.)

					Days when Attended.	MALES. The No.* of the Dietary on which placed.							FEMALES. The No.* of the Dietary on which placed.							Extras.			
Initials of Medical Officer in attendance on every case.	Name of the sick pauper.	When admitted to sick ward.	When discharged.	Nature of disease.		Sunday. Monday. Tuesday. Wednesday. Thursday. Friday. Saturday.							Sunday. Monday. Tuesday. Wednesday. Thursday. Friday. Saturday.							What ordered.	When ordered.	When discontinued.	State or termination of the case, and in the event of death, the apparent cause thereof.
					Total No. each day. ......}																		Total quantity consumed. }

* Dictaries for the sick are to be numbered thus :—No. 1, House Diet; No. 2, Full Diet; No. 3, Low Diet; No. 4, Fever Diet. As regards the sick paupers on diet No. 1 (house diet) the extras only should be entered in this book.

The following Form of Medical Relief Book has been ordered for the Township of Manchester.

Week ending —————— 18——

(A.) Filled up by ——————

Medical Officer.

(B.) Filled up by the Master of the Workhouse, with the articles actually given.

No. of Papers.	Ward.	Name of the Sick Pauper.	Age.	When admitted to the Sick Ward.	When discharged.	Nature of Disease.	Days when attended. S M T W T F S	The Number of the Dietary on which placed. Sunday 1 to 7	Monday 1 to 7	Tuesday 1 to 7	Wednesday 1 to 7	Thursday 1 to 7	Friday 1 to 7	Saturday 1 to 7	Extras ordered. What ordered. When ordered. When discontinued.	State or Termination of the Case, and in the Event of Death, the apparent cause thereof.	Extras provided. Ale. pts.	Porter. pts.	Wine. pts.	Brandy. pts.	Gin. pts.	Initials of Medical Officer in attendance on every Case.
1																						
2																						
3																						
4																						
5																						
6																						
7																						
8																						
9																						
10																						
11																						
12																						
13																						
14																						
15																						
16																						
17																						
18																						
19																						
Total Number each Day																	Totals					

The Number of the Paupers on each description of the Dietaries and according to *the several Sexes* is to be carried by the Master at the close of each week to a Summary at the end of the book, to be prepared in the following Form.

WEEKLY SUMMARY.

No. of the Dietary.	Description of Classes in the Diet Table.	Number of Patients each Day.							Collective Number of Days.	Quantity of Provisions consumed.															
		S	M	T	W	Th.	F	Sat.		Bread. lbs.	Gruel. pts.	Rice Pudding. lbs.	Rice Milk. pts.	Meat, Coarse. lbs.	Meat, Fine. lbs.	Broth. pts.	Potatoes. lbs.	Tea. pts.	Sugar, Raw. lbs.	Butter. oz.	Milk, Sweet. pts.	Milk, New. pts.	Arrowroot, with Milk. pts.	Sago, with Milk. pts.	Barley. lbs.
1	House Diet - { Adults - Children -																								
2	Full Diet - - { Adults - Children -																								
3	Low Diet - - { Adults - Children -																								
4	Fever Diet - { Adults - Children -																								
5	Milk Diet - { Adults - Children -																								
6	Mutton Diet - { Adults - Children -																								
7	Tea Diet - - { Adults - Children -																								
	Totals - - -																								

As regards the Sick on Diet No. 1 (House Diet) the extras only should be entered in this Book, since their ordinary Diet will appear in the "Daily Provisions Consumption Account," for which see Form 21 of the Order of the Poor Law Board, bearing date the 10th day of March, 1851.

14. It is doubtless an irksome duty to keep so extensive a record, but it is necessary to the proper administration of the law.

15. The whole of the entries need not be made by himself, but the nature of the disease, the day of visit, and the diet, and medical extras ordered, should be stated in his own handwriting, except when the visit is made by his deputy.

16. He must regard himself as responsible for the correctness of the entries when made by his assistant, and it is desirable that an assistant who is not his legally appointed deputy should not make the entries referred to.

17. In order to show by the entry that he has seen a particular inmate, it is not enough that he has seen him without having conversed with him. It implies that he has conversed with him personally.

18. The nature of the disease should not be stated in general terms, as debility, if a more particular term would more accurately describe it. Neither should the term used be repeated weekly without due consideration as to the present state of the patient.

19. When the inmate has two or more maladies of importance they should be indicated.

20. It will be found convenient to rule lines in the blank space, and to write headings for the medical extras which are the most frequently ordered, as gin, beer, &c.

21. The date of admission and discharge, and the date when a particular medical extra is discontinued, should be stated in every case.

22. The very extensive records of the prevalence of disease in every district of the country have not hitherto been analysed and published, and consequently a large amount of very useful information and of laborious care is withheld from sanitary and medical science. The magnitude of the store renders the utilisation of this work impossible, except by the aid of the government and by a considerable expenditure of public money ; but it may be hoped that ere long means will be provided for the preparation of parts of

them in duplicate, to be sent to the medical department of the Poor Law Board, or to a new department in the office of the Registrar General, for analysis and publication periodically.

SUDDEN DEATHS.

23. He is also required to inform the Poor Law Board of the occurrence of any case of sudden death in the workhouse by the following order :—

" He shall report in writing to the Poor Law Board the case of every sudden and every accidental death which may occur in the workhouse within twenty-four hours after he shall receive information of the same, and the cause of the death so far as he is able to explain it " [*G. O. April* 4, 1868].

24. No definition has been given of the meaning of the term " sudden death," and it is so far left to the discretion of the medical officer as to whether an attack of apoplexy or other unexpected disease which causes death in 12 to 24 hours, or deaths from any disease which occur unexpectedly within an hour, shall be so regarded. Any death which did not occur from the natural course of a disease, but was unexpected and rapid, should be deemed to be a " sudden death " for this purpose, provided the circumstances were such as to render the cause of death very doubtful.

NURSING.

25. The medical officer is required to report to the guardians any defect which he may observe in the performance of the duties of the nurses.

26. He has not the power to appoint a nurse, whether paid or otherwise, or to recommend an applicant for the appointment. In some Unions it is the practice of the guardians to take his opinion upon the fitness of an applicant, and this should be universal.

27. When he requires the aid of paupers he should request the master or matron to send a proper person into the sick wards. He has not the power to make a selection, and

the fewness of able-bodied women of good character in workhouses renders it sometimes difficult for the matron to supply the demand made by the medical officer ; but, where it is practicable, and he desires to have a particular person, he should consult the matron and seek to obtain her consent.

28. Where there is a paid nurse, or where the person who has charge of the sick is a pauper, the medical officer gives his directions to her [*C. O. Art.* 213], and she is expected to obey them ; but in all matters relating to the cleanliness of the wards the nurses of both classes are placed under the directions of the matron.

29. The medical officer should strive to maintain a friendly understanding with the master and matron in the discharge of his duties, and should not encourage the nurse to resist their authority.

Chapter XXXXX.

REMUNERATION.

———•———

1. The remuneration of the medical officer is fixed prior to his appointment, and is a stated annual sum to be paid quarterly on the usual quarter-days.

2. It may be increased by the guardians with the consent of the Poor Law Board, but it cannot be diminished without the consent of the medical officer.

3. The only additions are fees for midwifery, lunacy certificates, vaccination, and visits to lunatics in asylums, according to the terms of his contract; but it is held by the Consolidated Order that he is not entitled to charge for vaccinating the inmates, neither can he demand payment for some of the other duties mentioned, unless it has been agreed upon in the contract.

4. Where there is not a contract existing between the medical officer and the guardians, or if with a contract no reference is made to payment in midwifery cases, the medical officer is entitled to a fee of 10s. or 20s., at the discretion of the guardians, for attending a woman in or immediately after childbirth, provided the order is given by a person who is legally qualified to give it [C. O. Art. 182].

5. In such a case the medical officer should receive a written order from the master, or other competent person, but the same remuneration is payable if the medical officer in a case of difficulty or danger attend a woman at the workhouse without an order.

6. Unlike the district medical officer, he is not entitled to charge for the performance of surgical operations, since the

theory of the extra allowance is in payment of extra visits to the patient, which is supposed not to hold in the attendance of the medical officer at the workhouse. Moreover, the Poor Law Board discouraged the performance of important surgical operations in workhouses, as stated in the following extract from their 8th Report [*8th Rep. P. L. Crs., App. A.*] :

7. "The operations enumerated in Art. 10 are intended to provide for cases of urgency (principally those arising from accidents) which cannot be sent to a public hospital with safety and propriety. The payments for operations are limited to operations on out-door poor, and do not include those performed in the workhouse. It appears to the Commissioners that the continued attendance at the house of the patient, in severe surgical cases, usually forms the most burdensome part of the extra service of the medical man ; whereas, the constant visits of the medical officer to the workhouse enable him to attend a patient in the workhouse without always making a visit for that express purpose. Moreover, when a patient can be removed to a workhouse, or when he has long been the subject of medical treatment in the workhouse, he may in general be removed with safety or propriety to an infirmary or hospital ; and the Commissioners think it desirable that, where the distance or other circumstances do not present serious obstacles, paupers should enjoy the practised skill and combined judgment of the medical men usually connected with such establishments. While, therefore, the Commissioners would discourage the performance of important surgical operations in workhouses, they are ready to sanction any reasonable subscription to an hospital or similar establishment by a Board of Guardians for the Union."

8. It merits consideration whether the law should not direct an extra fee to be given for the performance of certain capital operations in workhouses, where such operations may be properly performed, not only to add somewhat to an inadequate salary, but because such cases do demand additional visits to the workhouse.

9. He cannot claim the fee of £2 (which by *C. O. Art.* 183 is payable to district medical officers) for attendance on any case of difficult midwifery.

10. The guardians have now the power, with the consent of the Poor Law Board, to award to him, as to other officers, a gratuity for extraordinary or unforeseen services [*C. O. Art.* 172].

11. There is no uniform scale of remuneration in use throughout the country, neither has any basis been devised upon which an equitable and uniform scale might be established.

12. The only rule is that which controls nearly all pecuniary transactions, that of supply and demand; and when a medical officer accepts a given salary he raises the presumption that in the particular case an equitable arrangement has been made, which presumption is the stronger in that the medical officer, a man of education and intelligence, has deliberately and knowingly entered into the compact with the guardians.

13. It is well known that in the absence of any universally admitted basis, each medical officer has regard to the special circumstances as they affect him, and these vary with different medical men. One is at leisure, and desires the advantage of a *pseudo*-hospital, where he may treat medical and surgical cases; another is fully employed, but to prevent the advent of an additional competitor, seeks the appointment, or he has taken a junior partner upon whom he devolves much of the work; whilst a third is a young man aspiring to a position and seeks this appointment as a stepping-stone to private practice. In all these cases the medical officer hopes to receive that which to him is money's worth, although it be not paid in money, and the money payment may be an inadequate remuneration.

14. Whilst many medical officers express satisfaction at their emoluments, it cannot be matter of surprise that the small payment, the necessities of the medical officers, and the varied motives which actuated them in seeking the

appointment, lead to dissatisfaction, and to a sense that they are not duly remunerated.

15. In very numerous instances every year, the salaries are increased on the ground of additional duty, or of clearly insufficient remuneration, and it may not be doubted that the tendency to increase salaries will continue.

16. It is desirable that some basis of computation of salaries should be agreed upon by the medical profession and the public, since it must be arrived at on the ground of opinion, and not on natural fitness.

17. Number of inmates of the workhouse, whether on the books of the medical officer alone or otherwise, seems to be a proper guide ; and yet, as a visit paid to a workhouse, whether large or small, occupies a certain time, a payment for each visit, modified by the time which is required for attendance upon the cases, is a better guide.

18. No expenses should be incurred by the medical officer except those of transit, and all medicines and medical appliances should be provided at the cost of the guardians.

19. In the larger workhouses, where surgical operations are frequently performed, the medical officer may very properly ask the guardians to provide surgical instruments, but under other circumstances he could not expect them to do so.

20. Whether a dispenser would be required in addition to the medical officer must depend upon the number of sick cases, and, therefore, in general terms, upon the size of the workhouse, but one would not be required in the small country workhouses.

21. When the period shall arrive that the guardians will provide medicines and dispense them for all the outdoor poor, they will doubtless do the same for all indoor poor.

22. The medical officer is prohibited from receiving percentages or payments by way of commission on articles purchased by him for the guardians, and although it is customary to allow such commission to medical men on articles used by them, it is desirable that the medical officer should not accept them when acting as an officer of the guardians [*C. O. Art.* 218].

23. In numerous workhouses the guardians supply only a few drugs, as cod liver oil and quinine, and in a few this list is extended to laudanum, iodide of potassium, or similarly expensive drugs, and the guardians adopt one of three courses respecting them, viz., to instruct the medical officer to give an order for the quantity required for individual patients upon a druggist, to keep a stock at the workhouse to be dispensed there, or to authorise the medical officer to dispense them from a stock which he keeps for the guardians or from his ordinary stock of drugs, and charge the cost to the guardians.

24. The most desirable course is for the medical officer to purchase a stock of cod liver oil on the best terms for the guardians, to be kept at the workhouse and separately dispensed there, whilst quinine is dispensed with other drugs.

Dr. De Jongh's is the purest and best kind of cod liver oil, and as it is very rich in biliary products a small dose suffices, and it is thus economical in use. Being in bottles, it keeps well, and is dispensed easily and without waste.

25. The following form of stock book, to be made up periodically when any drugs are kept by or for the guardians, will be found convenient :—

Stock Book.

Name of Drug_____

_____ Workhouse.

Date.	Stock in hand.	*Patients supplied.	†Quantity dispensed.	Stock remaining.

* In this column may be placed either the total number of patients supplied within a stated period, or the name or initials of each patient.

† In this column may be placed either the total quantity of the drug supplied within a stated period, or the quantity supplied to each patient mentioned in the preceding column.

26. The present plan does not, however, give entire satisfaction, and the medical officers should not rest until the guardians provide all the drugs which the patients require.

THE CHAPLAIN:

Chapter XXXIII.

APPOINTMENT AND DUTIES.

1. There is not a chaplain appointed to every workhouse, neither has the Poor Law Board made such an appointment universally imperative, but they have expressed the opinion that such an officer is desirable, and in the case of the Carlisle Union issued an order for the appointment [*Order, March 6th, 1867*].

2. In some Unions, where there are many guardians who are not members of the Church of England, the religious services are conducted by ministers or laymen of Dissenting religious bodies, but in a large majority of the Unions in England a clergyman of the Church of England is duly appointed as chaplain, and sometimes the incumbent of the parish in which the workhouse is situate accepts the office without salary.

3. The chaplain is appointed by the guardians, with the assent in writing of the bishop of the diocese [*C. O. Art. 171*] and the Poor Law Board, but the assent of the incumbent of the parish is not necessary [*C. O. Art. 153 ; Instr. Letter, February, 1842; and Molyneux v. Bagshaw, 9 Jur. (N.S.) 553*].

4. The chaplain pays the fees of the bishop's secretary on obtaining the assent of the bishop of the diocese [*Off. Cir. No. 44*].

5. He must be a clergyman of the Church of England, but the appointment is not to a benefice, neither does the chaplain require a licence.

6. He holds his office during good behaviour [*C. O. Art.* 187], and cannot be suspended from his office by the guardians [*C. O. Art.* 192], or removed from his office by the bishop of the diocese [*ex parte Molyneux* 27, *J. P.* 56, & 4 & 5 *Wm. IV. c.* 76].

7. He is required to perform divine service on each Sunday, Good Friday, and Christmas Day, unless the guardians and the Poor Law Board direct otherwise ; also to examine the children in the workhouse, both as to their religious and general knowledge [53, *Off. Cir. N. S.* 21], and to catechise those who belong to the Church of England at least once a month, and to record in a book called "The Chaplain's Report Book," the dates of his attendance, the general progress of the children in education, and the moral and religious state of the inmates generally [*C. O. Art.* 211].

8. He must read prayers (but not necessarily the whole order of morning prayer, including the Litany, and part of the Communion Service) and deliver a sermon on Sundays, Good Friday, and Christmas Day. (*Opinion of Queen's Advocate.*)

9. If there is a workhouse chapel, the Communion may be celebrated in it, with the consent of the bishop of the diocese, but if the chapel be consecrated such consent is not required.

10. If there be not a room or chapel thus licensed, the chaplain should administer the Communion to the sick and disabled only, and he should not baptize children except under circumstances which would justify private baptism anywhere.

11. Churching of women, with the baptism of infants, and the usual celebration of the Holy Communion, should be performed at the parish church.

12. The chaplain is required to visit the sick in the work-

house at such periods as the guardians may appoint, and whenever he may be sent for, or as often as occasion may require [*C. O. Art.* 211 & 208, No. 14].

13. It is desirable that in the appointment of a chaplain a contract should be drawn up in which he would undertake to perform divine service twice on each Sunday and to visit the sick in the workhouse on a specified day or days weekly, when he will make himself acquainted with the moral state of the inmates generally, besides other days on which it may be necessary that he should visit particular sick persons.

14. It is also most desirable that there should be a regularly appointed chaplain to every workhouse, and that in the selection of that officer, contiguity of residence and love of that particular kind of work should be duly considered by the guardians.

15. There are but few appointments which offer to a zealous and prudent clergyman a greater opportunity of doing good, and there is perhaps no officer whose effective services are more desirable in the administration of the Poor Law.

16. There are many chaplains who, in addition to their defined duties, amuse and instruct the aged and the children by regular or occasional evening meetings at which persons attend to read, speak, or sing, and who take especial interest in the moral training of the children, and particularly of the girls, and watch over them when they may have left the workhouse.

17. The chaplain cannot delegate the performance of his official duties to his curate or to any other clergyman without the consent of the guardians [*Instr. Letter, Feb.* 5, 1842].

THE MATRON.

Chapter XXXV.

QUALIFICATIONS, APPOINTMENT, AND GENERAL DUTIES.

PERSONAL QUALIFICATIONS.

1. No limitation as to age at the period of election is imposed by the Poor Law Board, but it is not desirable that the matron should be very young, lest she should lack the requisite knowledge, judgment, and personal authority; neither should she be too old, lest she should be deficient in activity, or in bodily or mental power. The most suitable age is from 20 to 50 years.

2. Where there is not a master appointed to the workhouse she must be able to keep accounts [*C. O. Art.* 163], and the responsibilities of her office are necessarily increased.

3. She should be active, intelligent, and discreet; of kind and yet firm bearing, and not given to much talking or to speaking in loud tones or in a violent manner.

4. Whilst allowing herself to be accessible to every inmate, and being herself acquainted with every female adult and the children, she should not encourage a degree of familiarity which would tend to lessen the respect which is due to her office.

5. She should be dressed in a manner suitable both to her position and her duties, and be at all times cleanly and tidy in her person and habits.

6. She should rise early, devote her time to the duties of her office, and be not frequently absent from the workhouse, and she should not frequent public places of amusement.

7. The matron is usually the wife of the master, and as there is a similarity in the duties of the two officers, and they have a common interest in the discharge of them, the division of labour may be conveniently arranged by them.

8. When she has young children living with her she must necessarily devote some time and consideration to their requirements, but it is needful that this should be done with due subordination to the discharge of her official duties. It is to be regretted that the two sets of duties should almost necessarily be antagonistic, and that a matron with young children can rarely be a good officer.

9. When she is not the wife of the master it is desirable that she should strictly conform to the requirements of the Consolidated Order, and that she should strive to co-operate with the master in a friendly manner in the discharge of such duties as may affect them both.

APPOINTMENT.

10. The following is the document which the matron is required to sign on her appointment :—

————Union.

APPOINTMENT OF MATRON.

1. State the Christian name and surname of the person appointed as matron of the workhouse, in full.
2. Her place of residence immediately previous to her appointment.
3. Her age.
4. Whether she is married or single.
5. Whether she has any children ; and, if so, whether they are dependent on her, and where it is proposed that they shall reside.
6. Her religious persuasion.
7. Her previous occupations or callings.
8. Whether she has before held any paid office in any Union or parish ; and, if so, what office, and in what Union or parish. The cause of her leaving the same. And the date when she left.

9. Whether her whole time is given up to the service of the Union,
    or
Whether she continues in any other occupation or calling.

10. The day on which she was elected by the guardians.

11. The date from which her duties commence.

12 The amount of salary proposed.

13. Whether any rations or other emoluments are allowed ; and, if so, what.

14. If there be no master of the workhouse, the nature and amount of the security which she is to give for the due performance of her duties.

15. Whether she agrees to give the guardians one month's notice previous to resigning her office, or to forfeit one month's amount of salary, to be deducted from the amount of salary due at the time of resignation, pursuant to Article 167 of the General Consolidated Order.

16. What testimonials the guardians have received ; and whether they are satisfied thereby, or otherwise, that the person appointed is competent to perform efficiently all the duties of the office of matron.

17. The cause of the vacancy on account of which the appointment is made : if a resignation, the cause thereof, the date on which it took effect, and the name of the former officer.

———————*Signature of the Clerk.*
——————— *Signature of the Officer appointed.*
[The Christian name and surname being written in full.]

Reported to the Poor Law Board
    for their approval.   ——————— day of——————— 18

11. She is appointed for life, or until she resigns or becomes incompetent to discharge the duties of her office, or be removed by the Poor Law Board [*C. O. Art.* 187]. Should she be the wife of the master, and her husband should die, she vacates her office at the next quarter-day, but may be re-elected by the guardians with the consent of the Poor Law Board [*C. O. Art.* 189].

GENERAL STATEMENT OF DUTIES.

12. She is required to personally discharge the duties of her office except for a limited period with the assent of the guardians.

13. The classes of duties which devolve upon her are, the superintendence of the cleansing of the workhouse; the custody, making, mending, and washing of the linen, and some of the clothing of the inmates ; the cooking of food, and the superintendence of the female inmates and the children, whether sick or otherwise [*C. O. Art.* 210].

14. She assists the master in the general management and superintendence of the workhouse, and particularly in the observance of order, cleanliness, punctuality, industry, and decency, and decorum of the inmates [*C. O. Art.* 210, *No.* 13], in the cleansing and ventilation of the rooms, and in taking charge of all provisions and stores.

15. She reports to the master any negligence or other misconduct on the part of the female officers and servants, or of any restraint or compulsion used towards female paupers of unsound mind [*C. O. Art.* 210, *No.* 15].

16. She reports to the master any defect in the state of repair of the building, fittings, and furniture which she may notice, and any deficiency in the stores, with the quantity of any articles which she may recommend to be ordered.

17. She has not power to purchase anything for the use of the inmates without the authority of the guardians.

18. She takes care that clothing and other requisites are delivered at the workhouse according to contract, and suggests to the master and guardians desirable improvements in the quality and kind of articles to be contracted for.

P

Chapter XXIV.

ADMISSION, DISCHARGE, PUNISHMENTS, AND EMPLOYMENT.

ADMISSION OF PAUPERS.

1. She admits paupers to the workhouse in the absence, illness, or incapacity of the master [*C. O. Art.* 210, *No.* 1], and in reference to cases of an urgent nature she should not refuse admission except upon the clearest ground of the unfitness of the applicant.

2. If the applicant be sick and require the immediate attention of the medical officer, she should send for that officer and place the applicant in the receiving ward, or in the sick ward, according to the urgency of the case; but if she have reason to believe that the applicant is suffering from fever or small-pox, she should at once place the patient in the infectious ward.

3. If the applicants be not sick she admits them to the receiving ward [*C. O. Art.* 210, *No.* 1], and proceeds in the manner already directed in reference to the master.

4. She causes every female applicant, and every child under seven years of age, to be searched, cleansed, and dressed in the workhouse dress, and afterwards to be taken to their proper wards [*C. O. Art.* 210, *No.* 2], but she may not forcibly cut off the hair of any female inmate.

5. She searches, or directs a female servant to search, when necessary, any female pauper entering or quitting the workhouse whom the porter or other officer may suspect of having in her possession spirits or other fermented liquors, or prohibited articles, or any letters,

printed papers, or books of an immoral tendency, cards, dice, or matches [*C. O. Art.* 210, *No.* 14].

DISCHARGE OF PAUPERS.

6. She discharges the inmates in the absence of the master.

PUNISHMENTS OF PAUPERS.

7. She may not punish any adult inmate without the concurrence of the master. She has a concurrent power with the schoolmistress to punish any female child, but she may not inflict corporal punishment [*C. O. Art.* 138].

EMPLOYMENT.

8. She provides and enforces the employment of the able-bodied female inmates and the elder girls in the household work of the workhouse [*C. O. Art.* 210], and directs them to assist in cleaning, washing, and cooking, and the aged in mending and light work.

9. She superintends and gives such directions as may be necessary for the washing, drying, and getting-up of the clothes, linen, and bedding [*C. O. Art.* 210, *No.* 11], and does not allow the drying to be effected in the sleeping-rooms, sick-wards, or board-room.

10. She takes care that inmates at work in the wash-house have good shoes, and that there are boards on the floor so as to prevent the feet from becoming wet.

11. She does not allow the dirty clothes to be sorted upon the floor, but has them placed in baskets or on tables.

12. She does not allow the ironing-room to be so hot as to be injurious to health, or the steam to escape into the wash-house or ironing-room, but takes care that there is proper ventilation in the roof of both rooms. She does not, however, allow windows to be opened in cold weather very near to the place where the ironing is performed.

13. She sees that both the wash-house and ironing-room are kept in a clean and tidy state.

14. She should not employ the aged and partially disabled in any labour which may not be fitted to their age and feebleness, nor any inmate of whatever class who may then be, or within one week have been, upon the workhouse medical relief book, except with the sanction of the medical officer.

15. It is desirable that she should provide suitable employment for the girls who are over seven years of age (and with the concurrence of the master, for the boys also), of a domestic nature, so far as may be consistent with their attendance at school, and that she should train them in habits of industry, tidiness, and cleanliness, and instruct them in needlework, cooking, and cleaning [*C. O. Art.* 210, *No.* 3]. She should co-operate with the schoolmistress in making them fit for domestic service, and she should pay great attention to their moral conduct. In certain schools the boys are taught to knit, darn, and mend their clothes, with very good results.

16. She should employ the harmless female imbeciles in labour suited to their mental capacity, and not in such as may be beyond their intelligence and sense of responsibility, without due superintendence, as, for example, taking care of infants or using hot water at the baths.

17. In the selection of inmates to assist in nursing the sick and in cleaning the sick-wards, she should choose those of good moral conduct, of cleanly and tidy habits, and of good temper, and, if possible, those who may have had knowledge of such duties. It is also desirable that she should strive to train suitable inmates as nurses.

18. She is not herself required to perform menial work, and should there not be a sufficiency of inmates who are capable of performing such work, she should apply to the guardians for paid servants, and without such application she could not be excused for any defect in the state of the workhouse.

Chapter XXXVI.

VISITATION OF WARDS, STORES, CLEANING, AND BATHING.

VISITATION OF WARDS.

1. She calls over the names of every able-bodied female pauper and of every female child above seven years of age in their several wards half an hour after the bell has been rung in the morning, and inspects those inmates as to their cleanliness and dress; or she may request the schoolmistress to call over the names of the female children between seven and fifteen years of age [*C. O. Art.* 210, *No.* 4; *C. O. Art.* 103].

2. If there be not a master, or if the master be absent, ill, or incapacitated, she causes the same to be done with respect to the male able-bodied paupers, and the male children over seven years of age.

3. She visits the sleeping-wards of the females twice daily, to see that they are properly cleansed and ventilated—viz., at eleven a.m. and before nine p.m. [*C. O. Art.* 210, *Nos.* 5 & 6]; but in order that she may inform herself as to the state of cleanliness of the other wards, it is desirable that she should visit the whole workhouse daily.

4. She visits all the wards of the females and children every night before nine o'clock, and ascertains that all the inmates are in bed and all fires and lights extinguished, except those which may be necessary for the use of the sick, suckling women, and children [*C. O. Art.* 210, *No.* 6].

5. She should not visit the wards for males, whether sick

or otherwise, at night, without being accompanied by the master, nurse, or a female assistant.

6. When making her visits, she should notice the state of cleanliness of the floors, counterpanes, sheets, pillows, and bedding generally, as well as of the chamber utensils of every kind, the lavatories, night-stools, and water-closets, and ascertain that nothing is concealed under the beds or bedsteads, and that the clothes of the inmates are placed upon chairs in an orderly manner.

SUPPLY OF STORES AND CLOTHING.

7. She should supply clean sheets and towels whenever required for the sick and dirty cases, and also the towels and other appliances in the ordinary lavatories in the proportion which are required by the Poor Law Board in their " Instructions " respecting fittings.

8. She should examine the clothes, and particularly the stockings of the inmates, as to their state of repair and cleanliness, and supply stockings to all classes (including children), and clean linen and stockings to every inmate once in each week, and as often as may be required to dirty cases, and under special circumstances. She should supply soap and combs and brushes to all classes.

9. She should be watchful that the stock of every requisite is sufficient.

10. She should cut out the clothing and linen herself, or direct an assistant or trustworthy inmate to do so, under her immediate superintendence and on her own responsibility [*Art.* 210, *No.* 8]; and she should mark or cause to be marked all the clothing, with the proper number and with the name of the Union on the inside only [55 *Geo. III. c.* 137, *s.* 2].

11. Such clothes, both outer and under clothing, as may be made in the workhouse, and the mending of old clothes and of linen, may be properly the task of the aged and pregnant women, and the elder girls, according to their ability.

12. She delivers the proper supply of clothing and other requisites for the children to the schoolmaster and school-mistress weekly, and examines the heads and skins of the children from time to time, to note their freedom from disease and their state of cleanliness, and satisfies herself that the children carefully wash themselves, or are properly washed, daily.

CLEANING.

13. In reference to the cleaning of the floors and furniture, she should see that they are not merely washed but cleansed, and that as little water as possible is left upon them or allowed to run underneath and between the boards.

14. The water should be clean and warm, and changed as often as it may become dirty. In many workhouses nearly the whole washing of a room is done with dirty water, and a very disagreeable smell is caused by and left after the operation.

15. The cloths and brushes should not be dirty or greasy.

16. It is not enough to throw a cloth full of water upon the floor and then wipe it up again ; neither is it sufficient to employ a weakly person, as a child or an old woman, in cleaning the floors. The floors should be scrubbed with a brush, aided by soap, and as little water used as possible.

17. Where greasy matters are not thrown upon the floors, and there is not much dirt carried in by the feet, as in sick-wards, it is very desirable to avoid the use of water, and to employ rubbing with dry white sandstone, as a usual mode of cleaning, by which the floors would look clean and white.

18. Where the floors are painted they may be kept clean by dry rubbing, with or without wax, and washed occasionally only.

19. Superintendence by the matron, or other responsible officer, is quite necessary during the cleaning of the floors.

20. All vessels, and particularly the urinals, should be washed well in hot water.

21. Tin vessels lose the tinning by continued use and cleaning, and when they look dark-coloured they should be re-tinned, or new ones supplied.

BATHING OF INMATES.

22. She takes care that all the female inmates, except the sick and disabled, are bathed at stated periods of one or two weeks, and that a proper supply of hot and cold water, soap and towels, is provided.

23. She should not allow imbeciles to have charge of the hot water which is used for this purpose, or to be bathed, or to bathe others, except under the supervision of a trust-worthy person.

Chapter XXXVIII.

COOKING AND SERVING FOOD.

1. The matron should be a good cook of plain food, and devote attention to the cooking of the food in an efficient and economical manner, and prevent waste.

2. Food of every kind should be so cooked that it may be masticated easily, and yet not made so soft that it loses its proper appearance. Meat should not be salted, except in hot weather, but hung in a properly ventilated larder; inasmuch as salted meat is less nutritious and less easy to masticate and digest than fresh meat. She should not boil it so fast as to make it hard, and it is better not to raise the water to the boiling point, but to keep it for a sufficient time at 180 to 200 degs. It should, however, be put at first into boiling water, so as to harden the outside a little and prevent too much of the juices from escaping.

3. In roasting meat she should, if possible, cook it in large joints, with as little of the fibre cut across as possible. She should put it at first before a hot fire, and have it well turned round so as to harden the outside, and then draw it from the fire and cook it slowly.

4. When the meat is baked in an oven, as it must be when roasted in large quantities, the oven should not be too hot, and some one should regulate the heat. Means should be taken to allow the escape of the steam.

5. Care should be taken to prevent too much waste in peeling potatoes, and they should not be so much cooked as to fall to pieces.

6. Rice should be boiled in a cloth, with plenty of space

allowed for the swelling of it, and it should not be made so soft as to be somewhat pasty, or allowed to escape into the water.

7. Oatmeal in gruel should be well boiled, and if it be Scotch oatmeal it can scarcely be boiled too much.

8. Milk need not be boiled, but will be sufficiently cooked if heated to 160 degs., or, when made with oatmeal and water, if added to the boiling oatmeal and water.

9. Suet for suet-pudding should be finely cut, but not so that the inmates cannot see it, and properly mixed with the flour, and the pudding should not be made too stiff. Baked suet-puddings are more agreeable than boiled, and each kind should be supplied alternately.

10. A cheap and simple gravy or sauce should be served with suet-pudding when broth is not eaten with it. It may consist of hot meat liquor, or treacle, vinegar, and water.

11. Bones should be sawn into small pieces and boiled in a digester for twelve hours, and the liquor derived therefrom added to that of the meat.

12. Soup and broth should be well boiled, and yet not so much as to entirely break down the peas, barley, or potato.

13. Broth should not be made for the sick by simply adding a lump of cooked meat to hot meat liquor, but be properly prepared with vegetables and seasoning.

14. Both soup and broth should be made palatable by herbs, other fresh vegetables, and seasoning.

15. Tea should be made by enclosing the proper quantity of tea in a large bag, with open meshes, and stirring it about in boiling water, or it should be thrown loose into the copper or other vessel and stirred : it should not be kept boiling. A pinch of carbonate of soda should be added.

16. Sugar should not be boiled in the tea, but both sugar and milk should be added when it is ready to be served.

17. To render food palatable is not only to make it more agreeable to the taste, but to render its action more efficient, and thereby to prevent waste.

18. The matron should take care that food is served hot,

and as quickly as possible. Whenever she observes that certain children and aged people habitually leave a particular food, she should endeavour to induce them to eat it, or she should provide some change of food for them ; both that they may be properly nourished and that food be not wasted.

19. She should take care that there is at hand a sufficient supply of all kinds of utensils for cooking, serving, and eating food, and if there be a deficiency of them to report it to the master and the guardians.

20. She should notice that the food is supplied by the tradesmen of good quality ; that the meat is tender, and without an undue proportion of fat ; the peas split, and of proper size and soundness ; the rice of good colour and size ; the tea of proper flavour and strength, and not containing much stalk ; the milk without water, the flour capable of taking up a proper quantity of water without becoming too soft, and the oatmeal not gritty.

Chapter XXXVIII.

SICK CHILDREN AND VAGRANTS.

1. She should especially watch over the sick, and also the infants and children under seven years of age, and take care that they are kept warm, clean, well clad, and well fed, and have proper exercise in the open air [*Art.* 210, *No.* 12]. She should supply proper diet to the sick, suckling women, and infants, under the direction of the medical officer.

2. She should confer with the medical officer and the paid nurse on all other matters appertaining to the nursing and care of the sick in a considerate and friendly spirit, and, whilst exercising a degree of supervision over the sick-wards and over the general conduct of the nurse and inmates, should pay due respect to the authority and position of the medical officer, and leave the responsibility with him.

3. There is in many workhouses a want of due harmony of action between the matron on the one side and the nurse and the medical officer on the other, which is prejudicial to the sick inmates, and particularly to the good management of the workhouse. Whilst not forgetting her authority or responsibility, the matron should recognise the fact that the nurse is appointed by the guardians to perform special duties, and to act chiefly under the direction of the medical officer; and she should not enforce her own views or interfere beyond a general supervision in such a way as to thwart the wishes of the medical officer.

4. When she has sufficient grounds of complaint against either of those officers, it is desirable that she should take the directions of the guardians rather than act in a hostile spirit.

5. Where there are not special female officers in charge of the vagrants she should observe the state of the female vagrant-wards, and the beds, bedding, and means of cleanliness, and see the female vagrants before they are dismissed in the morning; and should any of them be ill she should call the attention of the medical officer to the case, and make proper provision for her accommodation and care.

6. She should particularly ascertain whether any female vagrant, who is evidently pregnant, may be very near her confinement when she enters the vagrant-wards.

7. She should superintend the labour of the female vagrants, and see that they clean their wards and fold up the blankets.

SCHOOLMASTER AND SCHOOL-MISTRESS.

Chapter XXXIX.

APPOINTMENT, SALARY, AND DUTIES.

1. There are numerous workhouses in which only one of these officers is appointed, and in such a case it is usual to appoint a schoolmistress.

2. Where the number of children to be taught is very small, it would not be proper to appoint two officers; but even in such a school there may be boys over twelve years of age who are not properly restrained by a woman; and it is desirable that where a schoolmistress only is appointed the elder boys should, where possible, be sent to the national schools.

3. In some workhouses the schoolmaster and school-mistress are man and wife, and if they have not young children of their own the arrangement is to be desired. When children live with them in the workhouse it is usual for them to be educated with the workhouse children, and to associate with them.

4. The following document is signed by the schoolmaster on his appointment :—

——— Union.

1. State the Christian name and surname of the person appointed as schoolmaster of the workhouse, in full.

2. His place of residence immediately previous to his appointment.

3. His age.

4. Whether he is married or single; also whether he has any children; and, if so, whether they are dependent on him, and where it is proposed that they shall reside.

5. His religious persuasion.

6. His previous occupations or callings.

Whether he has been in the army, navy, excise, police, or other public service; and, if so, which service,

The cause of his leaving the same,

And the date when he left.

7. Whether he has before held any paid office in any Union or parish; and, if so, what office, and in what Union or parish,

The cause of his leaving the same,

And the date when he left.

8. Whether he has had any experience in teaching, or any training for it; and, if so, what.

9. Whether he holds a certificate from the Committee of Council on Education, or the Poor Law Board; and, if so, the class of such certificate, the date thereof, and in what school it was obtained.

10. Whether his whole time is given up to the service of the Union.

11. The day on which he was elected by the guardians.

12. The day on which his duties commence.

13. Whether he is to reside in the workhouse.

14. The amount of salary proposed; and

Whether any rations or other emoluments are allowed; and, if so, what.

15. Whether he agrees to give the guardians one month's notice previous to resigning his office, or to forfeit one month's amount of salary to be deducted therefrom, pursuant to Article 167 of the General Consolidated Order.

16. What testimonials the guardians have received, and whether they are satisfied thereby, or otherwise, that the person appointed is competent to fulfil the office of schoolmaster of the workhouse, and to perform efficiently the duties required by Articles 114 and 212 of the General Consolidated Order.

17. The cause of the vacancy on account of which the appointment is made; if a resignation, the cause of such resignation, and the name of the former officer, and on what day the resignation took effect.

Note.—The schoolmaster will be required to pass an examination by Her Majesty's Inspector of Schools when he next visits the work-house. *

——————————————————————*Signature of the Clerk.*

——————————————————————*Signature of the Officer appointed.*

[The Christian name and surname being written in full.]

Reported to the Poor Law Board for their approval,

——————— day of—————————18

* The clerk to the guardians should direct the special attention of the officer to this paragraph.

5. The following document is signed by the schoolmistress on her appointment :—

——— Union.

1. State the Christian name and surname of the person appointed as schoolmistress of the workhouse, in full.

2. Her place of residence immediately previous to her appointment.

3. Her age.

4. Whether married or single.

5. Whether she has any children ; and, if so, whether they are dependent on her, and where it is proposed that they shall reside.

6. Her religious persuasion.

7. Her previous occupations or callings.

8. Whether she has had any experience in teaching, or any training for it ; and, if so, what.

9. Whether she holds a certificate from the Committee of Council on Education ; and, if so, what is the class of such certificate.

10. Whether she has before held any paid office in any Union or parish ; and, if so, what office and in what Union or parish,

      The cause of her leaving the same,

      And the date when she left.

11. Whether her whole time is given up to the service of the Union.

12. The day on which she was elected.

13. The date from which her duties commence.

14. Whether she is to reside in the workhouse.

15. The amount of salary proposed, and

      Whether any rations or other emoluments are allowed ; and, if so, what.

16. Whether she agrees to give the guardians one month's notice previous to resigning her office, or to forfeit one month's amount of salary, to be deducted therefrom, pursuant to Article 167 of the General Consolidated Order.

17. What testimonials the guardians have received, and whether they are satisfied thereby, or otherwise, that she is competent to fulfil the office of schoolmistress of the workhouse, and to perform efficiently

the duties required by Articles 114 and 212 of the General Consolidated Order.

18. State the cause of the vacancy on account of which the appointment is made ; if a resignation, the cause of such resignation, and the name of the former officer.

Note.—The schoolmistress will be required to pass an examination by Her Majesty's Inspector of Schools when he next visits the workhouse. *

——————————————————— *Signature of the Clerk.*

——————————————————*Signature of the Officer appointed.*

[The Christian name and surname to be written in full.]

Reported to the Poor Law Board for their approval,

————————day of—————————— 18

* The clerk to the guardians should direct the special attention of the officer to this paragraph.

6. They hold office during good behaviour, or until they die, resign, or be proved to be incompetent to discharge their duties [*C. O. Art.* 187], and they should give one month's notice of their intention to resign their appointment [*C. O. Art.* 167].

7. They may be suspended by the guardians [*C. O. Art.* 192], and removed by the Poor Law Board [*C. O. Art.* 187].

8. There is no one standard of efficiency laid down by the Poor Law Board, but several are acknowledged—viz., permission, probation, competency, and efficiency, and each teacher is assigned to one or another by the Inspector of Workhouse Schools after examination.

9. The remuneration of these officers depends, in part, upon their efficiency, for whilst the guardians, with the consent of the Poor Law Board, determine the salary to be given to them, a payment is made by the Government out of the Consolidated Fund, which varies with the efficiency of those officers and the number of their scholars, all of which must be handed over to them by the guardians. [*For the scale see page* 10.]

10. Hence an inducement is offered to guardians to appoint competent officers, and in large schools considerable

Q

advantages accrue to those officers who obtain certificates of the higher grades.

11. They are also entitled, after sixty years of age, to such superannuation allowance as the guardians may give and the Poor Law Board sanction (not, however, exceeding two-thirds of the value of their salary and emoluments) after twenty years' service in one Union [27 & 28 *Vic. c.* 42].

12. Suitable furnished apartments (consisting almost invariably of two rooms for each officer) with rations similar to those allowed to the master, are to be provided and allowed, or if the officers reside out of the workhouse, each is entitled to have an allowance of £15 per year in lieu thereof.

13. They are not required to perform menial duties—not necessarily even to wash the children—and proper assistance should be afforded to them, in order that the children and their clothes and apartments may be kept clean and in good order.

14. They are required to superintend the washing and cleansing of the children, and should apply to the matron for towels, sheets, clothing, and all requisites.

15. They have the charge of the children, both during school hours and when out of school, except those who may be temporarily in the charge of industrial trainers or other officers.

16. They accompany the children to the dining-hall, and are present at their meals, and the schoolmaster says grace in the absence of the master [*C. O. Art.* 208, *No.* 9], but they do not take their meals with them.

17. They are required to instruct the children in reading, writing, arithmetic, and the principles of the Christian religion, and such other instruction as may fit them for service, and train them to habits of usefulness, industry, and virtue [*C. O. Art.* 114].

18. They regulate the discipline and arrangements of the school according to the directions of the guardians, accompany the children when they quit the workhouse for

exercise, or at public worship, keep the children clean in their persons, and orderly and decorous in their conduct, and assist the master and matron respectively in maintaining due subordination [*C. O. Art.* 212]. The school-master should read prayers in the absence of the master.

19. Hence their duties are of a very responsible nature, and upon the right discharge of them will greatly depend the future success in life of the children, and the relief or the burden of the poor-rates. In multitudes of instances these officers have had the gratification of knowing that their pupils have themselves become teachers, ministers of religion, or prosperous men of business in this or other countries.

20. The greatest care should be taken to instil habits of obedience, truthfulness, industry, sobriety, order, kindness, and cleanliness, and the schoolmaster and schoolmistress should feel that however important a knowledge of the elements of education may be, the formation of right habits should be a chief aim.

21. They should carefully watch the state of health of the children, and report to the master, matron, or medical officer any defect of appetite or general health which they may observe.

22. They should inspect the heads and bodies of each child at least weekly, and see that the children are bathed weekly in water and in a bath-room which is not too cold, and with proper means of drying the children.

23. They should obtain from the matron a proper supply of towels for daily washing, have them dried after the morning's and evening's use, and kept out of the dirt by the use of rollers ; also a supply of fine and coarse combs and hair-brushes, and see that they are used, kept clean, and fit for use.

24. The lavatory should be kept clean and dry, and if the floor be of stone or brick and is wet, there should be boards upon which the children may stand.

25. They should take care that each child washes in a

separate quantity of clean water, and is allowed the use of soap.

26. The habit of washing in dirty water, and the use of inferior soap, without an abundant supply of water and dry towels, frequently produce diseased eyes in children.

27. They should take care that the school-room, particularly, and also the day rooms and dormitories, are properly ventilated, but they must not expose the children to cold draughts, which would be likely to give them cold. They should call the attention of the master and visiting committee to any overcrowding or want of accommodation for the children.

28. In wet weather the children should not remain in wet clothes, and the schoolmaster and schoolmistress should take care that the boots and shoes are in good order and fit for use.

29. They should also take care that there is woollen clothing, and a proper amount of warmth in the various apartments in cold weather.

30. They should allow and insist upon plenty of exercise in the open air, and not be content to take the children into the lanes and fields [*C. O. Art.* 212, *No.* 3] once a week only, but twice or thrice a week, and on each occasion should allow them to run about freely in proper places.

31. They should notice whether the dietary is proper for the children, and whether the children leave any kind of food, or have not enough at any meal, and report to the master or medical officer. They should see that growing children have plenty of bread.

32. It is very desirable that they should give especial attention to exceptional cases, whether of feeble health or of bad habits, and endeavour to supply any defect or correct any existing evil.

33. In their general treatment of the children they should be kind and gentle, yet firm and just, and should never exhibit violence by voice or gesture, and never correct in anger.

34. They must not inflict corporal punishment on any female child [*C. O. Art.* 138], nor on any male child over fourteen years of age [*C. O. Art.* 142], except, perhaps, a caning over the clothes.

35. The schoolmaster must not inflict such punishment within two hours after the commission of the offence [*C. O. Art.* 140], and, if possible, the master should also be present [*C. O. Art.* 141] during the punishment. The particulars of the offence and punishment must be forthwith reported by the master, to be entered by him in the "punishment-book" [*C. O. Art.* 144].

36. The rod or other instrument of punishment must be approved by the guardians or the visiting committee [*C. O. Art.* 139], and no child may be punished by confinement in a dark room, or in any room by night [*C. O. Art.* 136].

37. Whilst maintaining due authority, the aim should be to obtain obedience by the respect and affection of the children rather than by frequent punishments.

38. They have not authority to grant leave of absence to the children, and in the discharge of all their duties they should be careful to co-operate with the master and matron in a friendly and efficient manner.

39. They are not required to ask the master or matron for leave of absence when they wish to leave the workhouse temporarily, but it is desirable that they should inform him of their intention to go out, and they will be held responsible for any neglect of duty during their absence.

THE NURSE.

Chapter IX.

APPOINTMENT AND DUTIES.

1. The following is the document which the nurse is required to sign on her appointment :—

1. State the Christian name and surname of the person appointed as nurse at the Union workhouse, in full.

2. Her place of residence immediately previous to her appointment.

3. Her age.

4. Whether married or single.

5. Whether she has any children ; and, if so, whether they are dependent on her, and where it is proposed that they shall reside.

6. Her previous occupations or callings.

7. Whether she has before held any office in any Union or parish ; and, if so, what office, and in what Union or parish.

8. The cause of her leaving the same, and
　　The date at which she left.

9. The day on which she was elected to her present office.

10. The date from which her duties commence.

11. The amount of salary proposed.

12. Whether any rations or other emoluments are allowed ; and, if so, what.

13. Whether she is competent to read and understand correctly the written directions of the medical officer, and otherwise to fulfil the office of nurse with watchfulness and care.

14. The cause of the vacancy on account of which the appointment

is made ; if a resignation or dismissal, the cause thereof, the name of the former officer, and the day on which she ceased to hold office.

_____ *Signature of the Clerk.*

_____*Signature of the Person appointed as Nurse.*

[The Christian name and surname to be written in full.]

Reported to the Poor Law Board for their approval,

_____ day of _____18

2. She holds office during the pleasure of the board of guardians [*C. O. Art.* 188], but it is usual to give and demand one month's notice of removal.

3. When she is dismissed by the guardians the fact is to be communicated to the Poor Law Board [*C. O. Art.* 188].

4. The nurse in some workhouses is improperly required to perform menial labour, such as scrubbing floors and washing clothes ; whilst in others she also fills the office of assistant-matron, and in a very few workhouses she is the wife of the schoolmaster or of the porter.

5. She should not be required to perform menial labour, and her duties should be strictly confined to the care of the sick, the lying-in [*C. O. Art.* 213, *No.* 1], the lunatics (where there is not a special attendant for that purpose), the aged and infirm who need her help, and the young children ; but the extent of her duties must depend very much upon the number of sick inmates.

6. She should be a single woman, or a widow without incumbrance, and should devote the whole of her time to the discharge of her duties.

7. She must be able to read written directions [*C. O. Art.* 165] and should be practically acquainted with the duties of her office.

8. The necessity for the appointment of a paid and trained nurse in each workhouse has increased of late years with the proportionately larger number of sick and the aged and infirm inmates ; and as it is very rarely possible that the

matron can efficiently discharge these important duties in addition to her own, it is desirable that such an appointment should be made in almost every workhouse.

9. Having regard to the class of sick cases which exist in provincial workhouses generally, one paid nurse will suffice for an infirmary with thirty to forty beds (some of which are nearly always empty), provided she can obtain a sufficient number of helpers. In the large towns, however, where the cases are of a more serious character, a trained assistant nurse would be required.

10. The fever and infectious wards in workhouses generally have too few inmates to require the appointment of a separate paid nurse, and hence the ordinary nurse must superintend the pauper nurses who have immediate charge of that important class of sick cases.

11. Her apartments should be in connection with the ordinary sick-wards, and not with those of the infectious-wards ; and, whilst careful that every attention should be paid to the latter class of cases, she should not go from one class of wards to the other unnecessarily; and she should be careful to entirely cleanse her hands and clothes from any stain of the excretions of fever patients.

12. When it is possible, she should keep a special dress for use in the infectious-wards, and she should always wash her hands on leaving those wards.

13. She should see that the most scrupulous cleanliness is observed in the infectious-wards, and particularly that the sputa, urine, and other evacuations, are quickly and entirely removed.

14. The linen, towels, &c., which may have been soiled by the evacuations, should be removed and put into boiling water ; and all night-stools and similar vessels should be well scalded with boiling water, and wiped with cloths kept exclusively for that purpose.

15. She should not allow any patient who is extremely ill to sit up for any purpose without the direction of the medical officer, and particularly at night ; and she should

take care that warm food and sufficient clothing are supplied in the night to persons so circumstanced.

16. She should keep all sick-wards, bath-rooms, water-closets, and passages well ventilated, but not in such a manner as to cause a cold draught to be felt by the inmates.

17. She must not open windows widely near to any patient, except, perhaps, in hot weather; but she should admit air in small quantities by small openings in various parts of the ward, both night and day.

18. To open the upper sashes to the extent of half an inch would probably suffice if done continually, but it is better that there should be proper ventilators, covered with finely perforated zinc, to allow the constant entrance and exit of air in very small quantities in one place.

19. She should pay attention to the direction of the wind and to the state of the weather, bearing in mind that the air will chiefly enter by those ventilators and openings which are on the windward side; and she should admit more air, if possible, on the opposite side.

20. She should take care that the sick beds are soft and in good order, and that there is sufficient bed-clothing.

21. Waterproof sheeting, both with and without funnels, should be used by her to dirty cases, and the most scrupulous cleanliness in such cases should be observed.

22. She is specially to act under the direction of two officers, viz., the medical officer and the matron, and she should be respectful to both, and, if possible, avoid allying herself with either.

23. She must obey the instructions of the medical officer in the administration of medicines and the general management of the sick [*C. O. Art.* 213, *No.* 1], and those of the matron in matters of order and cleanliness. The food to be given to the sick will be supplied by the matron, but ordered by the medical officer, and she will, as far as possible, carry out the directions of the medical officer.

24. In serious cases she should receive the directions of the medical officer in writing.

25. She must report to the medical officer any defect which she may observe in the arrangements of the sick and lying-in wards, and take care that a light is kept at night in the sick-wards [*C. O. Art.* 213, *Nos.* 2 *&* 3].

26. She should also take care that there is a fire both night and day when necessary, and that some one sits up with a patient who is dangerously ill.

27. If she observes a patient becoming seriously ill or approaching death, she should inform the master or matron.

28. Hot water and a proper supply of utensils and linen should be kept at hand.

29. She should not leave a lying-in case for at least one hour after delivery, and should be careful that no needless exertion is made by the latter. She should be particularly careful that very young children are kept warm.

30. It is very undesirable that she should drink any kind of intoxicating liquors.

31. She should, as far as possible, instruct suitable inmates in the discharge of the duties of nurse.

32. She should be well remunerated [*Instr. Letter,* 5*th May,* 1865], and probably not less, but more, than £20 per year should be paid to her, besides the use of two suitable rooms and the allowance of proper rations.

THE PORTER.

[**Chapter XLI.**

APPOINTMENT AND DUTIES.

1. The following is the document which a person who has been elected by the guardians to the office of porter is required to sign :—

1. State the Christian name and surname of the person appointed as porter of the workhouse, in full.

2. His place of residence immediately previous to his appointment.

3. His age.

4. Whether he is married or single.

5. Whether he has any children dependent on him; and, if so, where it is proposed that they shall reside.

6. His previous occupations or callings.

    Whether he has been in the army, navy, excise, police, or other public service; and, if so, what service,

    The cause of his leaving the same,

    And the date when he left.

7. Whether he has before held any office in any other Union or parish; and, if so, what office, and in what Union or parish.

    The cause of his leaving the same,

    And the date when he left.

8. Whether his whole time is given up to the service of the Union, or,

    Whether he continues in any other occupation or calling.

9. The day on which he was elected.

10. The date from which his duties commence.

11. The amount of salary proposed.

12. Whether any rations or other emoluments are allowed; and, if so, what.

13. Whether he agrees to give the guardians one month's notice previous to resigning his office, or to forfeit one month's amount of salary, to be deducted therefrom, pursuant to Article 167 of the General Consolidated Order.

14. Whether the guardians are satisfied by his testimonials, or otherwise, that he is competent to fulfil the office of porter of the workhouse, and to perform efficiently the duties required by Article 214 of the Order.

15. The cause of the vacancy on account of which the appointment is made : if a resignation or dismissal, the cause and date thereof, and the name of the former officer.

———————————————*Signature of the Clerk.*

———————————————*Signature of the Officer appointed.*

[The Christian name and surname to be written in full.]

Reported to the Poor Law Board for their approval,

—————— day of —————— 18

2. There is no limitation as to age, neither are any special qualifications prescribed by the Poor Law Board other than the capability to read and write.

3. In many of the smaller workhouses a paid porter is not appointed, but the duties are performed by the master, or by a pauper ; but as a certain amount of responsibility attaches to the office, it is desirable that a paid and competent official should be appointed.

4. The porter is usually a single man, but in some of the larger workhouses he is required to be married, and both himself and his wife are paid to perform the prescribed duties.

5. He usually occupies a room or rooms at the lodge or other entrance to the workhouse, and in near proximity to the receiving and vagrant wards, but in some instances his apartments are within the workhouse, to the inconvenience of the administration.

6. He is supplied with rations on a given scale, and usually his food is cooked apart from that of the master and other officers ; but sometimes the meat is cooked with the master's food, and sent from the master's table. The former is the more satisfactory plan.

7. He is not appointed for life, but holds office during the pleasure of the board of guardians. He must, on his appointment, agree to give the usual notice of one month, and when he is dismissed by the guardians, the fact must be reported to the Poor Law Board [*C. O. Art.* 167 & 188].

8. He is required to keep a book, which is known as "the porter's book," in which he must enter the names and business of all persons entering or leaving the workhouse, however many may be the times they enter or leave in a day, together with the time of such persons going in and out [*C. O. Art.* 214, *No.* 2].

9. This requirement applies to all persons, whether they have a legal right to enter the workhouse, or only attend there on business connected with the workhouse; but it does not appear that he can refuse to admit any person having a legal right to enter who may refuse to give his name.

10. He must admit the officers of the workhouse; the officers and guardians of the Union at proper times; Inspectors of Poor Law, Inspectors of Schools, Lunacy Commissioners, and county magistrates at all times; the coroner when there is a dead body in the workhouse; and his jurymen when an inquest is about to be held there by him; pauper applicants for admission properly authorised; persons desiring to see the register, when that book is kept at the workhouse; ministers of religion (other than the chaplain) when sent for, or duly authorised to enter; applicants for relief on board days, and other persons having business to transact at the workhouse.

11. He receives all applicants for admission, and takes them to the receiving-ward, or to such other ward as may be indicated by the master and matron [*C. O. Art.* 214, *No.* 3].

12. In the absence, illness, or incapacity of the master and matron, he admits applicants for admission presenting a legal order, and others on sudden or urgent necessity. He places all ordinary cases in the receiving-ward [*C. O. Art.* 214, *No.* 3]; but cases of fever or small-pox are taken by him to the infectious-ward.

13. He allows all persons other than the pauper inmates to leave the workhouse, and pauper inmates on the authority of the board of guardians, master, or matron.

14. He has charge of the gate [*C. O. Art.* 214, *No.* 1], and examines all packages of goods before admission, and prevents the introduction of spirituous and fermented liquors, and other articles for the introduction of which he has not received due authority [*C. O. Art.* 214, *No.* 4]. He does not prevent the introduction of such articles by the officers for their own use. He also examines all parcels about to be removed from the workhouse by pauper inmates, unless he have received the authority of the master or matron to allow them to pass [*C. O. Art.* 214, *No.* 6].

15. He should file every written authority which he may receive from the master and matron.

16. He searches any male pauper who may enter or leave the workhouse whom he suspects of having spirituous or fermented liquors, cards, dice, indecent publications, or other prohibited articles in his possession; and he causes the matron to be called to search any female about whom the like suspicion exists [*C. O. Art.* 214, *No.* 5]. He reports to the master any inmate who is drunk on returning to the workhouse.

17. He has usually the immediate charge of the receiving and vagrant wards, and superintends the bathing of the male applicants. He also delivers the food to such inmates.

18. He usually superintends the labour of the vagrants where there is not an officer specially appointed to that duty.

19. He searches all male vagrants, and removes their clothes until the morning; and, when necessary, dries the clothes before returning them, and keeps order in the vagrant-ward.

20. He notices carefully if any of them are ill, and reports the fact to the master.

21. He usually has charge of the room containing the inmates' own clothes, and should he find money or other valuable articles he reports the fact to the master.

22. He locks all the outer doors, and delivers the keys to the master at 9 p.m., from whom he receives them at 6 a.m. [*C. O. Art.* 214, *No.* 7], unless there be a night porter, to whom he transfers them at night and from whom he receives them in the morning.

23. Should any person apply for admission after that hour, he reports the fact to the master or matron [*C. O. Art.* 214, *No.* 7], and, in the absence of the master and matron at any time, he admits them into the receiving-ward [*C. O. Art.* 214, *No.* 3].

24. In many workhouses he is required to act as industrial trainer to the boys, either as tailor or shoemaker, or in cultivating the garden or the land; and in the smaller ones this is done with propriety.

25. He may be required to accompany the children when taking exercise, or going to a place of worship, in the absence of other officers; and, in the absence of the master, matron, and schoolmaster, it would be his duty to read prayers.

26. He is generally to assist the master and matron to preserve order, and he informs the master of any want of order or security in the workhouse, or of any other defects which he may notice; and acts in due subordination to the master and matron [*C. O. Art.* 214, *Nos.* 8 & 9].

PART III.

—◆—

THE CONSOLIDATED ORDER OF
THE POOR LAW BOARD.

𝕿𝖔 𝖙𝖍𝖊 𝕲𝖚𝖆𝖗𝖉𝖎𝖆𝖓𝖘 𝖔𝖋 𝖙𝖍𝖊 𝕻𝖔𝖔𝖗 *of the several Unions named in the Schedule hereunto annexed;*—

To the Churchwardens and Overseers of the several Parishes and Places comprised within the said Unions;—

To the Clerk or Clerks to the Justices of the Petty Sessions held for the Division or Divisions in which the Parishes and Places comprised within the said Unions are situate;—

And to all others whom it may concern.

WE, THE POOR LAW COMMISSIONERS, in pursuance of the authorities vested in Us by an Act passed in the fifth year of the reign of His late Majesty King William the Fourth, intituled "*An Act for the Amendment and better Administration of the Laws relating to the Poor in England and Wales,*" and by all other Acts amending the same, do hereby rescind every Order, whether General or Special, heretofore issued by the Poor Law Commissioners to the Unions named in the Schedule hereunto annexed, which relates to the several subjects herein provided for, except so far as the same may have related to the apprenticeship of any poor person not yet completed, or may have required or authorised the appointment of any officer, or the giving of any security, or the making of any contract not yet executed, or the making of any orders by the Guardians for contributions and payments not yet obeyed, or may have defined the salaries of any officers, or have prescribed the districts within which the duties of any officer shall be performed, or may have provided for the class of paupers or their number to be received into any particular Workhouse, or may have provided for the election of Guardians in any case where such election shall not have been completed when this Order shall come into force, and except the Order regulating the mode of election of Guardians, bearing date the Sixth day of March One thousand eight hundred and forty-six, and addressed to the Guardians of the Poor of the Nottingham Union.

And We do hereby Order, Direct, and Declare, with respect to each of the said Unions as follows :—

ELECTION OF GUARDIANS.

Article 1.—The Overseers of every Parish in the Union shall, before the Twenty-sixth day of March in every year, distinguish in the rate-book the name of every ratepayer in their parish who has been rated to the relief of the poor for the whole year immediately preceding the said day, and has paid the poor rates made and assessed upon him for the period of one whole year, except those which have been made or become due within the six months immediately preceding the said day.

Art. 2.—The Clerk shall at every future annual election of Guardians perform the duties hereby imposed upon him, and all other duties suitable to his office which it may be requisite for him to perform in conducting and completing such election ; and in case the office of Clerk shall be vacant.

R.

at the time when any duty relative to such election is imposed on the Clerk by this Order, or in case the Clerk, from illness or other sufficient cause, shall be unable to discharge such duties, the Guardians shall appoint some person to perform such of the said duties as then remain to be performed, and the person so appointed shall perform such duties.

Art 3.—The Guardians shall, before or during every such election, appoint a competent number of persons to assist the Clerk in conducting and completing the election in conformity with this Order ; but if the Guardians do not make such appointment within the requisite time, the Clerk shall take such measures for securing the necessary assistance as he may deem advisable.

Art. 4.—The persons appointed under Article 3 shall obey all the directions relative to the conduct of the election, which may be given by the Clerk for the execution of this Order.

Art. 5.—The Overseers of every Parish in the Union, and every Officer having the custody of the poor-rate books of any such Parish, shall attend the Clerk at such times as he shall require their attendance, until the completion of the election of Guardians, and shall, if required by him, produce to him such rate-books, and the registers of owners and proxies, together with the statements of owners, and appointments and statements of proxies, and all books and papers relating to such rates in their possession or power.

Provided that, where any register of owners shall have been prepared in any Parish containing a population exceeding two thousand persons, it shall not be necessary to produce the statements of owners.

Art. 6.—The Clerk shall prepare and sign a notice, which may be in the Form marked (A.) hereunto annexed, and which shall contain the following particulars :—

1st. The number of Guardians to be elected for each Parish in the Union.

2nd. The qualification of Guardians.

3rd. The persons by whom, and the places where, the

Nomination Papers in respect of each Parish are to be received, and the last day on which they are to be sent.

4th. The mode of voting in case of a contest, and the days on which the Voting Papers will be delivered and collected [*See additions, G. O., Jan.* 14, 1867].

5th. The time and place for the examination and casting up of the votes.

And the Clerk shall cause such notice to be published on or before the Fifteenth day of March, in the following manner :—

1st. A printed copy of such notice shall be affixed on the principal external gate or door of every Workhouse in the Union, and shall from time to time be renewed, if necessary, until the Ninth day of April.

2nd. Printed copies of such notice shall likewise be affixed on such places in each of the Parishes of the Union as are ordinarily made use of for affixing thereon notices of parochial business.

Provided that whenever the day appointed in this Order for the performance of any act relating to or connected with the Election of Guardians shall be a Sunday or Good Friday, such act shall be performed on the day next following, and each subsequent proceeding shall be postponed one day.

Art. 7.—Any person entitled to vote in any Parish, may nominate for the office of Guardian thereof, himself, or any other person or number of persons (not exceeding the number of Guardians to be elected for such Parish), provided that the person or persons so nominated be legally qualified to be elected for that office.

Art. 8.—Every nomination shall be in writing in the Form marked (B.) hereunto annexed, and be signed by one person only, as the party nominating, and shall be sent after the Fourteenth and on or before the Twenty-sixth day of March, to the Clerk, or to such person or persons as may have been appointed to receive the same, and the Clerk or such person or persons shall, on the receipt thereof, mark thereon the date of its receipt, and also a number according to the order of its receipt ; provided that no nomination sent before the Fifteenth or after the said Twenty-sixth day of March shall be valid [*See G. O., Feb.*, 1857, *& Jan.*, 1867].

Art. 9.—If the number of the persons nominated for the office of Guardian for any Parish shall be the same as, or less than, the number of Guardians to be elected for such Parish, such persons, if duly qualified, shall be deemed to be the elected Guardians for such Parish for the ensuing year, and shall be certified as such by the Clerk under his hand as hereinafter provided in Art. 22.

Art. 10.—But if the number of the duly qualified persons nominated for the office of Guardian for any Parish shall exceed the number of Guardians to be elected therein, the Clerk shall cause Voting Papers, in the Form marked (C.) hereunto annexed, to be prepared and filled up, and shall insert therein the names of all the persons nominated, in the order in which the Nomination Papers were received, but it shall not be necessary to insert more than once the name of any person nominated [*See G. O., Jan.*, 1867].

Art. 11.—The Clerk shall on the Fifth day of April cause one of such Voting Papers to be delivered by the persons appointed for that purpose, to the address in such Parish of each ratepayer, owner, and proxy qualified to vote therein.

Art. 12.—If the Clerk consider that any person nominated is not duly qualified to be a Guardian, he shall state in the Voting Paper the fact that such person has been nominated, but that he considers such person not to be duly qualified.

Art. 13.—If any person put in nomination for the office of Guardian in any Parish shall tender to the Officer conducting the election his refusal, in writing, to serve such office, and if in consequence of such refusal the number of persons nominated for the office of Guardian for such Parish shall be the same as, or less than, the number of Guardians to be elected for such Parish, all or so many of the remaining Candidates as shall be duly qualified shall be deemed to be the elected Guardians for such Parish for the ensuing year, and shall be certified as such by the Clerk under his hand, as hereinafter provided in Art. 22.

Art. 14.—Each Voter shall write his initials in the Voting Paper delivered to him against the name or names of the person or persons (not exceeding the number of Guardians to be elected in the Parish) for whom he intends to vote, and shall sign such Voting Paper; and when any person votes as a proxy, he shall in like manner write his own initials and sign his own name, and state also, in writing, the name of the person for whom he is proxy.

Art. 15.—Provided that, if any Voter cannot write, he shall affix his mark at the foot of the Voting Paper in the presence of a witness, who shall attest the affixing thereof, and shall write the name of the Voter against such mark, as well as the initials of such Voter against the name of every Candidate for whom the Voter intends to vote.

Art. 16.—If the initials of the Voter be written against the names of more persons than are to be elected Guardians for the Parish, or if the Voter do not sign or affix his mark to the Voting Paper, or if his mark be not duly attested, or his name be not duly written by the witness, or if a proxy do not sign his own name, and state in writing the name of the person for whom he is proxy, such Voter shall be omitted in the calculation of votes.

Art. 17.— The Clerk shall cause the Voting Papers to be collected on the Seventh day of April, by the persons appointed or employed for that purpose, in such manner as he shall direct [*See G. O., Jan.* 14, 1867].

Art. 18.—No Voting Paper shall be received or admitted, unless the same have been delivered at the address in each Parish of the Voter, and collected by the persons appointed or employed for that purpose, except as is provided in Art. 19.

Art. 19.—Provided that every person qualified to vote, who shall not on the Fifth day of April have received a Voting Paper, shall, on application before the Eighth day of April to the Clerk at his office, be entitled to receive a

Voting Paper, and to fill up the same in the presence of the Clerk, and then and there to deliver the same to him.

Art. 20.—Provided also, that in case any Voting Paper duly delivered shall not have been collected through the default of the Clerk, or the persons appointed or employed for that purpose, the Voter in person may deliver the same to the Clerk before twelve o'clock at noon on the Eighth day of April.

Art. 21.—The Clerk shall, on the Ninth day of April, and on as many days immediately succeeding as may be necessary, attend at the Board Room of the Guardians of the Union, and ascertain the validity of the votes, by an examination of the rate-books, and the registers of owners and proxies, and such other documents as he may think necessary, and by examining such persons as he may see fit; and he shall cast up such of the votes as he shall find to be valid, and to have been duly given, collected, or received, and ascertain the number of such votes for each Candidate [*See G. O., Jan.* 14, 1867].

Art. 22.—The Candidates, to the number of Guardians to be elected for the Parish, who being duly qualified, shall have obtained the greatest number of votes, shall be deemed to be the elected Guardians for the Parish, and shall be certified as such by the Clerk under his hand.

Art. 23.—The Clerk, when he shall have ascertained that any Candidate is duly elected as Guardian, shall notify the fact of his having been so elected, by delivering or sending, or causing to be delivered or sent, to him a notice in the Form (D.) hereunto annexed.

Art. 24.—The Clerk shall make a list containing the names of the Candidates, together with (in case of a contest) the number of votes given for each, and the names of the elected Guardians, in the Form marked (E.) hereunto annexed, and shall sign and certify the same, and shall deliver such list, together with all the Nomination and Voting Papers which he shall have received, to the Guardians of the Union, at their next meeting, who shall preserve the same for a period of not less than two years.

Art. 25.—The Clerk shall cause copies of such list to be printed, and shall deliver or send, or cause to be delivered or sent, one or more of such copies to the Overseers of each Parish.

Art. 26.—The Overseers shall affix, or cause to be affixed, copies of such list, at the usual places for affixing in each Parish notices of parochial business.

Art. 27.—In case of the decease, necessary absence, refusal, or disqualification to act, during the proceedings of the election, of the Clerk or any other person appointed or employed to act in respect of such election, the delivery of the nominations, voting papers, or other documents to the successor of the Clerk or person so dying, absenting himself, refusing or disqualified to act, shall, notwithstanding the terms of any notice issued, be as valid and effectual as if they had been delivered to such Clerk or person.

MEETINGS OF THE GUARDIANS.

Art. 28.—The Guardians shall upon the day of the week, and at the time of day, and at the place already appointed for holding the ordinary meetings, hold an ordinary meeting once at the least in every week or fortnight for the execution of their duties; and may, when they think fit, change the period, time, and place of such ordinary meeting, with the consent of the Commissioners previously obtained.

Art. 29.—The Guardians shall at the first meeting after the Fifteenth Day of April, elect out of the whole number of Guardians a Chairman and a Vice-Chairman, who, provided they be Guardians at the time, shall continue respectively to act as such Chairman and Vice-Chairman for the Year next ensuing.

Art. 30.—The Guardians at any time may elect two Vice-Chairmen, and if such Vice-Chairmen be appointed at the same time, the Guardians shall determine their precedence; according to which precedence one of the said Vice-Chairmen shall thenceforth preside and act as in the case when only one Vice-Chairman is elected.

Art. 31.—If a Chairman or a Vice-Chairman cease to be a Guardian, or refuse, or become incapable, to act as Chairman, or Vice-Chairman, before the expiration of the term of office, the Guardians shall, within one month after the occurrence of the vacancy, refusal, or incapacity, elect some other Guardian to be Chairman or Vice-Chairman, as the case may be.

Art. 32.—Whereas no act of any meeting of the Guardians will be valid unless three Guardians be present and concur therein; if three Guardians be not present at any meeting, the Clerk shall make an entry of that fact in the minute-book, and the time for holding such meeting shall be deemed to have expired as soon as the said entry shall have been made. But one hour at least shall be allowed to elapse from the time fixed for the commencement of the meeting, before such entry shall be made.

Art. 33. —If three or four or more Guardians be present at any ordinary meeting, such three, or the majority of such four or more Guardians, may adjourn the same, to the day of the next ordinary meeting, or to some other day previous to the next ordinary meeting.

Art. 34.—An extraordinary meeting of the Guardians may be summoned to be held at any time, upon the requisition of any two Guardians, addressed to the Clerk. Every such requisition shall be made in writing, in the Form (F.) hereunto annexed, and no business, other than the business specified in the said requisition, shall be transacted at such extraordinary meeting.

Art. 35.—Notice of every change in the period, time, or place of holding any meeting, and notice of the adjournment of any meeting, and notice of every extraordinary meeting, shall be given in writing to every Guardian. Every such notice shall be respectively in the Forms (G.), (H.), and (I.), hereunto annexed, and shall be given or sent by the Clerk to every Guardian, or left at his place of abode two days, if practicable, before the day appointed for the meeting to which it relates.

Art. 36.—If any case of emergency arise, requiring that a meeting of the Guardians should immediately take place, they, or any three of them, may meet at the ordinary place of meeting, and take such case into consideration, and may make an order thereon.

PROCEEDINGS OF THE GUARDIANS.

Art. 37.—At every meeting the Chairman, or in his absence, a Vice-Chairman, shall preside; but if at the commencement of any meeting the Chairman and Vice-Chairman or Vice-Chairmen be absent, the Guardians present shall elect one of themselves to preside at such meeting as Chairman thereof, until the Chairman or a Vice-Chairman take the chair.

Art. 38.—Every question at any meeting consisting of more than three Guardians shall be determined by a majority of the votes of the Guardians present thereat, and voting on the question, and when there shall be an equal number of votes on any question, such question shall be deemed to have been lost.

Art. 39.—No resolution agreed to or adopted by the Guardians shall be rescinded or altered by them, unless some Guardian shall have given to the Board seven days' notice of a motion to rescind or alter such resolution, which notice shall be forthwith entered on the Minutes by the Clerk. Provided always, that this regulation shall not extend to any resolution which immediately concerns the allowance of relief to any person, or the punishment of any pauper, or to any resolution which the Commissioners may request the Guardians to reconsider or amend, or to any question of emergency.

Art. 40.—The Guardians may, from time to time (as occasion may require), appoint a Committee to consider and report on any special subject, and such Committee may meet at such times and places as to them may seem convenient; but no act or decision of any such Committee shall of itself be deemed to be the act of the Guardians.

Art. 41.—At every ordinary meeting of the Guardians, the business shall, as far as may be convenient, be conducted in the following order :—

Firstly.—The minutes of the last ordinary meeting, and of any other meeting which may have been held since such ordinary meeting, shall be read to the Guardians ; and, in order that such minutes may be recognised as a record of the acts of the Guardians at their last meeting, they shall be signed by the Chairman presiding at the meeting at which such minutes are read, and an entry of the same having been so read shall be made in the minutes of the day when read.

Secondly.—The Guardians shall dispose of such business as may arise out of the minutes so read, and shall give the necessary directions thereon.

Thirdly.—They shall proceed to give the necessary directions respecting all applications for relief made since the last ordinary meeting, and also respecting the amount and nature of relief to be given and continued to the paupers then in the receipt of relief, until the next ordinary meeting, or for such other time as such relief may be deemed to be necessary.

Fourthly.—They shall hear and consider any application for relief which may be then made, and determine thereon.

Fifthly.—They shall read the report of the state of the Workhouse or Workhouses, examine all books and accounts relative to the relief of the paupers of the Union, and give all needful directions concerning the management and discipline of the said Workhouse or Workhouses and the providing of furniture and stores and other articles.

Sixthly.—They shall examine the Treasurer's account, and shall, when necessary, make orders on the Overseers or other proper authorities of the several Parishes in the Union, for providing such sums as may be lawfully required by the Guardians on account of the respective Parishes.

Seventhly.—They shall transact any such business as may not fall within any of the above classes.

Art. 42.—When the Guardians have allowed relief in the Workhouse to any applicant, a written or printed order for his admission therein, signed by the Clerk, shall be forthwith delivered to the applicant, or to any person on his behalf.

Art. 43.—When the Guardians have allowed out-door relief, in money or kind, to any applicant, the particulars of such relief shall be entered, by the proper Relieving Officer, in a ticket according to Form (K.) hereunto annexed, and such ticket shall be delivered by him to the applicant, or to some person on his behalf.

CONTRACTS OF THE GUARDIANS.

Art. 44.—All contracts to be entered into on behalf of the Union relating to the maintenance, clothing, lodging, employment, or relief of the poor, or for any other purpose relating to or connected with the general management of the poor, shall be made and entered into by the Guardians.

Art. 45.—The Guardians shall require tenders to be made in some sealed paper for the supply of all provisions, fuel, clothing, furniture, or other goods, or materials, the consumption of which may be estimated, one month with another, to exceed ten pounds per month, and of all provisions, fuel, clothing, furniture, or other goods, or materials, the cost of which may be reasonably estimated to exceed fifty pounds in a single sum, and shall purchase the same upon contracts to be entered into after the receipt of such tenders.

Art. 46.—Any work or repairs to be executed in the Workhouse, or the premises connected with the Workhouse, or any fixtures to be put up therein, which may respectively be reasonably estimated to exceed the cost of fifty pounds in one sum, shall be contracted for by the Guardians, on sealed tenders, in the manner prescribed in Articles 45 and 47.

Art. 47.—Notice of the nature and conditions of the contract to be entered into, of the estimated amount of the articles required, of the last day on which tenders will be received, and the day on which the tenders will be opened, shall be given in some newspaper circulating in the Union, not less than ten days previous to the last day on which such tenders are to be received ; and no tender shall be opened by the Clerk, or any Guardian, or other person, prior to the day specified in such notice, or otherwise than at a meeting of the said Guardians.

Art. 48.—When any tender is accepted, the party making the tender shall, in pursuance of these regulations, enter into a contract, in writing, with the Guardians, containing the terms, conditions, and stipulations mutually agreed upon, and whenever the Guardians deem it advisable, the party contracting shall find one or more surety or sureties, who shall enter into a bond conditioned for the due performance of the contract, or shall otherwise secure the same.

Art. 49.—Provided always, that if from the peculiar nature of any provisions, fuel, clothing, furniture, goods, materials, or fixtures to be supplied, or of any work or repairs to be executed, it shall appear to the Guardians desirable that a specific person or persons be employed to supply or execute the same, without requiring sealed tenders as hereinbefore directed, it shall be lawful for such Guardians, with the consent of the Commissioners first obtained, to enter into a contract with the said person or persons and to require such sureties and securities as are specified in Art. 48.

Art. 50.—Every contract to be hereafter made by any Guardians shall contain a stipulation requiring the contractor to send in his bill or account of the sum due to him for goods or work, on or before some day to be named in the contract.

Art. 51.—The Guardians shall fix some day or days, not being more than twenty-one days after the end of each quarter, for the attendance of contractors and tradesmen, or their authorised agents, and the Clerk shall notify such day to every contractor or tradesman to whom money may be due, or to his agent, or he shall, under the direction of the Guardians, cause the same to be advertised in some newspaper.

APPRENTICESHIP OF PAUPER CHILDREN.
PARTIES.

Art. 52.—No child under the age of nine years, and no child (other than a deaf and dumb child) who cannot read and write his own name, shall be bound apprentice by the Guardians.

Art. 53.—No child shall be so bound to a person who is not a housekeeper, or assessed to the poor-rate in his own name.

Or who is a journeyman, or a person not carrying on trade or business on his own account;

Or who is under the age of twenty-one;

Or who is a married woman.

THE PREMIUM.

Art. 54.—No premium, other than clothing for the apprentice, shall be given upon the binding of any person above the age of sixteen years, unless such person be maimed, deformed, or suffering from some permanent bodily infirmity, such as may render him unfit for certain trades or sorts of work.

Art. 55.—Where any premium is given it shall in part consist of clothes supplied to the apprentice at the commencement of the binding, and in part of money, one moiety whereof shall be paid to the master at the binding, and the residue at the termination of the first year of the binding.

TERM.

Art. 56.—No apprentice shall be bound by the Guardians for more than eight years.

CONSENT.

Art. 57.—No person above fourteen years of age shall be so bound without his consent.

And no child under the age of sixteen years shall be so bound without the consent of the father of such child, or if the father be dead, or be disqualified to give such consent, as hereinafter provided, or if such child be a bastard, without the consent of the mother, if living, of such child.

Provided, that where such parent is transported beyond the seas, or is in custody of the law, having been convicted of some felony, or for the space of six calendar months before the time of executing the indenture has deserted such child, or for such space of time has been in the service of Her Majesty, or of the East India Company, in any place out of the United Kingdom, such parent, if the father, shall be deemed to be disqualified as hereinbefore stated, and if it be the mother, no such consent shall be required.

PLACE OF SERVICE.

Art. 58.—No child shall be bound to a master whose place of business, whereat the child is to work and live, is distant more than thirty miles from the place in which the child is residing at the time of the proposed binding, or at the time of his being sent on trial to such master;

Unless in any particular case the Commissioners shall, on application to them, otherwise permit.

PRELIMINARIES TO THE BINDING.

Art. 59.—If the child whom it is proposed to bind apprentice, be in the Workhouse, and under the age of fourteen years, the Guardians shall require a certificate in writing from the Medical Officer of the Workhouse as to the fitness in regard to bodily health and strength of such child to be bound apprentice to the proposed trade, and shall also ascertain from the Master of the Workhouse the capacity of the child for such binding in other respects.

Art. 60.—If the child be not in the Workhouse, but in the Union by the Guardians of which it is proposed that he shall be bound, the Relieving Officer of the district in which the child is residing shall examine into the circumstances of the case, the condition of the child, and of his parents, if any, and the residence of the proposed master, the nature of his trade, the number of other apprentices, if any, then bound to him, and generally as to the fitness of the particular binding, and shall report the result of his inquiry to the Guardians.

Art. 61.—If in any case within Article 60, the Guardians think proper to proceed with the binding, they shall, when the child is under the age of fourteen years, direct the Relieving Officer to take the child to the Medical Officer of the district, to be examined as to his fitness in respect of bodily health and strength for the proposed trade or business ; and such Medical Officer shall certify in writing according to his judgment in the matter, which certificate shall be produced by the said Relieving Officer to the next meeting of the Guardians.

Art. 62.—If the child be not residing within the Union, the Guardians who propose to bind him shall not proceed to do so unless they receive such a report as is required in Article 60 from the Relieving Officer of the district in which such child is residing, and a certificate from some medical man practising in the neighbourhood of the child's residence to the effect required in Article 61.

Art. 63.—When it is proposed to give a premium other than clothing upon the binding of any person above the age of sixteen years, the Guardians shall require a certificate in writing from some medical practitioner, certifying that the person is maimed, deformed, or disabled, to the extent specified in such Article, and shall cause a copy of such certificate to be entered on their minutes before they proceed to execute the indenture.

Art. 64.—When such certificate as is required by Articles 59, 61, 62, and 63, is received, or in case from the age of the child no such certificate is required, the Guardians shall direct that the child and the proposed master, or some person on his behalf, and in case the child be under the age of sixteen, that the parent or person in whose custody such child shall be then living, attend some meeting of the Board to be then appointed.

Art. 65.—At such meeting, if such parties appear, the Guardians shall examine into the circumstances of the case ; and if, after making all due inquiries, and hearing the objections (if any be made) on the part of the relatives or friends of such child, they deem it proper that the binding be effected, they may forthwith cause the indenture to be prepared, and, if the master be present, to be executed, but if he be not present they shall cause the same to be transmitted to him for execution ; and when executed by him, and returned to the Guardians, the same shall be executed by the latter, and shall be signed by the child, as provided in Article 67.

Art. 66.—If the proposed master reside out of the Union, but in some other Union or Parish under a Board of Guardians, whether formed under the provisions of the first-recited Act, or of the Act of the twenty-second year of the reign of King George the Third, intituled " *An Act for the better Relief and Employment of the Poor,*" or of any local Act, the Guardians shall, before proceeding to effect the binding, communicate in writing the proposal to the Guardians of such other Union or Parish, and request to be informed whether such binding is open to any objection, and if no objection be reported by such Guardians within the space of one calendar month, or, if the objection does not appear to the Guardians proposing to bind the child to be sufficient to prevent the binding, the same may be proceeded with ; and when the indenture shall have been executed, the Clerk to the Guardians who executed the same shall send notice thereof in writing to the Guardians of the Union or Parish wherein the said apprentice is to reside.

INDENTURE.

Art. 67.—The indenture shall be executed in duplicate, by the master and the Guardians, and shall not be valid unless signed by the proposed apprentice with his name, or, if deaf and dumb, with his mark, in the presence of the said Guardians; and the consent of the parent, where requisite, shall be testified by such parent signing with his name or mark, to be properly attested, at the foot of the said indenture; and where such consent is dispensed with under Article 57, the cause of such dispensation shall be stated at the foot of the indenture by the Clerk.

Art. 68.—The name of the place or places at which the apprentice is to work and live shall be inserted in the indenture.

Art. 69.—One part of such indenture, when executed, shall be kept by the Guardians; the other shall be delivered to the master.

DUTIES OF THE MASTER OF A PAUPER APPRENTICE.

Art. 70.—And We do hereby prescribe the duties of the master to whom such poor child may be apprenticed, and the terms and conditions to be inserted in the said indenture, to be as follows:

No. 1. The master shall teach the child the trade, business, or employment set forth in the indenture, unless the Guardians authorise the substitution of another trade, business, or employment.

No. 2. He shall maintain the said child with proper food and nourishment.

No. 3. He shall provide a proper lodging for the said child.

No. 4. He shall supply the said child with proper clothing during the term of the binding, together with the necessary provision of linen.

No. 5. He shall, in case the said child be affected with any disease or sickness, or meet with any accident, procure, at his own cost, adequate medical or surgical assistance, from some duly qualified medical man, for such child.

No. 6. He shall, once at least on every Sunday, cause the child to attend some place of divine worship, if there be any such within a reasonable distance, according to the religious persuasion in which the child has been brought up, so, however, that no child shall be required by the master to attend any place of worship to which his parents or surviving parent may object, nor when he shall be above the age of sixteen, any place to which he may himself object.

No. 7. Where such parents or parent or next of kin desire it, he shall allow the said child to attend any Sunday or other school which shall be situated within the same parish, or within two miles distance from his residence, on every Sunday, and, if there be no such school which such child can attend, he shall, at some reasonable hour on every Sunday, allow any minister of the religious persuasion of the child to have access to such child for the purpose of imparting religious instruction.

No. 8. Where the apprentice continues bound after the age of seventeen years the master shall, in every case where the Guardians require him so to do, pay to such apprentice, for and in respect of every week that he duly and properly serves the said master, as a remuneration, a sum to be inserted in the indenture, or to be agreed upon by the Guardians and the said master when that time arrives, or, if they cannot agree, to be settled by some person to be then chosen by the said master and such Guardians, and, until such sum be agreed upon or settled, not less than one fourth of the amount then commonly paid as wages to journeymen in the said trade, business, or employment.

No. 9. The master shall himself, or by his agent, produce the apprentice to the Guardians by whom such apprentice was bound at their ordinary meeting next preceding the end of the first year of the binding, and before the receipt of the remainder of the premium, if any be due, and shall in like manner produce the said apprentice at some one of their ordinary meetings, to be held at or about the middle of the term, and whenever afterwards required to do so by the said Guardians : Provided, that if the apprentice reside out of the Union by the Guardians whereof he was bound, the apprentice shall be produced, as hereinbefore directed, to the Guardians of the Union or Parish, as described in Article 66, in which the apprentice may be residing.

No. 10. The master shall not cause the said apprentice to work or live more than ten miles from the place or places mentioned in the indenture, according to Article 68, without the leave of the Guardians so binding him, to be given under their common seal : Provided, that such Guardians may in such licence so to be given under their common seal, by express words to that effect, if they think fit, authorise the master, at any time during the residue of the term of the apprenticeship, to change the place of the abode or service of the apprentice, without any further application to them or their successors.

Art. 71.—These duties of the master set forth in Art. 70 shall be enforced by covenants and conditions to be inserted in the indenture to be executed by him.

Art. 72.—The master shall also covenant, under a penalty to be specified in the covenant, not to assign or cancel the indenture, without the consent of the Guardians, under their common seal, previously obtained, and to pay to the said Guardians all cost and expenses that they may incur in consequence of the said apprentice not being supplied with medical or surgical assistance by the master, in case the same shall be at any time requisite.

Art. 73.—The indenture shall be made subject to the following provisoes :—

No. 1. That if the master take the benefit of any Act for the relief of insolvent debtors or be discharged under any such Act, such indenture shall forthwith become of no further force or effect.

No. 2. That if, on a conviction for a breach of any one of the aforesaid covenants and conditions before a Justice of the Peace, the Guardians who may be parties to the said indenture declare by a resolution that the indenture is determined, and transmit a copy of such resolution, under the hand of their Clerk, by the post or otherwise, to the said master, such indenture shall, except in respect of all rights and liabilities then accrued, forthwith become of no further force or effect.

Art. 74.—Nothing contained in this Order shall apply to the apprenticing of poor children to the sea service.

MODE OF OBTAINING MEDICAL RELIEF BY PERMANENT PAUPERS.

Art. 75.—The Guardians shall, once at least in every year, cause to be prepared by the Clerk or Relieving Officers a list of all such aged and infirm persons, and persons permanently sick or disabled, as may be actually receiving relief from such Guardians, and residing within the district of each Medical Officer of the Union, and shall from time to time furnish to each District Medical Officer a copy of the list aforesaid.

Art. 76.—Every person whose name is inserted in such list shall receive a ticket in the Form (L.) hereunto annexed, and shall be entitled on the exhibition of such ticket to the Medical Officer of his district to obtain such advice, attendance, and medicines as his case may require, in the same manner as if he had received an order from the Guardians, and such ticket shall remain in force for the time specified therein, unless such person shall cease to be in the receipt of relief before the expiration of such time.

RELIEF OF NON-SETTLED AND NON-RESIDENT POOR.

Art. 77.—If any Board of Guardians undertake to administer relief allowed to a non-settled pauper living within the Union for which they act, on behalf of the Officers, or of the Board of Guardians, of the Parish or Union in which such pauper is deemed to be settled, every such undertaking shall be made in conformity with the rules and regulations of the Commissioners in force at the time.

Art. 78.—No money shall be transmitted to any Guardians or to any Officer of a Parish or Union, to be applied to the relief of any non-resident pauper, except in conformity with the provisions of this Order.

Art. 79.—No money shall be paid on account of any non-resident pauper to the Guardians or to the Officer of any Union or Parish in which the relief is administered by a Board of Guardians, except in one of the three following ways :—

No. 1. By post-office order payable to the Treasurer of the Union or Parish to the account of which the money is to be paid, or to the banker of such Treasurer.

No. 2. By cheque or order payable to the Treasurer of such Parish or Union, or to his order.

No. 3. By cheque payable to bearer (where the same may lawfully be drawn), and crossed as payable through the Treasurer of such Parish or Union, or his banker, or through the agent of such Treasurer or banker ; and every such cheque shall be so crossed by the Clerk before it is signed by the presiding Chairman.

Art. 80.—Every account for relief duly administered to non-resident poor shall be discharged by the Guardians, within two calendar months from the receipt of such account, by the transmission of the amount due, in one of the modes prescribed in Art. 79.

ORDERS FOR CONTRIBUTIONS AND PAYMENTS.

Art. 81 *(amended).*—The Clerk shall, as soon as convenient before the 25th day of March next, and thenceforth four weeks at least before the 29th day of September and the 25th day of March respectively in each year, estimate the probable amount of the expenditure in the relief of the Poor, and other charges by the Guardians on behalf of the Union, as well as any separate expenditure chargeable against any Parish therein during the then next ensuing half year, and estimate the probable balance due to or from each Parish at the end of the current half year, and shall apportion the sums to be contributed by the several Parishes comprised in the Union, according to the law for the time being in force therein, and shall prepare the orders on the Overseers or other proper authorities of the several Parishes for the payment of such respective contributions, and of any such separate expenditure as aforesaid, and the orders so prepared shall be laid before the Guardians for their consideration a reasonable time before the expiration of the current half year [*G. O., Feb.* 26, 1866].

Art. 82 *(amended).*—The Guardians shall make orders on the Overseers or other proper authorities of every Parish in the Union at the commencement of each half year ending on the days above mentioned, and from time to time as occasion may arise, for the Payment to the Guardians of all such sums as may be required by them as the contribution of the Parish to the common fund of the Union, and for any other expenses separately chargeable by the Guardians on the Parish; and in such orders the contributions shall be directed to be paid in one sum or by instalments, on days to be specified in such orders, as to the Guardians may seem fit [*G. O., Feb.* 26, 1866].

Art. 83.—Every such order shall be made according to the Form (M.) hereunto annexed. It shall be signed by the presiding Chairman of the meeting, and two other Guardians present thereat, and shall be countersigned by the Clerk.

Art. 84.—The Guardians shall pay every sum greater than Five Pounds by an order, which shall be drawn upon the Treasurer of the Union, and shall be signed by the presiding Chairman and two other Guardians at a meeting, and shall be countersigned by the Clerk.

Art. 85.—The Guardians shall examine at their Board, or shall cause to be examined by some Committee or Guardian authorised by them for the purpose, every bill exceeding in amount one pound (except the salaries of officers) brought against the Union; and when any such bill has been allowed by the Board, or by such Committee or Guardian, a note of the allowance thereof shall be made on the face of the bill before the amount is paid.

CUSTODY OF BONDS.

Art. 86.—The Guardians shall provide for the safe custody of all bonds given in pursuance of the Regulations of the Commissioners, so always that no bond given by any person shall remain in the custody of such person himself.

Art. 87.—The Guardians shall, at the audit next after the Twenty-fifth day of March in every year, cause every person having the custody of bonds given by any officer of the Union to produce such bonds to the Auditor for his inspection.

GOVERNMENT OF THE WORKHOUSE.

ADMISSION OF PAUPERS.

Art. 88.—Every pauper who shall be admitted into the Workhouse, either upon his first or any subsequent admission, shall be admitted in some one of the following modes only; that is to say:—

By a written or printed order of the Board of Guardians, signed by their Clerk according to Art. 42.

By a provisional written or printed order, signed by a Relieving Officer or an Overseer.

By the Master of the Workhouse (or, during his absence, or inability to act, by the Matron), without any order, in any case of sudden or urgent necessity.

Provided that the Master may admit any pauper delivered at the Workhouse under an order of removal to a Parish in the Union.

Art. 89.—No pauper shall be admitted under any written or printed order as mentioned in Art. 88, if the same bear date more than six days before the pauper presents it at the Workhouse.

Art. 90.—If a pauper be admitted otherwise than by an order of the Board of Guardians, the admission of such pauper shall be brought before the Board of Guardians at their next ordinary meeting, who shall decide on the propriety of the pauper's continuing in the Workhouse or otherwise, and make an order accordingly.

Art. 91.—As soon as the pauper is admitted, he shall be placed in some room to be appropriated to the reception of paupers on admission, and shall then be examined by the Medical Officer.

Art. 92.—If the Medical Officer upon such examination pronounce the pauper to be labouring under any disease of body or mind, the pauper shall be placed in the sick-ward, or in such other ward as the Medical Officer shall direct.

Art. 93.—If the Medical Officer pronounce the pauper to be free from any such disease, the pauper shall be placed in the part of the Workhouse assigned to the class to which he may belong.

Art. 94.—No pauper shall be detained in a receiving-ward for a longer time than is necessary for carrying into effect the regulations in Arts. 91, 92, and 93, if there be room in the proper ward for his reception.

Art. 95.—Before being removed from the receiving-ward, the pauper shall be thoroughly cleansed, and shall be clothed in a workhouse dress, and the clothes which he wore at the time of his admission shall be purified, and deposited in a place appropriated for that purpose, with the pauper's name affixed thereto. Such clothes shall be restored to the pauper when he leaves the Workhouse.

Art. 96.—Every pauper shall, upon his admission into the Workhouse, be searched by or under the inspection of the proper officer, and all articles prohibited by any Act of Parliament, or by this Order, which may be found upon his person, shall be taken from him, and, so far as may be proper, restored to him at his departure from the Workhouse.

Art. 97.—Provided always, that the regulations respecting the admission, clothing, and searching of paupers shall not apply to any casual poor wayfarer, unless the Guardians shall so direct, or unless he is compelled to remain in the Workhouse from illness or other sufficient cause, in which case he shall be admitted regularly as an inmate.

CLASSIFICATION OF THE PAUPERS.

Art. 98.—The paupers, so far as the Workhouse admits thereof, shall be classed as follows :—

Class 1. Men infirm through age or any other cause.

Class 2. Able-bodied men, and youths above the age of fifteen years.

Class 3. Boys above the age of seven years, and under that of fifteen.

Class 4. Women infirm through age or any other cause.

Class 5. Able-bodied women, and girls above the age of fifteen years.

Class 6. Girls above the age of seven years, and under that of fifteen.

Class 7. Children under seven years of age.

To each class shall be assigned that ward or separate building and yard which may be best fitted for the reception of such class, and each class of paupers shall remain therein, without communication with those of any other class.

Art. 99.—Provided,

Firstly. That the Guardians shall from time to time, after consulting the Medical Officer, make such arrangements as they may deem necessary with regard to persons labouring under any disease of body or mind.

Secondly. The Guardians shall, so far as circumstances will permit, further subdivide any of the classes enumerated in Art. 98, with reference to the moral character, or behaviour, or the previous habits of the inmates, or to such other grounds as may seem expedient.

Thirdly. That nothing in this order shall compel the Guardians to separate any married couple, being both paupers of the first and fourth classes respectively, provided the Guardians shall set apart for the exclusive use of every such couple a sleeping apartment separate from that of the other paupers.

Fourthly. That any paupers of the fifth and sixth classes may be employed constantly or occasionally in any of the female sick-wards, or in the care of infants, or as assistants in the household work; and the Master and Matron shall make such arrangements as may enable the paupers of the fifth and sixth classes to be employed in the household work, without communication with the paupers of the second and third classes.

Fifthly. That any pauper of the fourth class, whom the Master may deem fit to perform any of the duties of a nurse or assistant to the Matron, may be so employed in the sick-wards, or those of the fourth, fifth, sixth, or seventh classes, and any pauper of the first class, who may by the Master be deemed fit, may be placed in the ward of the third class, to aid in the management, and superintend the behaviour, of the paupers of such class, or may be employed in the male sick-ward.

Sixthly. That the Guardians, for a special reason to be entered on their minutes, may place any boy or girl between the ages of ten and sixteen years, in a male or female ward respectively, different from that to which he or she properly belongs, unless the Commissioners shall otherwise direct.

Seventhly. That the paupers of the seventh class may be placed in such of the wards appropriated to the female paupers as shall be deemed expedient, and the mothers of such paupers shall be permitted to have access to them at all reasonable times.

Eighthly. That the Master (subject to any directions given or regulations made by the Guardians) shall allow the father or mother of any child in the same Workhouse, who may be desirous of seeing such child, to have an interview with such child at some one time in each day, in a room in the said Workhouse to be appointed for that purpose. And the Guardians shall make arrangements for permitting the members of the same family who may be in different Workhouses of the Union to have occasional interviews with each other, at such times and in such manner as may best suit the discipline of the several Workhouses.

Ninthly. That casual poor wayfarers admitted by the Master or Matron shall be kept in a separate ward of the Workhouse, and shall be dieted and set to work in such manner and under such regulations as the Guardians by any resolution now in force, or to be made hereafter, may direct.

Art. 100.—The Guardians shall not admit into the Workhouse, or any ward of the same, or retain therein, a larger number or a different class of paupers than that heretofore or hereafter from time to time to be fixed by the Commissioners ; and in case such number shall at any time be exceeded, the fact of such excess shall be forthwith reported to the Commissioners by the Clerk.

Art. 101.—No pauper of unsound mind, who may be dangerous, or who may have been reported as such by the Medical Officer, or who may require habitual or frequent restraint, shall be detained in the Workhouse for any period exceeding fourteen days, and the Guardians shall cause the proper steps to be taken for the removal of every such pauper to some asylum or licensed house as soon as may be practicable.

DISCIPLINE AND DIET OF THE PAUPERS.

Art. 102.—All the paupers in the Workhouse, except the sick and insane, and the paupers of the first, fourth, and seventh classes, shall rise, be set to work, leave off work, and go to bed at the times mentioned in the Form (N.) hereunto annexed, and shall be allowed such intervals for their meals as are therein stated, and these several times shall be notified by the ringing of a bell ; provided always, that the Guardians may, with the consent of the Commissioners, make such alterations in any of the said times or intervals as the Guardians may think fit.

Art. 103.—Half an hour after the bell shall have been rung for rising, the names of the paupers shall be called over by the Master and Matron respectively, in the several wards provided for the second, third, fifth, and sixth classes, when every pauper belonging to the respective wards shall be present, and shall answer to his name, and be inspected by the Master and Matron respectively, provided that the paupers of the third and sixth class may be called over and inspected by the Schoolmaster and Schoolmistress.

Art. 104.—The meals shall be taken by all the paupers, except the sick, the children, persons of unsound mind, casual poor wayfarers, women suckling their children, and the paupers of the first and fourth classes, in the dining-hall or day-room, and in no other place whatever, and during the time of meals, order and decorum shall be maintained.

Art. 105.—No pauper of the second, third, fifth, or sixth classes shall go to or remain in his sleeping-room, either in the time hereby appointed for work, or in the intervals allowed for meals, except by the permission of the Master or Matron.

Art. 106.—The Master and Matron shall (subject to the directions of the Guardians) fix the hours of rising and going to bed, for the paupers of the first, fourth, and seventh classes, and determine the occupation and employment of which they may be capable ; and the meals for such paupers shall be provided at such times and in such manner as the Guardians may from time to time direct.

Art. 107.—The paupers shall be dieted with the food and in the manner set forth in the Dietary Table which may be prescribed for the use of the Workhouse, and no pauper shall have or consume any liquor, or any food or provision other than is allowed in the said Dietary Table, except on Christmas Day or by the direction in writing of the Medical Officer, as provided in Article 108.

Art. 108.—Provided,

First. That the Medical Officer may direct in writing such diet for any individual pauper as he may deem necessary, and the Master shall obey such direction until the next ordinary meeting of the Guardians, when he shall report the same in writing to the Guardians.

Secondly. That if the Medical Officer at any time certify that he deems a temporary change in the diet essential to the health of the paupers in the Workhouse, or of any class or classes thereof, the Guardians shall cause a copy of such certificate to be entered on the minutes of their proceedings, and may forthwith order, by a resolution, the said diet to be temporarily changed, according to the recommendation of the Medical Officer, and shall forthwith transmit a copy of such certificate and resolution to the Commissioners.

Thirdly. That the Medical Officer shall be consulted by the Matron as to the nature of the food of the infants, and of their mothers when suckling, and the time at which such infants should be weaned.

Fourthly. That the Guardians may, without any direction of the Medical Officer, make such allowance of food as may be necessary to paupers employed as nurses or in the household work ; but they shall not allow to such paupers any fermented or spirituous liquors on account of the performance of such work, unless in pursuance of a written recommendation of the Medical Officer.

Art. 109.—If any pauper require the Master or Matron

to weigh the allowance of provisions served out at any meal, the Master or Matron shall forthwith weigh such allowance in the presence of the pauper complaining, and of two other persons.

Art. 110.—The clothing to be worn by the paupers in the Workhouse shall be made of such materials as the Board of Guardians may determine.

Art. 111.—More than two paupers, any one of whom is above the age of seven years, shall not be allowed to occupy the same bed, unless in the case of a mother and infant children.

Art. 112.—The paupers of the several classes shall be kept employed according to their capacity and ability; and no pauper shall receive any compensation for his labour.

Art. 113.—No pauper in the Workhouse shall be employed or set to work in pounding, grinding, or otherwise breaking bones, or in preparing bone dust.

Art. 114.—The boys and girls who are inmates of the Workhouse shall, for three of the working hours, at least, every day, be instructed in reading, writing, arithmetic, and the principles of the Christian Religion, and such other instruction shall be imparted to them as may fit them for service, and train them to habits of usefulness, industry, and virtue.

Art. 115.—Any pauper may quit the Workhouse upon giving to the Master, or (during his absence or inability to act) to the Matron, a reasonable notice of his wish to do so; and in the event of any able-bodied pauper, having a family, so quitting the house, the whole of such family shall be sent with him, unless the Guardians shall, for any special reason, otherwise direct; and such directions shall be in conformity with the regulations of the Commissioners with respect to relief in force at the time.

Art. 116.—Provided nevertheless, that the Guardians may, by any general or special direction, authorise the Master to allow a pauper, without giving any such notice as is required in Art. 115, to quit the Workhouse, and to return after a temporary absence only ; and every such allowance shall be reported by the Master to the Guardians at their next ordinary meeting.

Art. 117.—Prov'ded also, that nothing herein contained shall prevent the Master from allowing the paupers of each sex under the age of fifteen, subject to such restrictions as the Guardians may impose, to quit the Workhouse, under the care and guidance of himself, or the Matron, Schoolmaster, Schoolmistress, Porter, or some one of the assistants and servants of the Workhouse, for the purpose of exercise.

Art. 118.—Any person may visit any pauper in the Workhouse by permission of the Master, or (in his absence) of the Matron, subject to such conditions and restrictions as the Guardians may prescribe ; such interview shall take place in a room separate from the other inmates of the Workhouse, and in the presence of the Master, Matron, or Porter, except where a sick pauper is visited.

Art. 119.—No written or printed paper of an improper tendency, or which may be likely to produce insubordination, shall be allowed to circulate, or be read aloud, among the inmates of the Workhouse.

Art. 120.—No pauper shall play at cards, or at any game of chance, in the Workhouse ; and the Master may take from any pauper, and keep until his departure from the Workhouse, any cards, dice, or other articles applicable to games of chance, which may be in his possession.

Art. 121.—No pauper shall smoke in any room of the Workhouse, except by the special direction of the Medical Officer, or shall have any matches or other articles of a highly combustible nature in his possession, and the Master may take from any person any articles of such a nature.

Art. 122.—Any licensed minister of the religious persuasion of an inmate of the Workhouse, who may at any time in the day, on the request of any inmate, enter the Workhouse for the purpose of affording religious assistance to him, or for the purpose of instructing his child or children in the principles of his religion, shall give such assistance or instruction so as not to interfere with the good order and discipline of the other inmates of the Workhouse, and such religious assistance or instruction shall be strictly confined to inmates who are of the religious persuasion of such minister, and to the children of such inmates, except in the cases in which the Guardians may lawfully permit religious assistance and instruction to be given to any paupers who are Protestant Dissenters, by licensed ministers who are Protestant Dissenters.

Art. 123.—No work, except the necessary household work and cooking, shall be performed by the paupers on Sunday, Good Friday, and Christmas Day.

Art. 124.—Prayers shall be read before breakfast and after supper every day, and Divine Service shall be performed every Sunday, Good Friday, and Christmas Day in the Workhouse (unless the Guardians, with the consent of the Commissioners, otherwise direct), and at such prayers and Divine Service all the paupers shall attend, except the sick, persons of unsound mind, the young children, and such as are too infirm to do so ; provided that those paupers who may object so to attend, on account of their professing religious principles differing from those of the Established Church, shall also be exempt from such attendance.

Art. 125.—The Guardians may authorise any inmates of the Workhouse, being members of the Established Church, to attend Public Worship at a parish church or chapel, on every Sunday, Good Friday, and Christmas Day, under the control and inspection of the Master or Porter, or other officer.

Art. 126.—The Guardians may also authorise any inmates of the Workhouse, being Dissenters from the Established Church, to attend Public Worship at any Dissenting chapel in the neighbourhood of the Workhouse, on every Sunday, Good Friday, and Christmas Day.

PUNISHMENTS FOR MISBEHAVIOUR OF THE PAUPERS.

Art. 127.—Any pauper, being an inmate of the Workhouse, who shall neglect to observe such of the regulations in this Order as are applicable to him as such inmate ;—

> Or who shall make any noise when silence is ordered to be kept ;
>
> Or shall use obscene or profane language ;
>
> Or shall by word or deed insult or revile any person ;
>
> Or shall threaten to strike or to assault any person ;
>
> Or shall not duly cleanse his person ;
>
> Or shall refuse or neglect to work, after having been required to do so ;
>
> Or shall pretend sickness ;
>
> Or shall play at cards or other game of chance ;
>
> Or shall refuse to go into his proper ward or yard, or shall enter or attempt to enter, without permission, the ward or yard appropriated to any class of paupers other than that to which he belongs ;
>
> Or shall climb over any fence or boundary wall surrounding any portion of the Workhouse premises, or shall attempt to leave the Workhouse otherwise than through the ordinary entrance ;
>
> Or shall misbehave in going to, at, or returning from Public Worship out of the Workhouse, or at Divine Service or Prayers in the Workhouse ;
>
> Or having received temporary leave of absence, and wearing the Workhouse clothes, shall return to the Workhouse after the appointed time of absence, without reasonable cause for the delay ;
>
> Or shall wilfully disobey any lawful order of any officer of the Workhouse ;

Shall be deemed DISORDERLY.

Art. 128.—Any pauper, being an inmate of the Workhouse, who shall, within seven days, repeat any one, or commit more than one, of the offences specified in Art. 127 ;

> Or who shall by word or deed insult or revile the Master or Matron, or any other officer of the Workhouse, or any of the Guardians ;

T

Or shall wilfully disobey any lawful order of the Master
　　or Matron after such order shall have been repeated;

Or shall unlawfully strike or otherwise unlawfully assault
　　any person;

Or shall wilfully or mischievously damage or soil any
　　property whatsoever belonging to the Guardians;

Or shall wilfully waste or spoil any provisions, stock,
　　tools, or materials for work, belonging to the Guar-
　　dians;

Or shall be drunk;

Or shall act or write indecently or obscenely;

Or shall wilfully disturb other persons at Public Worship
　　out of the Workhouse, or at Divine Service or Prayers
　　in the Workhouse;

Shall be deemed REFRACTORY.

Art. 129.—The Master may, with or without the direction of the Guardians, punish any disorderly pauper by
substituting, during a time not greater than forty-eight
hours, for his dinner, as prescribed by the Dietary, a meal
consisting of eight ounces of bread, or one pound of cooked
potatoes or boiled rice, and also by withholding from him,
during the same period, all butter, cheese, tea, sugar, or
broth, which such pauper would otherwise receive, at any
meal during the time aforesaid.

Art. 130.—The Guardians may, by a special direction to
be entered on their minutes, order any refractory pauper to
be punished by confinement in a separate room, with or
without an alteration of diet, similar in kind and duration
to that prescribed in Art. 129 for disorderly paupers; but
no pauper shall be so confined for a longer period than
twenty-four hours, or, if it be deemed right that such pauper
should be carried before a Justice of the Peace, and if such
period of twenty-four hours should be insufficient for that
purpose, then for such further time as may be necessary for
such purpose.

Art. 131.—If any offence, whereby a pauper becomes refractory under Art. 128, be accompanied by any of the fol-

lowing circumstances of aggravation—that is to say, if such pauper

> Persist in using violence against any person;
>
> Or persist in creating a noise or disturbance, so as to annoy other inmates;
>
> Or endeavour to excite other paupers to acts of insubordination;
>
> Or persist in acting indecently or obscenely in the presence of any other inmate;
>
> Or persist in mischievously breaking or damaging any goods or property of the Guardians;

the Master may, without any direction of the Guardians, immediately place such refractory pauper in confinement for any time not exceeding twelve hours; which confinement shall, however, be reckoned as part of any punishment afterwards imposed by the Guardians for the same offence.

Art. 132.—Every refractory pauper shall be deemed to be also disorderly, and may be punished as such; but no pauper who may have been punished for any offence as disorderly, shall afterwards be punished for the same offence as refractory, and no pauper who may have been punished for any offence as refractory, shall afterwards be punished for the same offence as disorderly.

Art. 133.—No pauper shall be punished by confinement or alteration in diet for any offence not committed in the Workhouse since his last admission, except in such cases as are expressly specified in Articles 127 and 128.

Art. 134.—No pauper who may have been under medical care, or who may have been entered in the medical weekly return as sick or infirm, at any time in the course of the seven days next preceding the punishment, or who may be reasonably supposed to be under twelve, or above sixty years of age, or who may be pronounced by the Medical Officer to be pregnant, or who may be suckling a child, shall be punished by alteration of diet, or by confinement, unless the Medical Officer shall have previously certified in writing that no injury to the health of such pauper is reasonably to be apprehended from the proposed punishment and any modification diminishing such punishment which the Medical Officer may suggest, shall be adopted by the Master.

Art. 135.—No pauper shall be confined between eight o'clock in the evening, and six o'clock in the morning, without being furnished with a bed and bedding suitable to the season, and with the other proper conveniences.

Art. 136.—No child under twelve years of age shall be punished by confinement in a dark room, or during the night.

Art. 137.—No corporal punishment shall be inflicted on any male child, except by the Schoolmaster or Master.

Art. 138.—No corporal punishment shall be inflicted on any female child.

Art. 139.—No corporal punishment shall be inflicted on any male child, except with a rod or other instrument, such as may have been approved of by the Guardians or the Visiting Committee.

Art. 140.—No corporal punishment shall be inflicted on any male child until two hours shall have elapsed from the commission of the offence for which such punishment is inflicted.

Art. 141.—Whenever any male child is punished by corporal correction, the Master and Schoolmaster shall (if possible) be both present.

Art. 142.—No male child shall be punished by flogging whose age may be reasonably supposed to exceed fourteen years.

Art. 143.—The Master shall keep a book to be furnished him by the Guardians, in the Form (O.) hereunto annexed, in which he shall duly enter,

Firstly, All cases of refractory or disorderly paupers, whether children or adults, reported to the Guardians for their decision thereon.

Secondly, All cases of paupers, whether children or adults, who may have been punished without the direction of the Guardians, with the particulars of their respective offences and punishments.

Art. 144.—The person who punishes any child with corporal correction shall forthwith report to the Master the particulars of the offence and punishment; and the Master shall enter the same in the book specified in Art. 143.

Art. 145.—Such book shall be laid on the table at every ordinary meeting of the Guardians; and every entry made in such book since the last ordinary meeting shall be read to the Board by the Clerk.

The Guardians shall thereupon, in the first place, give direction as to the confinement or other punishment of any refractory or disorderly pauper reported for their decision, and such direction shall be entered on the minutes of the proceedings of the day, and a copy thereof shall be inserted by the Clerk in the book specified in Art. 143.

The Guardians, in the second place, shall take into their consideration the cases in which punishments are reported to have been already inflicted by the Master or other officer, and shall require the Master to bring before them any pauper so punished, who may have signified a wish to see the Guardians. If the Guardians in any case are of opinion that the officer has acted illegally or improperly, such opinion shall be entered on the minutes, and shall be communicated to the Master, and a copy of the minute of such opinion shall be forwarded to the Commissioners by the Clerk.

Art. 146.—If any pauper above the age of fourteen years unlawfully introduce or attempt to introduce any spirituous or fermented liquor into the Workhouse, or abscond from the Workhouse with clothes belonging to the Guardians, the Master may cause such pauper to be forthwith taken before a Justice of the Peace, to be dealt with according to law. And whether he do so or not, he shall report every such case to the Guardians at their next ordinary meeting.

Art. 147.—The Master shall cause a legible copy of Arts. 127, 128, 129, 130, and 131 to be kept suspended in the dining-hall of the Workhouse, or in the room in which the inmates usually eat their meals, and also in the Board-room of the Guardians.

VISITING COMMITTEE.

Art. 148.—The Guardians shall appoint one or more *Visiting Committees* from their own body ; and each of such committees shall carefully examine the Workhouse or Workhouses of the Union once in every week at the least, inspect the last reports of the Chaplain and Medical Officer, examine the stores, afford, so far as is practicable, to the inmates an opportunity of making any complaints, and investigate any complaints that may be made to them.

Art. 149.—The Visiting Committee shall from time to time write such answers as the facts may warrant to the following queries, which are to be printed in a book, entitled the "Visitors' Book," to be provided by the Guardians, and kept in every Workhouse for that purpose, and to be submitted regularly to the Guardians at their ordinary meetings :—

Q. 1. Is the Workhouse, with its wards, offices, yards, and appurtenances, clean and well ventilated in every part ?—and is the bedding in proper order ?—if not, state the defect or omission.

Q. 2. Do the inmates of the Workhouse, of all classes, appear clean in their persons, and decent and orderly in their behaviour ; and is their clothing regularly changed ?

Q. 3. Are the inmates of each sex employed and kept at work as directed by the Guardians, and is such work unobjectionable in its nature ?—if any improvement can be suggested in their employment, state the same.

Q. 4. Are the infirm of each sex properly attended to, according to their several conditions ?

Q. 5. Are the boys and girls in the school properly instructed as required by the regulations of the Commissioners, and is their industrial training properly attended to?

Q. 6. Are the young children properly nursed and taken care of, and do they appear in a clean and healthy state?—Is there any child not vaccinated?

Q. 7. Is regular attendance given by the Medical Officer? —Are the inmates of the Sick-wards properly tended? —Are the nurses efficient?—Is there any infectious disease in the Workhouse?

Q. 8. Is there any dangerous lunatic or idiot in the Workhouse?

Q. 9. Is Divine Service regularly performed? — Are prayers regularly read?

Q. 10. Is the established dietary duly observed?—and are the prescribed hours of meals regularly adhered to?

Q. 11. Are the provisions and other supplies of the qualities contracted for?

Q. 12. Is the classification properly observed according to Arts. 98 and 99?

Q. 13. Is any complaint made by any pauper against any officer, or in respect of the provisions or accommodations?—if so, state the name of the complainant, and the subject of the complaint.

Q. 14. Does the present number of inmates in the Workhouse exceed that fixed by the Poor Law Commissioners?

REPAIRS AND ALTERATIONS OF THE WORKHOUSE.

Art. 150.—The Guardians shall once at least in every year, and as often as may be necessary for cleanliness, cause all the rooms, wards, offices, and privies belonging to the Workhouse to be limewashed.

Art. 151.—The Guardians shall cause the Workhouse and all its furniture and appurtenances to be kept in good and substantial repair ; and shall, from time to time, remedy without delay any such defect in the repair of the house, its drainage, warmth, or ventilation, or in the furniture or fixtures thereof, as may tend to injure the health of the inmates.

GOVERNMENT OF THE WORKHOUSE BY THE GUARDIANS.

Art 152.—We do declare, that, subject to the Rules and Regulations herein contained, the guidance, government, and control of every Workhouse, and of the officers, servants, assistants, and paupers within such Workhouse, shall be exercised by the Guardians of the Union.

APPOINTMENT OF OFFICERS.

Art. 153.—The Guardians shall, whenever it may be requisite, or whenever a vacancy may occur, appoint fit persons to hold the undermentioned offices, and to perform the duties respectively assigned to them ; namely,

1. Clerk to the Guardians.
2. Treasurer of the Union.
3 Chaplain.
4. Medical Officer for the Workhouse.
5. District Medical Officer.
6. Master of the Workhouse.
7. Matron of the Workhouse.
8. Schoolmaster.
9. Schoolmistress.
10. Porter.
11. Nurse.
12. Relieving Officer.
13. Superintendent of Out-door Labour.

And also such assistants as the Guardians, with the consent of the Commissioners, may deem necessary for the efficient performance of the duties of any of the said offices.

[*To Unions formed since* 1847]. And the said Guardians shall from time to time afterwards, whenever a vacancy may occur, appoint a fit person to supply such vacancy, except in the case of the Superintendent of Out-door Labour, whose office shall be filled as and when the Guardians may find it requisite to employ such officer.

Art. 154.—The officers so appointed to or holding any of the said offices, as well as all persons temporarily discharging the duties of such offices, shall respectively perform such duties as may be required of them by the Rules and Regulations of the Commissioners in force at the time, together with all such other duties, conformable with the nature of their respective offices, as the Guardians may lawfully require them to perform.

[*Proviso omitted*].

MODE OF APPOINTMENT.

Art. 155. Every officer and assistant, to be appointed under this Order, shall be appointed by a majority of the Guardians present at a meeting of the Board, consisting of more than three Guardians, or by three Guardians if no more be · present. Every such appointment shall, as soon as the same has been made, be reported to the Commissioners by the Clerk.

Art. 156.—No appointment to any of the offices specified in Art. 153 shall be made under this Order, unless a notice that the question of making such appointment will be brought before the Board has been given and entered on the minutes, at one of the two ordinary meetings of the Board next preceding the meeting at which the appointment is made, or unless an advertisement giving notice of the consideration of such appointment shall have appeared in some public paper by the direction of the Guardians at least seven days before the day on which such appointment is made. Provided that no such notice or advertisement shall be necessary for the appointment of an assistant or temporary substitute.

Art. 157.—The Guardians shall not, by advertisement, or other public notice, printed or written, invite tenders for the supply of medicines, or for the medical attendance on the paupers of the Union, unless such advertisement or notice shall specify the district or place for which such supply of medicines and such attendance is required, together with the amount of salary or other remuneration.

Art. 158.—The Guardians may from time to time divide the Union into districts for general and medical relief, with the consent of the Commissioners; and on any change in the division of the Union into districts for general and medical relief, or in the assignment of Relieving Officers and Medical Officers to such districts, the Clerk shall report every such change to the Commissioners for their approbation.

Art. 159.—The Guardians shall not assign to any Medical Officer a district which exceeds in extent the area of fifteen thousand statute acres, or which contains a population exceeding the number of fifteen thousand persons, according to the then last enumeration of the population published by authority of Parliament.

Art. 160.—Provided that if it be impracticable, consistently with the proper attendance on the sick poor, for the Guardians to divide the Union into districts, containing respectively an area and population less than is specified in Art. 159, then and in such case the Guardians shall cause a special minute to be made and entered on the usual record of their proceedings, stating the reasons which, in their opinion, make it necessary to form a district exceeding the said limits, and shall transmit a copy of such minute to the Commissioners for their consideration; and if the Commissioners signify their approval thereof to such Guardians, then and in such case, but not otherwise, such Guardians may proceed to assign the said district to a Medical Officer.

Art. 161.—Provided also, that the limit of fifteen thousand statute acres, prescribed in Art. 159, shall not apply to any medical district situate wholly or in part within the principality of Wales; but no medical district situate wholly or in part within that principality shall be assigned to any Medical Officer residing more than seven miles from any part of any Parish included within such district, unless such district shall have been specially sanctioned by the Commissioners in the same manner as is directed in Art. 160 [*see G. O., May* 25, 1857].

QUALIFICATIONS OF OFFICERS.

Art. 162.—No person shall hold the office of Clerk, Treasurer, Master, or Relieving Officer under this Order who has not reached the age of twenty-one years.

Art. 163.—No person shall hold the office of Master of a Workhouse, or Matron of a Workhouse having no Master, unless he or she be able to keep accounts.

Art. 164.—No person shall hold the office of Relieving Officer unless he be able to keep accounts, and unless he reside in the district for which he may be appointed to act, devote his whole time to the performance of the duties of his office, and abstain from following any trade or profession, and from entering into any other service.

Art. 165.—No person shall hold the office of Nurse who is not able to read written directions upon medicines.

Art. 166.—Provided always, that the Guardians may with the consent of the Commissioners previously obtained, but not otherwise, dispense with any of the conditions specified in Articles 162, 163, 164, and 165.

Art. 167.—No person shall be appointed to the office of Master, Matron, Schoolmaster, Schoolmistress, Porter, or Relieving Officer, under this Order, who does not agree to give one month's notice previous to resigning the office, or to forfeit one month's amount of salary, to be deducted as liquidated damages from the amount of salary due at the time of such resignation.

Art. 168 [*amended*, 1859].—No person shall hold the office of Medical Officer under this Order unless he be duly registered under "The Medical Act of 1858," and be qualified by law to practise both medicine and surgery in England and Wales, such qualification being established by the production to the Board of Guardians of a diploma, certificate of a degree, licence, or other instrument granted or issued by competent legal authority, in Great Britain or Ireland, testifying to the medical or surgical or medical and surgical qualification or qualifications of the candidate for such office.

Provided that evidence that any candidate was in practice as an apothecary on the first day of August, One thousand eight hundred and fifteen, shall be taken to be equivalent to a certificate to practise from the Society of Apothecaries, London.

Provided also that any person being registered as aforesaid who shall possess a Warrant or Commission as surgeon or assistant-surgeon or apothecary in Her Majesty's Army, or as surgeon or assistant-surgeon in the service of the Honourable East India Company, dated previous to the first day of August, One thousand eight hundred and twenty-six, shall be qualified to be appointed to the office of Medical Officer as aforesaid.

Art. 169.—Provided always, that if it be impracticable, consistently with the proper attendance on the sick poor, for the Guardians to procure a person residing within the district in which he is to act, and duly qualified in one of the four modes recited in Art. 168, to attend on the poor in such district, or that the only person resident within such district, and so qualified, shall have been dismissed from office by the Commissioners, or shall be unfit or incompetent to hold the office of Medical Officer, then and in such case the Guardians shall cause a special minute to be made and entered on the usual record of their proceedings, stating the reasons which, in their opinion, make it necessary to employ a person not qualified as required by Art. 168, and shall forthwith transmit a copy of such minute to the Commissioners for their consideration; and the Commissioners may permit the employment by such Guardians of any person duly licensed to practise as a medical man, although such person be not qualified in one of the four modes required by Art. 168.

Art. 170.—Provided also, that the Guardians may, with the consent of the Commissioners, continue in office any Medical Officer duly licensed to practise as a medical man already employed by any such Guardians, although such Medical Officer may not be qualified in one of the four modes required by Art. 168. [*Now omitted.*]

Art. 171.—No person shall hold the office of Chaplain under this Order without the consent of the Bishop of the diocese to his appointment, signified in writing.

REMUNERATION OF THE OFFICERS.

Art. 172.—The Guardians shall pay to the several officers and assistants appointed to or holding any office or employment under this Order, such salaries or remuneration as the Commissioners may from time to time direct or approve.

Provided that the Guardians, with the approval of the Commissioners, may pay to any officer or person employed by such Guardians a reasonable compensation on account of extraordinary services, or other unforeseen circumstances connected with the duties of such officer or person or the necessities of the Union.

Art. 173 [*amended*].—The salary of every officer or assistant, appointed to, or holding any office or employment under this Order, shall be payable up to the day on which he ceases to hold such office or employment, and no longer, and shall be paid at the several quarters ending at the usual feast days in the year: namely, Midsummer Day, Michaelmas Day, Christmas Day, and Lady Day; provided, nevertheless, that in case of any officer whose duty it is to render accounts to the Board of Guardians, it shall be competent for the Guardians to defer in whole or in part the payment of the salary of any such officer until his accounts have been audited and allowed by the Auditor, after which audit and allowance the sum due up to the date of his accounts so audited shall be forthwith paid.

Art. 174.—If no remuneration or salary be expressly

assigned to the Treasurer, the profit arising from the use of money from time to time left in his hands shall be deemed to be the payment of his services.

Art. 175 [*amended*].—An officer who may be suspended, and who may upon such suspension be dismissed by the Poor Law Board, shall not be entitled to any salary from the date of such suspension; and no officer who shall be temporarily suspended from his office by reason of his services not being required, shall be entitled to any salary pending such temporary suspension.

Art. 176.—The Guardians shall not pay to any officer bound to account, to be hereafter appointed, who may have been removed, or who may be under suspension from his office, any salary claimed by such officer until his accounts shall have been audited by the Auditor.

The following are inserted in the recent issues of the Consolidated Order :—

(173) The Guardians shall pay as compensation to the Clerk, or to the person appointed under the authority of this Order to act as such in the performance of the duties hereby prescribed for the conduct of every election of Guardians, such a sum, not exceeding

pounds, as the Guardians shall determine, which sum shall include the remuneration of the persons who may have been appointed to assist him in conducting and completing the election, and shall be defrayed out of the common fund of the Union.

(174) The Guardians shall, in the case of every contested election, pay one farthing per head on the population of the Parish in which the contest shall have taken place, if the population shall be more than five hundred, to the said Clerk or other person as aforesaid, in addition to the compensation mentioned in Art. 173, which sum shall be charged by the said Guardians to the account of such Parish; and for the purpose of ascertaining the last-mentioned sums, the population of the Parish shall be taken to be as stated in the census

which at the time of such election shall have been last made under the authority of any Act of Parliament.

Art. 177.—No salary of any District Medical Officer shall include the remuneration for operations and services of the following classes performed by such Medical Officer in that capacity for any out-door pauper, but such operations and services shall be paid for by the Guardians, according to the rates specified in this Article.

	£	s.	d.
1. Treatment of Compound Fractures of the Thigh			
2. Treatment of Compound Fractures or Compound Dislocations of the Leg	5	0	0
3. Amputation of Leg, Arm, Foot, or Hand			
4. The Operation for Strangulated Hernia			
5. Treatment of Simple Fractures or Simple Dislocations of the Thigh or Leg	3	0	0
6. Amputation of a Finger or Toe	2	0	0
7. Treatment of Dislocations or Fractures of the Arm	1	0	0

The above rates shall include the payment for the supply of all kinds of apparatus and splints.

Art. 178.—Provided that except in cases of sudden accident immediately threatening life, no Medical Officer shall be entitled to receive such remuneration for any amputation, unless he shall have obtained at his own cost the advice of some member of the Royal College of Surgeons of London, or some fellow or licentiate of the Royal College of Physicians of London, before performing such amputation, and unless he shall also produce to the Guardians a certificate from such member of the Royal College of Surgeons, or such fellow or licentiate, stating that in his opinion it was right and proper that such amputation should be then performed.

Art. 179.—Provided also, that if in any case the patient has not survived the operation more than thirty-six hours, and has not required and received several attendances after the operation by the Medical Officer who has performed the same, such Medical Officer shall be entitled only to one half of the payments respectively prescribed above.

Art. 180.—Provided also, that if several of the fees specified in Art. 177 become payable with respect to the same person at the same time, and in consequence of the same cause or injury, the Medical Officer shall be entitled only to one of such fees, and if they be unequal, to the highest.

Art. 181.—In any surgical case, not provided for in Art. 177, which has presented peculiar difficulty, or required and received long attendance from the District Medical Officer, the Guardians may make to the said Medical Officer such reasonable extra allowance as they may think fit, and the Commissioners may approve.

Art. 182.—In cases in which any Medical Officer, either for the Workhouse or a District, shall be called on by order of a person legally qualified to make such order, to attend any woman in or immediately after childbirth, or shall, under circumstances of difficulty or danger, without any order, visit any such woman actually receiving relief, or whom the Guardians may subsequently decide to have been in a destitute condition, such Medical Officer shall be paid for his attendance and medicines by a sum of not less than ten shillings, nor more than twenty shillings, according as the Guardians may agree with such officer.

Art. 183.—Provided that in any special case in which great difficulty may have occurred in the delivery, or long subsequent attendance in respect of some puerperal malady or affection may have been requisite, any District Medical Officer shall receive the sum of two pounds.

SECURITY OF THE OFFICERS.

Art. 184.—Every Treasurer, Master, Matron of a Workhouse in which there is no Master, Collector, or Relieving Officer, every person hereafter appointed as Clerk, and every other officer whom the Guardians shall require so to do, shall respectively give a bond conditioned for the due and faithful performance of the duties of the office, with two sufficient sureties, not, in the case of any security to be here-after entered into, being officers of the same Union; and every officer who shall have entered into any such security shall give immediate notice to the Guardians of the death, insolvency, or bankruptcy of either of such sureties, and shall, when required by the Guardians, produce a certificate, signed by two householders, that his sureties are alive, and believed by them to be solvent, and such officer shall supply a fresh surety, in the place of any such surety who may die, or become bankrupt or insolvent.

Art. 185.—Provided that the Guardians may, if they think fit, take the security of any society or company expressly authorised by statute to guarantee or secure the faithful discharge of the duties of such officers.

Art. 186.—Provided also, that the Guardians may, with the consent of the Commissioners, dispense with such security in the case of any banking firm acting as Treasurer, or in the case of a Treasurer being a banker or partner of such firm.

CONTINUANCE IN OFFICE AND SUSPENSION OF OFFICERS.— SUPPLY OF VACANCIES.

Art. 187 [*amended*].—Every officer appointed to or holding any office under this Order, other than a Medical Officer, shall continue to hold the same until he die, or resign, or be proved to be insane, by evidence which the Board shall deem sufficient, or shall become legally disqualified to hold such office, or be removed by the Poor Law Board.

Art. 188.—Provided always, that every porter, nurse, assistant, or servant may be dismissed by the Guardians without the consent of the Commissioners; but every such dismissal, and the grounds thereof, shall be reported to the Commissioners.

Art. 189.—If any Master and Matron hereafter appointed be husband and wife, and one of them should be dismissed by Order of the Commissioners, or should otherwise vacate his or her office, or should die, the other or survivor shall, at

U

the expiration of the then current quarter, cease to hold his or her office of Master or Matron, as the case may be.

Art. 190.—No officer of a Workhouse who may have been dismissed by any Order of the Commissioners, shall, after such dismissal, remain upon the Workhouse premises, or enter therein for the purpose of interfering in the management of such Workhouse, unless the Commissioners have consented to his subsequent appointment to an office in such Workhouse, under the provisions of the said first-recited Act, or to his temporary employment therein.

Art. 191 [*amended*].—Every Medical Officer duly appointed shall hold his office according to the provisions contained in the General Order of the Board bearing date the twenty-fifth day of May, One thousand eight hundred and fifty-seven.

Art. 192.—The Guardians may at their discretion suspend from the discharge of his or her duties any Master, Matron, Schoolmaster, Schoolmistress, Medical Officer, Relieving Officer, or Superintendent of Out-door Labour; and the Guardians shall, in case of every such suspension, forthwith report the same, together with the cause thereof, to the Commissioners; and if the Commissioners remove the suspension of such officer by the Guardians, he or she shall forthwith resume the performance of his or her duties.

Art. 193.—If any officer or assistant, appointed to or holding any office or employment under this Order, be at any time prevented by sickness or accident, or other sufficient reason, from the performance of his duties, the Guardians may appoint a fit person to act as his temporary substitute, and may pay him a reasonable compensation for his services; and every such appointment shall be reported to the Commissioners as soon as the same shall have been made.

Art. 194.—The Vice-Chairman, or some Guardian to be appointed by the Guardians, may perform any of the duties assigned to the Clerk until any vacancy in the office shall have been filled, or until a substitute be appointed in the case of the sickness, accident, or absence of the Clerk.

Art. 195.—When any officer may die, resign, or become legally disqualified to perform the duties of his office, the Guardians shall, as soon as conveniently may be after such death, resignation, or disqualification, give notice thereof to the Commissioners, and proceed to make a new appointment to the office so vacant in the manner prescribed by the above Regulations.

Art. 196.—If any officer give notice of an intended resignation to take effect on a future day, the Guardians may elect a successor to such officer, in conformity with the above Regulations, at any time subsequent to such notice.

Art. 197.—In the case of any Medical Officer who holds his office for a specified term, the Guardians may provide for the continuance of such officer, or appoint his successor, within the three calendar months next before the expiration of such term.

PERSONAL DISCHARGE OF DUTIES.

Art. 198.—In every case not otherwise provided for by this Order, every officer shall perform his duties in person, and shall not intrust the same to a deputy, except with the special permission of the Commissioners on the application of the Guardians.

Art. 199.—Every Medical Officer shall be bound to visit and attend personally, as far as may be practicable, the poor persons intrusted to his care, and shall be responsible for the attendance on them.

Art. 200.—Every Medical Officer shall, as soon as may be after his appointment, name to the Guardians some legally qualified Medical Practitioner to whom application for medicines or attendance may be made in the case of his absence from home, or other hindrance to his personal attendance, and who will supply the same at the cost of such Medical Officer, and the name and residence of every Medical Practitioner so named shall be forwarded by the Clerk to each Relieving Officer, and to the Overseers of every Parish in the District of such Medical Officer.

DUTIES OF THE OFFICERS.

Art. 201.—And we do hereby define and specify the duties of the several Officers appointed to or holding their offices under this Order, and direct the execution thereof, to be as follows :—

DUTIES OF THE CLERK.

Art. 202.—The following shall be the duties of the Clerk [*see Assessment Committees Acts*] :—

No. 1. To attend all meetings of the Board of Guardians, and to keep punctually minutes of the proceedings at every meeting, to enter the said minutes in a book, and to submit the same so entered to the presiding Chairman at the succeeding meeting for his signature.

No. 2. To keep, check, and examine all accounts, books of accounts, minutes, books, and other documents, as required of him by the Regulations of the Commissioners, or relating to the business of the Guardians, and from time to time to produce all such books and documents, together with the necessary vouchers, and the bonds of any Officers, with any certificates relating thereto, which may be in his custody, to the Auditor of the Union, at the place of audit and at the time and in such manner as may be required by the Regulations of the Commissioners.

No. 3. To peruse and conduct the correspondence of the Guardians according to their directions, and to preserve the same, as well as all Orders of the Commissioners, and letters received, together with copies of all letters sent, and all letters, books, papers, and documents belonging to the Union, or intrusted to him by the Guardians, and to make all necessary copies thereof.

No. 4. To prepare all written contracts and agreements to be entered into by any parties with the Guardians, and to see that the same are duly executed, and to prepare all bonds or other securities to be given by any of the officers of the Union, and to see that the same are duly executed by such officers and their sureties.

No. 5. To receive all requisitions of Guardians for extra-ordinary meetings, and to summon such meetings accordingly ; and to make, sign, and send all notices required to be given to the Guardians, by this or any other Order of the Commissioners.

No. 6. To countersign all Orders legally made by the Guardians on Overseers, for the payment of money, and all Orders legally drawn by the Guardians upon the Treasurer.

No. 7. To ascertain, before every ordinary meeting of the Board, the balance due to or from the Union, in account with the Treasurer, and to enter the same in the minute book.

No. 8. At the first meeting of the Guardians in each quarter, to lay before the Guardians, or some Committee appointed by them, the non-settled poor account, and the non-resident poor account, posted in his ledger to the end of the preceding quarter, and to take the directions of the Guardians respecting the remittance of cheques or post-office orders to the Guardians of any other Union or Parish, or the transmission of accounts due from other Unions or Parishes, and requests for payment.

No. 9. Within fourteen days from the close of each quarter, to transmit by post all accounts of relief administered in the course of the preceding quarter to non-settled poor to the Guardians of the Unions and Parishes on account of which such relief was given ; and to state in every account so transmitted the names and classes of the several paupers to whom the relief in question has been administered.

No. 10. To communicate to the several officers and persons engaged in the administration of relief within the Union, all Orders and Directions of the Commissioners, or of the Guardians ; and, so far as may be, to give the instructions requisite for the prompt and correct execution of all such Orders and Directions, and to report to the Guardians any neglect or failure therein which may come to his knowledge.

No. 11 [*amended*]. To conduct all applications by or on behalf of the Guardians to any Justice or Justices at Petty or Special Sessions, or out of Sessions, and, if he be an attorney or solicitor, to perform and execute, without charge for anything beyond disbursements, all legal business connected with the Union, or in which the Guardians shall be engaged, except prosecutions at the Assizes or Quarter or General Sessions, or Central Criminal Court, all other proceedings at the said Quarter or General Sessions, actions and other proceedings in the Superior Courts of Law, suits and other proceedings in the Superior Courts of Equity, and Parliamentary business. He shall take care in every case that his bill for legal business against the Guardians shall be duly taxed before the same shall be paid.

No. 12. To prepare and transmit all reports, answers, or returns, as to any question or matter connected with or relating to the administration of the laws for the relief of the Poor in the Union, or to any other business of the Union, which are required by the Regulations of the Commissioners, or which the Commissioner or any Assistant Commissioner may lawfully require from him.

No. 13. To conduct duly and impartially, and in strict conformity with the Regulations in force at the time, the annual or any other Election of Guardians.

No. 14. To observe and execute all lawful orders and directions of the Guardians applicable to his office.

DUTIES OF THE TREASURER OF THE UNION.

Art. 203.—The following shall be the duties of the Treasurer of the Union :—

No. 1. To receive all monies tendered to be paid to the Guardians, and to place the same to their credit.

No. 2. To pay out of any monies for the time being in his hands belonging to the Guardians, all orders for money which shall be drawn upon him, in conformity with Art. 84, when the same shall be presented at the house or usual place of business of the Treasurer, and within the usual hours of business.

No. 3. To keep an account, under the proper dates, of all monies received and paid by him as such Treasurer, to balance the same at Lady Day and Michaelmas in every year, and to render an account of such monies to the Guardians, when required by them to do so.

No. 4. Whenever there are not funds belonging to the Guardians in his hands as Treasurer of the Union, to report in writing the fact of such deficiency to the Commissioners.

No. 5. To submit a proper account, together with the bonds of any officers which may be in his custody, to the Auditor at the place of audit, and at the time and in such manner as may be required by the Regulations of the Commissioners.

No. 6. To receive the monies payable to him as Treasurer of the Union, under any Act of Parliament or other authority of law.

Art. 204.—Provided that the Regulations in Art. 203 shall not be applicable to cases in which the Governor and Company of the Bank of England may act as Treasurer of the Union or Bankers to the Guardians.

DUTIES OF A MEDICAL OFFICER.

Art. 205.—The following shall be the duties of every Medical Officer appointed by the Guardians, whether he be the Medical Officer for a Workhouse or for a District :—

No. 1. To give to the Guardians, when required, any reasonable information respecting the case of any pauper who is or has been under his care ; to make any such written report relative to any sickness prevalent among the paupers under his care as the Guardians or the

Commissioners may require of him ; and to attend any meeting of the Board of Guardians when requested by them to do so.

No. 2. To give a certificate respecting children whom it is proposed to apprentice, in conformity with Articles 59 and 61.

No. 3. To give a certificate under his hand in every case to the Guardians, or the Relieving Officer, or the pauper on whom he is attending, of the sickness of such pauper or other cause of his attendance, when required to do so.

No. 4. In keeping the books prescribed by this Order, to employ, so far as is practicable, the terms used or recommended in the Regulations and Statistical Nosology issued by the Registrar General ; and also to show when the visit or attendance made or given to any pauper was made or given by any person employed by himself.

DUTIES OF A DISTRICT MEDICAL OFFICER.

Art. 206.—The following shall be the duties of a District Medical Officer :—

No. 1. To attend duly and punctually upon all poor persons requiring medical attendance within the District of the Union assigned to him, and according to his agreement to supply the requisite medicines to such persons whenever he may be lawfully required to furnish such attendance or medicines by a written or printed order of the Guardians, or of a Relieving Officer of the Union, or of an Overseer.

No. 2. On the exhibition to him of a ticket, according to Art. 76, and on application made on behalf of the party to whom such ticket was given, to afford such medical attendance and medicines as he would be bound to supply if he had received in each case an order from the Guardians to afford such attendance and medicines.

No. 3. To inform the Relieving Officer of any poor person whom he may attend without an order.

No. 4. To make a return to the Guardians at each ordinary meeting, in a book prepared according to the Form marked (P.), hereunto annexed, and to insert therein the date of every attendance, and the other particulars required by such Form, in conformity with Art. 205. No. 4.

Provided, however, that the Medical Officer may, with the consent of the Guardians, but not otherwise, make the entries which he is directed to make in such book on detached sheets of paper, according to the same Form, and cause the same to be laid before the Guardians at every ordinary meeting, instead of such book, and the Guardians shall, in that case, cause such sheets to be bound up at the end of the year.

DUTIES OF THE MEDICAL OFFICER FOR THE WORKHOUSE.

Art. 207.—The following shall be the duties of the Medical Officer for the Workhouse [*see also G. O., April* 4, 1866] :—

No. 1. To attend at the Workhouse at the periods fixed by the Guardians, and also when sent for by the Master or Matron.

No. 2. To attend duly and punctually upon all poor persons in the Workhouse requiring medical attendance, and according to his agreement to supply the requisite medicines to such persons.

No. 3. To examine the state of the paupers on their admission into the Workhouse, and to give the requisite directions to the Master according to Articles 91 and 92.

No. 4. To give directions and make suggestions as to the diet, classification, and treatment of the sick paupers, and paupers of unsound mind, and to report to the Guardians any pauper of unsound mind in the Workhouse whom he may deem to be dangerous, or fit to be sent to a Lunatic Asylum.

No. 5. To give all necessary instructions as to the diet or treatment of children and women suckling children, and to vaccinate such of the children as may require vaccination.

No. 6. To report in writing to the Guardians any defect in the diet, drainage, ventilation, warmth, or other arrangements of the Workhouse, or any excess in the number of any class of inmates, which he may deem to be detrimental to the health of the inmates.

No. 7. To report in writing to the Guardians any defect which he may observe in the arrangements of the infirmary, and in the performance of their duties by the nurses of the sick.

No. 8. To make a return to the Guardians, at each ordinary meeting, in a book prepared according to the Form (Q.) hereunto annexed, and to insert therein the date of every attendance, in conformity with Art. 205, and the other particulars required by such Form to be inserted by the Medical Officer, and to enter in such return the death of every pauper who shall die in the Workhouse, together with the apparent cause thereof.

No. 9. To enter in the commencement of such book, according to the Form marked (R.), hereunto annexed, the proper dietary for the sick paupers in the house in so many different scales as he shall deem expedient.

DUTIES OF THE MASTER.

Art. 208.—The following shall be the duties of the Master :—

No. 1. To admit paupers into the Workhouse, in obedience to the Orders specified in Art. 88, and also every person applying for admission who may appear to him to require relief through any sudden or urgent necessity, and to cause every pauper, upon admission, to be examined by the Medical Officer, as is directed in Art. 91.

No. 2. To cause every male pauper above the age of seven

years, upon admission, to be searched, cleansed, and clothed, and to be placed in the proper ward.

No. 3. To enforce industry, order, punctuality, and cleanliness, and the observance of all Regulations for the government of the Workhouse by the paupers, and by the several officers, assistants, and servants therein.

No. 4. To read prayers to the paupers before breakfast and after supper every day, or cause prayers to be read, according to Art. 124.

No. 5. To cause the paupers to be inspected, and their names called over, in conformity with Art. 103, in order that it may be seen that each individual is clean and in a proper state.

No. 6. To provide for and enforce the employment of the able-bodied adult paupers during the hours of labour; to assist in training the youths in such employment as will best fit them for gaining their own living; to keep the partially disabled paupers occupied to the extent of their ability; and to allow none who are capable of employment to be idle at any time.

No. 7. To visit the sleeping-wards of the male paupers at eleven o'clock in the forenoon of every day, and see that such wards have been all duly cleansed and are properly ventilated.

No. 8. To see that the meals of the paupers are duly provided, dressed, and served, according to the directions in Articles 104 and 107, and to superintend the distribution of the food.

No. 9. To say, or cause to be said, grace before and after meals.

No. 10. To visit all the wards of the male paupers before nine o'clock every night in winter, and ten o'clock in summer, and see that all the male paupers are in bed, and that all fires and lights therein are extinguished, except so far as may be necessary for the sick.

No. 11. To receive from the Porter the keys of the Workhouse at nine o'clock every night, and to deliver them to him again at six o'clock every morning, or at such hours as shall from time to time be fixed by the Guardians.

No. 12. To see that the male paupers are properly clothed, and that their clothes are kept in proper repair.

No. 13. To cause the birth of every child born in the Workhouse to be registered by the Registrar of Births and Deaths within the space of one week after such child shall have been born ; and also to enter such birth in a register kept according to Form (S.), hereunto annexed.

No. 14. To send for the Medical Officer in case any pauper is taken ill or becomes insane, and to take care that all sick and insane paupers are duly visited by the Medical Officer, and are provided with such medicines and attendance, diet and other necessaries, as the Medical Officer or the Guardians direct, and to apprise the nearest relation in the Workhouse of the sickness of any pauper, and, in the case of dangerous sickness, to send for the Chaplain, and any relative or friend of the pauper, resident within a reasonable distance, whom the pauper may desire to see.

No. 15. To take care that no pauper at the approach of death shall be left unattended either during the day or the night.

No. 16. To give immediate information of the death of any pauper in the Workhouse to the Medical Officer, and to the nearest relations of the deceased, who may be known to him, and who may reside within a reasonable distance ; and if the body be not removed within a reasonable time, to provide for the interment thereof.

No. 17. When requisite, to cause the death of every pauper dying in the Workhouse to be duly registered by the Registrar of Births and Deaths within five days after the day of such death ; and also to enter such death in a register kept according to Form (T.), hereunto annexed.

No. 18. To deliver an inventory of the clothes and other property of any pauper who may have died in the Workhouse, to the Guardians at their next ordinary meeting.

No. 19. To keep such portion of the Workhouse Medical Relief Book prescribed in this Order as is assigned to him in the Form marked (Q.), and to keep all books or accounts which he is, or hereafter may be, by any Order of the Commissioners, directed and required to keep, to allow the same to be constantly open to the inspection of any of the Guardians of the Union, and to submit the same to the Guardians at their ordinary meetings.

No. 20. To submit to the Guardians, at every ordinary meeting, an estimate of such provisions and other articles as are required for the use of the Workhouse, and to receive and execute the directions of the Guardians thereupon.

No. 21. To receive all provisions and other articles purchased or procured for the use of the Workhouse, and before placing them in store to examine and compare them with the bills of parcels or invoices severally relating thereto ; and after having proved the accuracy of such bills or invoices, to authenticate the same with his signature, and submit them to the Guardians at their next ordinary meeting.

No. 22. To receive and take charge of all provisions, clothing, linen, and other articles belonging to the Workhouse, or confided to his care by the Guardians, and issue the same to the Matron or other persons as may be required.

No. 23. To report to the Guardians from time to time the names of such children as the Schoolmaster may recommend as fit to be put out to service, or other employment, and to take the necessary steps for carry-

ing into effect the directions of the Guardians
thereon.

No. 24. To take care that the wards, rooms, larder,
kitchen, and all other offices of the Workhouse, and all
the utensils and furniture thereof, be kept clean and in
good order ; and as often as any defect in the same, or
in the state of the Workhouse, shall occur, to report
the same in writing to the Guardians at their next
ordinary meeting.

No. 25. To submit to the Guardians, at every ordinary meeting, a report of the number of the inmates in the Workhouse according to the Form (U.) hereunto annexed.

No. 26. To bring before the Visiting Committee or the
Guardians any pauper inmate desirous of making a
complaint or application to the Guardians.

No. 27. To report forthwith to the Medical Officer and
to the Guardians, in writing, all cases in which any
restraint or compulsion may have been used towards
any pauper inmate of unsound mind in the Workhouse.

No. 28. To keep a book, in which he shall enter all his
written reports to the Guardians or to the Medical
Officer, and to lay the same before the Guardians at
every ordinary meeting.

No. 29. To inform the Visiting Committee and the
Guardians of the state of the Workhouse in every
department, and to report in writing to the Guardians
any negligence or other misconduct on the part of any
of the subordinate officers or servants of the establishment; and generally to observe and fulfil all lawful
orders and directions of the Guardians suitable to his
office.

Art. 209.—The Master shall not, except in case of necessity, purchase or procure any articles for the use of the
Workhouse, nor order any alterations or repairs of any part
of the premises, or of the furniture or other articles belonging thereto, nor pay any monies on account of the Workhouse, or of the Union, without the authority of the Guar-

dians, nor apply any articles belonging to the Guardians to purposes other than those authorised or approved of by such Guardians.

DUTIES OF THE MATRON.

Art. 210.—The following shall be the duties of the Matron :—

No. 1. In the absence of the Master, or during his inability to act, to act as his substitute in the admission of paupers into the Workhouse, according to Articles 88 and 208, Nos. 1 and 2, and to cause every pauper upon such admission to be examined by the Medical Officer, as is directed in Art. 91.

No. 2. To cause the pauper children under the age of seven years, and the female paupers, to be searched, cleansed, and clothed upon their admission, and to be placed in their proper wards.

No. 3. To provide for and enforce the employment of the able-bodied female paupers during the hours of labour, and to keep the partially disabled female paupers occupied to the extent of their ability, and to assist the Schoolmistress in training up the children so as best to fit them for service.

No. 4. To call over the names of the paupers as is directed in Art. 103, to inspect their persons, and see that each individual is clean.

No. 5. To visit the sleeping-wards of the female paupers at eleven o'clock of the forenoon of every day, and to see that such wards have been all duly cleansed and are properly ventilated.

No. 6. To visit all the wards of the females and children every night before nine o'clock, and to ascertain that all the paupers in such wards are in bed, and all fires and lights not necessary for the sick or for women suckling their children therein extinguished.

No. 7. To pay particular attention to the moral conduct and orderly behaviour of the females and children, and to see that they are clean and decent in their dress and persons.

No. 8. To superintend and give the necessary directions for making and mending the linen and clothing supplied to the male paupers, and all the clothing supplied to the female paupers and children, and to take care that all such clothing be properly numbered and marked on the inside with the name of the Union.

No. 9. To see that every pauper in the Workhouse has clean linen and stockings once a week, and that all the beds and bedding be kept in a clean and wholesome state.

No. 10. To take charge of the linen and stockings for the use of the paupers, and the other linen in use in the Workhouse, and to apply the same to such purposes as shall be authorised or approved of by the Guardians, and to no other.

No. 11. To superintend and give the necessary directions concerning the washing, drying, and getting up of the linen, stockings, and blankets, and to see that the same be not dried in the sleeping-wards, or in the sick-wards.

No. 12. To take proper care of the children and sick paupers, and to provide the proper diet for the same, and for women suckling infants, and to furnish them with such changes of clothes and linen as may be necessary.

No. 13. To assist the Master in the general management and superintendence of the Workhouse, and especially in—

Enforcing the observance of good order, cleanliness, punctuality, industry, and decency of demeanour among the paupers ;—

Cleansing and ventilating the sleeping-wards and the dining-hall, and all other parts of the premises ;—

Placing in store and taking charge of the provisions,

clothing, linen, and other articles belonging to the Union.

No. 14. When requested by the Porter, in pursuance of Art. 214, No. 5, to search any female entering or leaving the Workhouse under the circumstances described in that article.

No. 15. To report to the Master any negligence or other misconduct on the part of any of the female officers or servants of the establishment, or any case in which restraint or compulsion may have been used towards any female inmate of unsound mind.

No. 16. And generally to observe and fulfil all lawful orders and directions of the Guardians suitable to her office.

DUTIES OF THE CHAPLAIN.

Art. 211.—The following shall be the duties of the Chaplain :—

No. 1. To read prayers and preach a sermon to the paupers and other inmates of the Workhouse on every Sunday, and on Good Friday and Christmas Day, unless the Guardians, with the consent of the Commissioners, may otherwise direct.

No. 2. To examine the children, and to catechise such as belong to the Church of England, at least once in every month, and to make a record of the same, and state the dates of his attendance, the general progress and condition of the children, and the moral and religious state of the inmates generally, in a book to be kept for that purpose, to be laid before the Guardians at their next ordinary meeting, and to be termed " THE CHAPLAIN'S REPORT."

No. 3. To visit the sick paupers, and to administer religious consolation to them in the Workhouse, at such periods as the Guardians may appoint, and when applied to for that purpose by the Master or Matron.

X

Duties of the Schoolmaster and Schoolmistress.

Art. 212.—The following shall be the duties of the Schoolmaster and Schoolmistress for the Workhouse, or either of them :—

No. 1. To instruct the boys and girls according to the directions in Art. 114.

No. 2. To regulate the discipline and arrangements of the school, and the industrial and moral training of the children, subject to the direction of the Guardians.

No. 3. To accompany the children when they quit the Workhouse for exercise, or for attendance at public worship, unless the Guardians shall otherwise direct.

No. 4. To keep the children clean in their persons, and orderly and decorous in their conduct.

No. 5. To assist the Master and Matron respectively in maintaining due subordination in the Workhouse.

Duties of a Nurse.

Art. 213.—The following shall be the duties of a Nurse for the Workhouse : —

No. 1. To attend upon the sick in the sick and lying-in wards, and to administer to them all medicines and medical applications, according to the directions of the Medical Officer.

No. 2. To inform the Medical Officer of any defects which may be observed in the arrangements of the sick or lying-in ward.

No. 3. To take care that a light is kept at night in the sick-ward.

Duties of the Porter.

Art. 214.—The following shall be the duties of the Porter of the Workhouse :—

No. 1. To keep the gate, and to prevent any person not being an officer of the Workhouse, or of the Union, an

Assistant Poor Law Commissioner, or any person authorised by law, or by the Commissioners, or Guardians, from entering into or going out of the house without the leave of the Master or Matron.

No. 2. To keep a book in which he shall enter the name and business of every officer or other person who shall go into the Workhouse, and the name of every officer or other person who shall go out thereof, together with the time of such officer's or person's going in or out.

No. 3. To receive all paupers who apply or present themselves for admission in conformity with Art. 88, and if the Master and Matron be both absent, to place such paupers in the receiving-ward until the Master or Matron return.

No. 4. To examine all parcels and goods before they are received into the Workhouse, and prevent the admission of any spirituous or fermented liquors, or other articles contrary to any of the Regulations contained in this Order, or otherwise contrary to law.

No. 5. To search any male pauper entering or leaving the Workhouse whom he may suspect of having possession of any spirits or other prohibited articles, and to require any other person entering the Workhouse whom he may suspect of having possession of any such spirits or prohibited articles, to satisfy him to the contrary before he permit such person to be admitted, and in the case of any female, to cause the Matron to be called for the purpose of searching her, if necessary.

No. 6. To examine all parcels taken by any pauper out of the Workhouse, and to prevent the undue removal of any article from the premises.

No. 7. To lock all the outer doors, and take the keys to the Master, at nine o'clock every night, and to receive them back from him every morning at six o'clock, or at such hours as shall from time to time be fixed by the Guardians; and if any application for admission to the

Workhouse be made after the keys shall have been so taken to the Master, to apprise the Master forthwith of such application.

No. 8. To assist the Master and Matron in preserving order, and in enforcing obedience and due subordination in the Workhouse.

No. 9. To inform the Master of all things affecting the security and order of the Workhouse, and to obey all lawful directions of the Master or Matron, and of the Guardians, suitable to his office.

DUTIES OF A RELIEVING OFFICER.

Art. 215.—The following shall be the duties of a Relieving Officer :—

No. 1. To attend all ordinary meetings of the Guardians, and to attend all other meetings when summoned by the Clerk.

No. 2. To receive all applications for relief made to him within his district, or relating to any Parish situated within his district, and forthwith to examine into the circumstances of every case by visiting the house of the applicant (if situated within his district), and by making all necessary inquiries into the state of health, the ability to work, the condition and family, and the means of such applicant, and to report the result of such inquiries in the prescribed form to the Guardians at their next ordinary meeting, and also to visit from time to time, as requisite, all paupers receiving relief, and to report concerning the same as the Guardians may direct.

No. 3. In any case of sickness or accident requiring relief by medical attendance, to procure such attendance by giving an order on the District Medical Officer, in the Form (V.) hereunto annexed, or by such other means as the urgency of the case may require.

No. 4. To ascertain from time to time from the District

Medical Officer the names of any poor persons whom such Medical Officer may have attended or supplied with Medicines, without having received an order from himself to that effect.

No. 5. In every case of a poor person receiving medical relief, as soon as may be, and from time to time afterwards, to visit the house of such person, and, until the next ordinary meeting of the Guardians, to supply such relief (not being in money) as the case on his own view, or on the certificate of the District Medical Officer, may seem to require.

No. 6. In every case of sudden or urgent necessity, to afford such relief to the destitute person as may be requisite, either by giving such person an order of admission into the Workhouse, and conveying him thereto, if necessary, or by affording him relief out of the Workhouse, provided that the same be not given in money, whether such destitute person be settled in any Parish comprised in the Union or not.

No. 7. To report to the Guardians at their next ordinary meeting all cases reported to him by an Overseer in conformity with Art. 218, and to obey the directions of the Guardians with reference to the relief administered in such cases.

No. 8. To perform the duties with respect to pauper apprentices prescribed by Arts. 60, 61, and 62.

No. 9. To give all reasonable aid and assistance at the request of any other Relieving Officer of the Union, by examining into the case of any applicant for relief, or administering relief to any pauper whose name has been entered on the books of such other Relieving Officer, and who may be within his own district.

No. 10. Duly and punctually to supply the weekly allowances of all paupers belonging to his district, or being within the same, and to pay or administer the relief of all paupers within his district to the amount and in the manner in which he may have been lawfully ordered by the Guardians to pay or administer the same.

No. 11. To visit, relieve, and otherwise attend to non-settled poor, being within his district, according to the directions of the Guardians, whose officer he is, and in no other way, subject always to the obligation imposed on him in cases of sudden or urgent necessity.

No. 12. To set apart one or more pages in his out-door relief list, in which he shall duly and punctually enter up the payments made by authority of his own Board of Guardians to non-settled poor, and to take credit for such payments in his receipt and expenditure book.

No. 13. To present his weekly accounts to the Clerk for his inspection and authentication before every ordinary meeting of the Guardians, and to the Guardians, at such meeting, for their approval.

No. 14. To submit to the Auditor of the Union all his books, accounts, and vouchers, at the place of audit, and at such time and in such manner as may be required by the Regulations of the Commissioners.

No. 15. To assist the Clerk in conducting and completing the annual or other election of Guardians, according to the Regulations of the Commissioners.

No. 16. To observe and execute all lawful orders and directions of the Guardians applicable to his office.

Art. 216.—The Relieving Officer shall in no case take credit in his accounts, or enter as paid or given by way of relief, any money or other articles which have not been paid or given previously to the taking of such credit or the making of such entry ; and he shall not take credit in such accounts for any money paid to any tradesman or other person without producing, at the next ordinary meeting of the Guardians, a bill from such tradesman or person, with voucher of payment.

DUTIES OF A SUPERINTENDENT OF OUT-DOOR LABOUR.

Art. 217.—The duties of a Superintendent of Out-door Labour shall be to superintend any able-bodied paupers not inmates of the Workhouse who may be set to work by the Guardians, to take care that they perform the work respectively assigned to them, and to report truly to the Guardians respecting the performance of such work.

RECEIPT AND PAYMENT OF MONEY BY OFFICERS.

Art. 218.—No Clerk, Relieving Officer, Master, or other officer appointed to or holding any office under this Order, shall, directly or indirectly, receive or bargain to receive any gratuity, per-centage, or allowance of any kind with reference to any contract with the Guardians, or in respect of any payment made or to be made for goods supplied or work executed according to the order of such Guardians or on their behalf.

Art. 219.—No Clerk shall directly or indirectly cause to be paid to himself, or shall pay away on his own account or for his own benefit, any cheque drawn by the Guardians, and made payable to any person other than himself.

Art. 220.—Every Clerk receiving any cheque or money from the Guardians on account of any other party, shall transmit the same within fourteen days to the proper persons, and shall produce the receipt or acknowledgment for the same at the next ordinary meeting after the same has come to his hands.

Art. 221.—Every officer of the Union who may receive money on behalf of the Guardians thereof, shall forthwith pay the same into the hands of the Treasurer of the Union, to the credit of the Guardians, notwithstanding that any salary or balance may be due from the Union to such officer.

Art. 222.—No Relieving Officer, or other officer of any Guardians, nor any Assistant Overseer or Collector, shall receive money for the relief of any non-settled pauper on behalf of any officer, or of the Guardians, of any other Parish or Union, or shall constitute himself in any way the agent of any officer or Guardians of such other Parish or Union, except as is provided in this Order.

Art. 223.—If any money be transmitted to any officer, contrary to the provisions of this Order, such officer shall forthwith pay such money into the hands of the Treasurer of the Union whose officer he is, and shall report to the Guardians at their next meeting the fact that such money has been so received and paid, and shall make a true entry accordingly in his accounts.

EXPLANATION OF TERMS.

Art. 224.—Whenever the word " Parish " is used in this Order, it shall be taken to include any place maintaining its own poor, whether parochial or extra-parochial.

Art. 225.—Whenever the word " Overseer " is used in this Order, it shall be taken to include any person acting or legally bound to act in the discharge of any of the duties usually performed by Overseers of the Poor, so far as such duties are referred to in this Order.

Art. 226. [*Omitted in recent Order.*]

Art. 227.—Whenever the word " medicines " is used in this Order, it shall be taken to include all medical and surgical appliances ; whenever the words " medical attendance " are used in this Order, they shall be taken to include surgical attendance ; and whenever the words " medical relief " are used in this Order, they shall be taken to include relief by surgical as well as medical attendance.

Art. 228.—Whenever the words " Medical Officer " are used in this Order, they shall be taken to include any person duly licensed as a medical man, who may have contracted or agreed with any Guardians for the supply of medicines, or for medical attendance.

Art. 229.—Whenever the words Clerk, Master, or Matron are used in this Order, they shall be taken to mean the Clerk to the Guardians, and the Master or Matron of the Workhouse respectively.

Art.—230. The term "non-resident poor" in this Order shall be taken to mean all paupers in receipt of relief allowed on account of any Union in relation to which the term is used, but not residing therein.

Art. 231.—The term "non-settled poor" in this Order shall be taken to mean all paupers residing in the Union in relation to which the term is used, but to whom relief is allowed on account of some Parish or Union other than that in which they reside.

Art. 232.—Whenever in describing any person or party, matter or thing, the word importing the singular number or the masculine gender only is used in this Order, the same shall be taken to include, and shall be applied to, several persons or parties as well as one person or party, and females as well as males, and several matters or things as well as one matter or thing, respectively, unless there be something in the subject or context repugnant to such construction.

Art. 233.—Whenever in this Order any Article is referred to by its number, the Article of this Order bearing that number shall be taken to be signified thereby.

FORMS REFERRED TO IN THE FOREGOING ORDER.

FORM A.—*Election Amendment Order, 21st Feb., 1868.*

FIRST SCHEDULE.

NOTICE OF ELECTION.

FOR UNIONS.

Election of Guardians of the Poor for the year 186 .

———— UNION.

I, the undersigned, Clerk to the Guardians of the Poor of the above-named Union, with reference to the ensuing Election of Guardians of the Poor for the several Parishes in the said Union, do hereby give notice as follows :—

1.—The number of Guardians of the Poor to be elected for the Parishes in the said Union is as follows :—

For the Parish of   Guardians.
For the Parish of   Guardians.
For the Parish of   Guardians.

2.—Any person, not otherwise disqualified by law, who shall be rated to the Poor Rate in any Parish in the Union in respect of hereditaments of the annual rateable value of not less than   Pounds, is qualified to be nominated for the office of Guardian at the said Election by any person then qualified to vote.

3.—Nominations of Guardians must be made according to the Form below, which is the Form prescribed by the Poor Law Board. Such nominations must be sent after the Fourteenth, but on or before the   day of March instant, to me,   , or to Mr.

at   for the Parish of   , or to Mr.

at   for the Parish of   , who

alone are authorised to receive the same. Nominations sent before the said Fourteenth (*a*), or after the said day of March instant, or sent to any other person, will be invalid; and so also if they be delivered at the address, office, or residence of the Clerk or other persons above named, before the hour of nine o'clock in the morning or after the hour of eight o'clock in the evening, unless sent through the post.

4.—On the day of I shall cause a list of the names of the persons nominated as Candidates for the several Parishes to be suspended in the Board Room of the Guardians, and to be affixed to the principal door of the Workhouse at .

5.—If more than the above-mentioned number of Guardians be nominated for any Parish, I shall cause a list of the Candidates and of the names and addresses of their several Nominators to be made out, and to be kept in the Board Room of the Union, which list will be open to the inspection of every person qualified to vote on any day when the Board of Guardians are not holding their Meeting, between the hours mentioned above. I shall also cause Voting Papers to be delivered on the day of April at the address in such Parish of each Ratepayer, Owner, and Proxy qualified to vote; and on the day of April I shall cause such Voting Papers to be collected.

6.—On the day of April I shall attend at the Board Room of this Union at the hour of , and I shall on that day, and, if necessary, the following days, proceed to ascertain the number of votes given for each Candidate.

7.—If any Voter do not receive a Voting Paper on the said day of April, he may apply to me before the day of April for one; and if any Voting Paper be not collected on the said day of April through

---

(*a*) This should be the 15th, and the notice when issued should be altered accordingly.

the default of the Collector, the Voter in person may deliver it to me before noon on the   day of April.

8.—Any person put in nomination for the Office of Guardian may, at any time during the proceedings in the Election, tender to me in writing his refusal to serve the office, and the Election, so far as regards that person, will be no further proceeded with.

Form of Nomination Paper.

Parish of   ⎫
————————   ⎬   This   day of   , 186
———————— Union. ⎭

Names of Persons nominated to be Guardians,	Residence of the Persons nominated.	Quality or Calling of Persons nominated.

I, being*   duly qualified to vote in the Parish aforesaid, nominate the above to be Guardian [*or* Guardians] for the said Parish.

———————————— Signature   ⎫
———————————— Address   ⎬ of Nominator.

*Note.—Only one person is empowered to sign this paper, and after the word *being* he must insert (*a ratepayer*) or (*owner of property*) according to his qualification.
One of these words only must be used.

Given under my hand, this   day of March, 186 .
———————— Clerk to the said Guardians.

WARNING.—It is enacted by the Statute 14 & 15 Vict. c. 105, s. 3, that—" If any person, pending or after the Election of any Guardian or Guardians, shall wilfully, fraudulently, and with intent to affect the result of such Election, commit any of the acts following ; that is to say, fabricate in whole or in part, alter, deface, destroy, abstract, or purloin any Nomination or Voting Paper used therein ; or personate any person entitled to vote at such Election ; or falsely assume to act in the name or on the behalf of any person so entitled to vote ; or interrupt the distribution or collection of the Voting Papers ; or distribute or collect the same under a false pretence of being lawfully authorised to do so," he will be liable to be sent to prison for three months with hard labour.

Form A.

Second Schedule.

NOTICE OF ELECTION.

FOR PARISHES AND TOWNSHIPS.

Election of Guardians of the Poor for the year 186 .

—— Parish [*or* Township].

I, the undersigned, Clerk to the Guardians of the Poor of the above-named Parish [*or* Township], with reference to the ensuing Election of Guardians of the Poor for the said Parish [*or* Township], do hereby give notice as follows :—

1.—The number of Guardians of the Poor to be elected for the said Parish [*or* Township] is —

[*Where the Parish is divided into Wards, the number of Guardians for each Ward is to be stated.*]

2.—Any person not otherwise disqualified by law, who shall be rated to the Poor Rate in the Parish [*or* Township] in respect of hereditaments of the annual rateable value of not less than   Pounds, is qualified to be nominated for the office of Guardian at the said Election by any person then qualified to vote.

3.—Nominations of Guardians must be made according to the Form below, which is the Form prescribed by the Poor Law Board. Such nominations must be sent after the Fourteenth, but on or before the   day of March instant, to me,   , or to Mr.   , at   , or to Mr.   at   , who alone are authorised to receive the same. Nominations sent before the said Fourteenth (*a*), or after the said   day of

---

(*a*) This should be the 15th, and the notice when issued should be altered accordingly.

March instant, or sent to any other person, will be invalid ; and so also if they be delivered at the address, office, or residence of the Clerk or other persons above named, before the hour of nine o'clock in the morning or after the hour of eight o'clock in the evening, unless sent by the post.

4.—On the   day of   I shall cause a list of the names of the persons nominated as Candidates for the Parish [*or* Township] to be suspended in the Board Room of the Guardians, and to be affixed to the principal door of the Workhouse at   .

5.—If more than the above-mentioned number of Guardians be nominated for the Parish [Township *or* Ward], I shall cause a list of the Candidates and of the names and addresses of their several Nominators to be made out, and to be kept in the Board Room of the Parish [*or* Township], which list will be open to the inspection of every person qualified to vote on any day when the Board of Guardians are not holding their Meeting, between the hours mentioned above. I shall· also cause Voting Papers to be delivered on the   day of April, at the address in the Parish [Township *or* Ward] of each Ratepayer, Owner, and Proxy qualified to vote ; and on the   day of April I shall cause such Voting Papers to be collected.

6.—On the   day of April I shall attend at the Board Room of this Parish [*or* Township] at the hour of   , and I shall on that day, and, if necessary, the following days, proceed to ascertain the number of votes given for each Candidate.

7.—If any Voter do not receive a Voting Paper on the said   day of April, he may apply to me before the   day of April for one; and if any Voting Paper be not collected on the said   day of April through the default of the Collector, the Voter in person may deliver it to me before noon on the   day of April.

8.—Any person put in nomination for the office of Guardian may, at any time during the proceedings in the Election, tender to me in writing his refusal to serve the office, and the Election, so far as regards that person, will be no further proceeded with.

```
┌─────────────────────────────────────────────────────────────┐
│                  Form of Nomination Paper.                   │
│  Parish (or Township) of  ⎫                                  │
│  ─────────────────────    ⎬  This        day of    , 186 .  │
│  *─────────────── Ward.    ⎭                                 │
│  ┌──────────────┬──────────────────┬──────────────────┐     │
│  │ Names of Persons│ Residence of the│ Quality or Calling│   │
│  │ nominated to be │ Persons nominated.│ of Persons nomi-│   │
│  │  Guardians.     │                  │    nated.        │   │
│  ├──────────────┼──────────────────┼──────────────────┤     │
│  │              │                  │                  │      │
│  └──────────────┴──────────────────┴──────────────────┘     │
│  I, being†            duly qualified to vote in the Parish [Township or│
│  Ward] aforesaid, nominate the above to be Guardian [or Guardians] for │
│  the said Parish [Township or Ward].                         │
│             ───────────────────── Signature ⎫ of Nominator.  │
│             ───────────────────── Address   ⎭                │
│  * Where the Parish is divided into Wards, insert the name of the Ward.│
│  † Note.—Only one person is empowered to sign this paper, and after the│
│  word being he must insert (a ratepayer) or (owner of property) according│
│  to his qualification.                                       │
│  One of these words only must be used.                       │
└─────────────────────────────────────────────────────────────┘
```

Given under my hand, this   day of March, 186 .

———————, Clerk to the said Guardians.

WARNING.—It is enacted by the Statute 14 & 15 Vict. c. 105, s. 3, that—" If any person, pending or after the Election of any Guardian or Guardians, shall wilfully, fraudulently, and with intent to affect the result of such Election, commit any of the acts following; that is to say, fabricate in whole or in part, alter, deface, destroy, abstract, or purloin any Nomination or Voting Paper used therein; or personate any person entitled to vote at such Election; or falsely assume to act in the name or on the behalf of any person so entitled to vote; or interrupt the distribution or collection of the Voting Papers; or distribute or collect the same under a false pretence of being lawfully authorised to do so," he will be liable to be sent to prison for three months with hard labour.

FORM B.—*Nomination Paper.* (See Art. 8.)

(*See substituted Form on pp.* 316, 319.)

＊Form B.—(*Election of Guardians Amendment Order, Jan. 14, 1867.*) *Voting Paper for the Election of Guardians for the year* 186 .

——————— Union.

Voting Paper for the Parish of

No of Voting Paper.	Name and Address of Voter.	Number of Votes.	
		As Owner.	As Ratepayer.

Directions to the Voters.

The Voter is entitled to vote for   Guardian [*or* Guardians], and no more.

The Voter, if able to write, must himself write his initials against the name of every person for whom he votes, and must himself sign this paper.

The name of a Firm or Partnership will be of no avail. The signature by a wife for her husband, whether in his name or her own, will be useless.

If the Voter cannot write, he must affix his mark, but such mark must be attested, and the name of the Voter filled in by a witness, and such witness must write the initials of the Voter against the name of every person for whom the Voter intends to vote.

If a Proxy vote, he must in like manner write his own initials, sign his own name, and state in writing the name of the person for whom he is Proxy; thus—*John Smith* for *Richard Williams.*

This paper must be carefully preserved by the Voter, as no second paper will be given. When it is filled up, it must be kept ready for delivery to Mr.   , who will call for the Voting Paper on the   day of   , between the hours of   before noon, and of   afternoon. No other person is authorised to receive the Voting Paper.

—————————————————

* This is substituted for Form C. referred to in Art. 10.

The Voter may deliver the paper open or sealed up in an envelope, and may himself deposit it in the box or bag used for the collection.

If the Voting Paper be not ready for the person appointed to collect it when called for, the vote will be lost. It will also be lost if more than name be returned in the list, with the initials of the Voter placed against such name , or if the Voting Paper be not signed by the Voter, or if the mark of the Voter be not attested when attestation is required.

Initials of the Voter against the Name of the Person for whom the vote is intended to be given.	Names of the Persons nominated as Guardians.	Residence of the Persons nominated.	Quality or Calling of the Persons nominated.	Opinion of the Clerk as to the disqualification.

I vote for the persons in the above list against whose names the initials are placed as above.

(Place for Signature of the Voter)

(Place for the mark if the Voter cannot write)

Name of the Voter who cannot write

Witness to the mark

Address of the Witness

(Place for Signature where the Voter votes by Proxy)

for

WARNING.—It is enacted by the Statute 14 & 15 Vict. c. 105, s. 3, that—" If any person, pending or after the Election of any Guardian or Guardians, shall wilfully, fraudulently, and with intent to affect the result of such Election, commit any of the Acts following ; that is to say, fabricate in whole or in part, alter, deface, destroy, abstract, or purloin any Nomination or Voting Paper used therein ; or personate any person entitled to vote at such Election ; or falsely assume to act in the name or on the behalf of any person so entitled to vote ; or interrupt the distribution or collection of the Voting Papers ; or distribute or collect the same under a false pretence of being lawfully authorised to do

Y

so," he will be liable to be sent to prison for three months with hard labour.

FORM C.—(*Rescinded, and Form B. substituted.*)

FORM D.—*Notice to Guardians Elected.*   (See Art. 23.)

——— UNION.

Parish [*or* Township] of ———.

Sir,—I do hereby give you notice, and declare that you have been duly elected a Guardian of the Poor for the Parish [*or* Township] of —— in the —— Union, and that the first meeting of the Board of Guardians of the said Union at which you will be lawfully entitled to attend and act as Guardian will be held at —— on —— day, the — [*add* instant, *or* April next], at the hour of——.

Signed this —— day of ——.

 —— Clerk to the Guardians of the Poor of the —— Union.

To Mr. —— of ——.

FORM E.   (See Art. 24.)

——— Union.

I do hereby certify that the Election of Guardians of the Poor for the several Parishes in the ——— Union was conducted in conformity with the Order of the Poor Law Commissioners, and that the Entries contained in the Schedule hereunto written are true.

Parishes (arranged alphabetically.)	Names of Persons nominated as Guardians.	Residence.	Quality or Calling.	No. of Votes given for each Candidate.	Names of the Guardians elected.	Names of the Guardians qualified to act in the Parishes where no Guardian has been elected.

Given under my hand this ——— day of —— ·——

 ——— Clerk to the Guardians of the Poor of the ——— Union.

FORM F. (See Art. 34.)

To the Clerk of the Guardians of the ———— Union.

Requisition for an Extraordinary Meeting of Guardians.

We, the undersigned, being two of the Guardians of the Poor of the ———— Union, do hereby require an Extraordinary Meeting of the Guardians of the said ———— Union to be summoned, to be holden at ———— on ———— the ———— day of ———— 18—, at ———— o'clock in the forenoon, to take into consideration [*set out the business*].

————
———— } Guardians.

FORM G.—*Notice of Change of Period, Time or Place of Meeting.* (See Art. 35.)

———— day of ———— 18—.

To *A. B.*, Guardian of the Poor of the ———— Union.

Sir,—You are hereby informed that the next Ordinary Meeting of the Guardians of the Poor of the ———— Union will take place at ———— on ———— day the ———— day of ———— 18—, at ———— o'clock in the ————noon, for the transaction of business; and that the Ordinary Meetings of the said Guardians will henceforth be held [*weekly or fortnightly, as the case may be*] at the same place, on the same day of the week, and at the same hour.

———— Signature of Clerk to the Guardians.

FORM H.—*Notice of an Adjourned Meeting of Guardians.* (See Art. 35.)

———— day of ———— 18 —.

To *A. B.*, Guardian of the Poor of the ———— Union.

Sir,—This is to give you notice, that an adjourned meeting of the Guardians of the Poor of the ———— Union will be held at ———— on ———— the ———— day of ———— 18,— which meeting you are hereby requested to attend.

———— Signature of Clerk to the Guardians.

FORM I.—*Notice of an Extraordinary Meeting of Guardians.*
(See Art. 35.)

———— day of ———— 18—.

To *A. B.*, Guardian of the Poor of the ———— Union.

Sir,—I am directed by *C. D.* and *E. F.*, two of the Guardians of the Poor of the ———— Union, to summon an Extraordinary Meeting of the Guardians of the Poor of the said Union, at ———— on ———— the ———— day of ———— 18—, at ———— o'clock in the forenoon, to take into consideration [*set out the business*], which meeting you are hereby requested to attend.

———— Signature of Clerk to the Guardians.

FORM K.—*Out-Relief Ticket.*   (See Art. 43.)

———— UNION.
Weekly Relief ordered the ———— day of ———— 18—,

Name.	Money.	Loaves. lb. each.	For what Period.
	Other Articles.		

———— Signature of Relieving Officer.

FORM L.—*Ticket for Permanent Medical List.*
(See Art. 76.)

————————————UNION.
Date————
Good until the ———————— day of———————— 18————
Name of Pauper————
Residence of Pauper————
Name of Medical Officer————
Residence————
Usual hour at which he is at home————

FORM M.—*Order for Contributions.*   (See Art. 83.)
(*See p. 16.*)

FORM N.—(*See p. 112.*)

FORM O.—(*See p. 120.*)

FORM P.—*District Medical Officer's Relief Book.*

—— UNION.

—— Medical Officer of the District.

Name of Pauper.	Age.	Residence.	Nature of Disease.	Week ending —— day of 186 .			Week ending —— day of 186 .			Week ending —— day of 186 .			Week ending —— day of 186 .			Observations.
				Days when attended, or when Medicines were furnished. *	Necessaries ordered to be given to the Patient.	Present State or Termination of the Case.	Days when attended, or when Medicines were furnished. *	Necessaries ordered to be given to the Patient.	Present State or Termination of the Case.	Days when attended, or when Medicines were furnished. *	Necessaries ordered to be given to the Patient.	Present State or Termination of the Case.	Days when attended, or when Medicines were furnished. *	Necessaries ordered to be given to the Patient.	Present State or Termination of the Case.	
				S M T W Th F Sat			S M T W Th F Sat			S M T W Th F Sat			S M T W Th F Sat			

* Attendances at the Patient's own house are to be denoted by the Letter (H.). Attendances at the Surgery or Medical Officer's residence by the Letter (S.). Medicine supplied without seeing the Patient, by the Letter (M.) Any attendance given by a Substitute or other Person instead of the Medical Officer, is to be entered in *red* ink.

FORM Q.—*Workhouse*

(A) To be filled up by the Medical Officer.

Initials of Medical Officer in attendance on every case.	Name of the sick pauper.	When admitted to sick ward.	When discharged.	Nature of disease.	Days when Attended.							MALES. The No.* of the Dietary on which placed.							FEMALES. The No.* of the Dietary on which placed.							Extras. What ordered.	When ordered.	When discontinued.	State or termination of the case, and in the event of death, the apparent cause of.
					Sunday.	Monday.	Tuesday.	Wednesday.	Thursday.	Friday.	Saturday.	Sunday.	Monday.	Tuesday.	Wednesday.	Thursday.	Friday.	Saturday.	Sunday.	Monday.	Tuesday.	Wednesday.	Thursday.	Friday.	Saturday.				
					Total No. each day. ......}																								Total quantity consumed.}

* Dietaries for the sick are to be numbered thus :—No. 1, House

As regards the Sick Paupers on Diet No. 1 (House Diet), the extras only should be entered in this book, since their ordinary Diet will appear in the "Daily Provisions' Consumption Account," for which see Form 26 of the General Order of the Commissioners, bearing date the 17th day of March, 1847.

The Number of the Paupers on each description of the Dietaries, and according to the several Sexes, is to be carried by the Master at the close of each week to a Summary at the end of the Book, to be prepared in the following Form :—

		WEEKLY SUMMARY.								
No. of the Dietary.	Description of Classes in the Diet Table.	Number of Patients each Day.							Collective Number of Days.
		S	M	T	W	Th.	F	Sat.	
1	House Diet.—Males . .								
1	House Diet.—Females .								
2	Full Diet.—Males . . .								
2	Full Diet.—Females . .								
3	Low Diet.—Males . . .								
3	Low Diet.—Females . .								
4	Fever Diet.—Males. . .								
4	Fever Diet.—Females . .								
	Total Number of Sick Paupers								

Medical Relief Book.

B.) To be filled up by the Master of the Workhouse, with the Articles
actually given.

Quantity of Provisions consumed.									Extras provided.							Remarks.
Bread.	Meat.	Bacon.	Cheese.	Rice.	Oatmeal.	Milk.			Ale.	Porter.	Wine.	Brandy.	Gin.			
lbs.	lbs.	lbs.	lbs.	lbs.	lbs.	pts.			pts.	pts.	pts.	pts.	pts.			

Diet. No. 2. Full Diet. No. 3. Low Diet. No. 4. Fever Diet.

FORM R.—*See p.* 182.

FORM R.—*See p.* 182.

FORM S.—*Register of Births in the*   *Workhouse.*
——— UNION.   ——— *Master.*

Date of Birth.	Whether Male or Female.	Name of Parents, or Mother.	From what Parish Parent admitted.*	When and where baptized.	In what Name baptized.	Remarks.

  * *Note.*—In the case of a Vagrant admitted into the Workhouse who
becomes a Mother therein, the word Vagrant must be inserted.

FORM T.—*Register of Deaths in the*   *Workhouse.*
——— UNION.   ——— *Master.*

Date of Death.	Name.	Age.	From what Parish admitted.*	Where buried.

  * *Note.*—In the case of a Vagrant admitted into the Workhouse who dies
therein, the words admitted as a Vagrant should be inserted.

FORM U.—(See Art. 208, No. 25.)

—— UNION WORKHOUSE. *Week ending* ____ 18 .

WARDS.	Beds therein.	Number of Occupants each Night.							Total.	Observations.
		S.	M.	T.	W.	Th.	F.	Sat.		
Able-bodied Men ..										
Old Men										
Boys										
Male Infirmary....										
—— Infectious....										
—— Receiving										
Total										
Able-bodied Women										
Old Women										
Girls										
Female Infirmary..										
Lying-in-Ward										
Female Infectious..										
—— Receiving..										
Total......										

The foregoing is a true statement.

—— Master.

_____

—— Matron.

FORM V.—*The Medical Relief Order Check Book.*
(See Art. 215, No. 3.)

No.——

   To——, Medical Officer.

Name, _____

Age, _____

Residence, _____

Nature of Case,_____

   Forwarded by —— at ——

o'clock in the —— of the——

day of —— 18—.

   —— Relieving Officer.

No.——

   To ——, Medical Officer, —— Union.

Sir,

   You are hereby requested to visit and undertake the treatment of the undermentioned cases.

   Name, _____

   Age, _____

   Residence, _____

   Nature of Case,* _____

   Forwarded by —— at —— o'clock in the —— of the —— day of —— 18—.

   —— Relieving Officer.

  * This is to be filled up so as to distinguish—
     1. Midwifery Cases.
     2. Fractures and Accidents.
     3. Cases of urgency, which require immediate attention.

INDEX.

PARTS I. AND II.

The Index of Part III., or the Consolidated Order, see page 337.

INDEX TO PART III.

THE CONSOLIDATED ORDER.

Note.—*The numbers referred to are not those of the pages of the Book, but of the Articles of the Consolidated Order.*

LONDON : R. K. BURT AND CO., PRINTERS, WINE OFFICE COURT, CITY.

RACK & SIMPLE BEDSTEADS

FOR

INFIRMARIES AND WORKHOUSES.

THOMAS CHRISPIN,

IRON BEDSTEAD, MATTRESS,

AND

𝔚𝔞𝔰𝔥𝔦𝔫𝔤 𝔐𝔞𝔠𝔥𝔦𝔫𝔢 𝔐𝔞𝔨𝔢𝔯,

28, KING STREET, & 1 & 2, QUEEN STREET,

HUDDERSFIELD,

BEGS to inform Guardians, Medical Men, and others, that he has always on hand, ready for immediate dispatch, a large assortment of Iron and Brass Bedsteads, Mattresses in Straw, Flock, Hair, and Spring; Feather and Flock Beds, Pillows and Bolsters in sets, as also Woollen Flocks for Beds and Mattresses.

The Bedsteads may be had of any width and length for both adults and children.

The Rack Bedstead, for use in Infirmaries, is recommended by the Medical Officer of the Poor Law Board, and by it the patient may be raised up by the strength of a child.

A Catalogue with prices and patterns sent on application.

ESTIMATES GIVEN.

THOMAS CHRISPIN,
WASHING, WRINGING, & MANGLING MACHINE MAKER,
1 & 2, QUEEN STREET, & 28, KING STREET,
HUDDERSFIELD.

The patent combined Washing, Wringing, and Mangling Machine effects a great saving in labour and material, and is particularly fitted for workhouses and workhouse infirmaries, where labour is insufficient at certain seasons of the year.

The dash-wheel inside the tub is made to turn a circle with reversible action. The clothes are placed inside the drum or dash-wheel, which has six rows of brushes put towards the clothes if coarse and dirty, or outside if for fine things.

The quick reversing action and rubbing of the clothes against the inside of the dash-wheel being amply sufficient to cleanse any article.

This machine, by altering the position of the brushes, is equally adapted for the heaviest linens or blankets, or the finest clothes, as there is nothing in the inside of the drum which can possibly injure them, whilst the large amount of motion given to the clothes cleanses the same in about five minutes.

As the clothes are at no time nearer than 3 in. to the bottom of the tub, they are always above the sediment and dirt, whereas in all other machines the clothes lie in the dirty water and sediment.

The action for washing is easily thrown out of gear; this being done, the rollers are put into a working position for wringing or mangling.

This machine will wash from ten to twelve shirts at a time. There is a cover to the tub by which the heat is retained in the water, and the annoyance of steam and effluvia is avoided. The width of the rollers is 26 inches; weight, about 5 cwt. Price £7.

There are also larger machines made, any of which can have a pulley attached so that they can be worked by the same steam-power which is used for any other purpose.

Full directions supplied with each machine.

Besides the above, the following machines of larger size are made:—

30 in. rollers, £8; 36 in. rollers, with pulley for steam-power, £17; 42 in. rollers, with pulley for steam-power, £28.

Washing Machines alone—

26 in. wide, £5; 30 in. wide, £5 10s.; 36 in. wide, with pulley for steam-power, £10; 42 in. wide, with pulley for steam-power, £18.

The above prices are Carriage Paid to any Railway Station in England.

A Catalogue with other patterns of machines, &c., and prices sent on application.

DANKS & NIXON

SOLICIT ATTENTION TO THEIR

PATENT VENTILATING & HEAT ECONOMISING GRATES,

 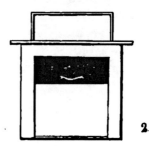

1.   2.

For producing a pure and healthy atmosphere in Public Buildings, Hospitals, School-rooms, &c.

1. THE contrivance is as simple as it is effectual. The air when admitted is from 65 to 70 degrees of heat, and the supply is so copious that, besides rendering the fire independent of the doors and windows for its draught, it secures the proper action of any outlet that may be made for *foul air*. It stands unrivalled for producing a pure and healthy atmosphere, is really economical in use, and the first cost very moderate.

2. *Our* draught Regulator, designed by S. T. Barber, Esq., Architect, of Eastwood, Notts, and manufactured by us, is also an invention of considerable importance, and invaluable as a preventive to Smoky Chimneys. It is now in use at the Basford Union Poorhouse, near Nottingham, and many other places. By its use the draught in a chimney can be increased or decreased at pleasure, and it can be so secured at any time as to prevent accidents occurring from fire in Lunatic Wards, or any other apartments. One may be seen at the Poor Law Offices in London.

Drawings and Prices forwarded on application

TO

DANKS & NIXON,

NOTTINGHAM.

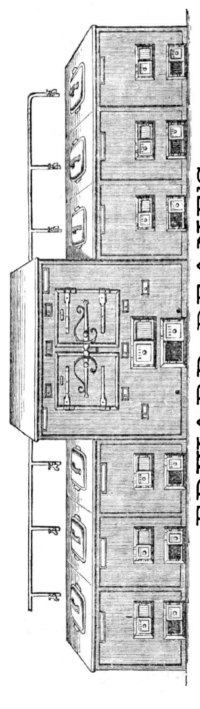

T. & W. EARLY,

Manufacturers,

HIGH STREET & FARM MILLS,

WITNEY, OXFORDSHIRE,

Manufacturers of All-Wool Blankets,

SERGES, FLANNEL, CLOTH, COVERLIDS,

HOUSE-FLANNEL, BED AND CASUAL RUGS.

T. & W. EARLY having given the requirements of Workhouses and Public Institutions, both for ordinary inmates and sick wards, their special attention for the last three years, can with confidence recommend their goods.

The White Blankets, Grey Rugs, and Black-and-Yellow Rugs, are especially adapted for the purpose, and have given the greatest satisfaction in every instance.

These goods are all approved by the Medical Officer of the Poor Law Board.

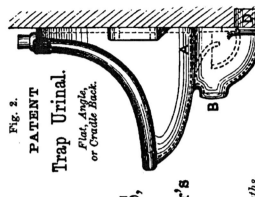

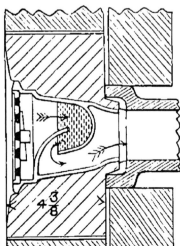

HOOPER'S
WATER OR AIR BEDS AND CUSHIONS.

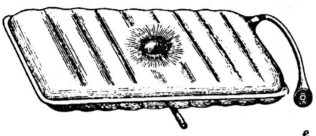

			£	s.	d.
Full Length	33	×	72	9	9	0*
Three-Quarter	30	×	40	6	16	6
Half..............................	27	×	30	5	0	0

With Central Tube for dirty cases about 10s. extra (*see above Cut*).

Circular Cushions, with Depressed Centre { 18 in. diameter 30s.
 20 in. do. 35s.

Square ditto   ditto ....18 × 18, 40s. ; 20 × 20, 45s.

Horse Shoe Shape for Sacrum ....35s. ; extra size, 45s.

HOOPER'S WATERPROOF SHEETS
WITH OR WITHOUT CENTRAL TUBE.

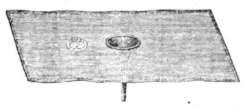

With Tube (*see Cut*) .... 36 × 48, 10s. 6d. ; 36 × 72, 16s.

Without Tube ...... 36 × 36, 5s. 6d. ; 36 × 72, 10s. 6d. ; 42 × 72, 12s. 6d.

Do. do. ...... 1¼ yards square, 8s. 6d. ; 1½ yards square, 12s. 6d.

HOOPER'S INDIA-RUBBER URINALS.

Day use .... Male, 15s. .... Female, 17s. 6d.

Night use .... „ 21s. .... „ 25s.

* All the prices are subject to 25 per cent. Discount to Boards of Guardians.

7, PALL MALL EAST, LONDON.

CPSIA information can be obtained at www.ICGtesting.com
Printed in the USA
BVOW02s1208260814

364295BV00020B/877/P